God Is Change

D1319896

God Is Change

_Religious Practices and Ideologies in
the Works of Octavia Butler_

Edited by Aparajita Nanda
and Shelby L. Crosby

TEMPLE UNIVERSITY PRESS
Philadelphia • Rome • Tokyo

TEMPLE UNIVERSITY PRESS
Philadelphia, Pennsylvania 19122
tupress.temple.edu

Library of Congress Cataloging-in-Publication Data

Names: Nanda, Aparajita, editor. | Crosby, Shelby, 1974– editor.
Title: God is change : religious practices and ideologies in the works of
  Octavia Butler / edited by Aparajita Nanda and Shelby L. Crosby.
Description: Philadelphia : Temple University Press, 2021. | Includes
  bibliographical references and index. | Summary: "Octavia Butler's
  fictional worlds show the potential of religion to connect, heal, or
  liberate. Contributors explore the bases of these potentials in the many
  religious traditions Butler draws on, the forms they take in her
  stories, and the work they do to heal trauma and violence"—Provided by
  publisher.
Identifiers: LCCN 2020043395 (print) | LCCN 2020043396 (ebook) | ISBN
  9781439921111 (cloth) | ISBN 9781439921128 (paperback) | ISBN
  9781439921135 (pdf)
Subjects: LCSH: Butler, Octavia E.—Criticism and interpretation. |
  Religion in literature.
Classification: LCC PS3552.U827 Z68 2021 (print) | LCC PS3552.U827
  (ebook) | DDC 813/.54—dc23
LC record available at https://lccn.loc.gov/2020043395
LC ebook record available at https://lccn.loc.gov/2020043396

♾ The paper used in this publication meets the requirements of the
American National Standard for Information Sciences—Permanence
of Paper for Printed Library Materials, ANSI Z39.48-1992

Printed in the United States of America

9 8 7 6 5 4 3 2 1

Contents

Acknowledgments

The editors of this volume are humbled and grateful to the estate of Dr. Gregory Hampton, who graciously allowed Dr. Hampton's essay to be included in this volume after his passing in 2020.

Dr. Nanda would like to thank my esteemed colleagues and my family for all their support in the completion of this project. With deep gratitude I remember all the help I got from Professor Hertha Wong, my former chair and associate dean of arts and humanities, University of California, Berkeley, right from the inception of this book to its finish. This volume would never have seen the light of day without the very generous support and unstinting help I got from Professors Amy Shachter (senior associate provost for research and faculty affairs), Andrew Keener, Mary Grover, and especially my research assistant, Derek Sikkema.

Dr. Crosby would like to thank my family for all of their support during the process of completing this project. I am eternally gratefully to Dr. Alexis Masani Deveaux, who first introduced me to Octavia Butler; without her, I may not have found Butler. Thank you to Susannah Bartlow for her endless support and help throughout this project. You rock the tomato! I appreciate the support I have received from the chair of my department, Dr. Joshua Phillips, and the University of Memphis. This book has been such an incredible experience. Thank you to all of my students for reading and learning about Octavia Butler with me. Their helpful feedback and conversations enriched this collection immeasurably.

Drs. Nanda and Crosby would like to thank Ryan Mulligan, editor, Temple University Press, for his continued support and guidance.

God Is Change

Introduction

APARAJITA NANDA AND SHELBY L. CROSBY

At the 1992 Republican National Convention, the conservative politician Pat Buchanan declared, "There is a religious war going on in this country. It is a cultural war, as critical to the kind of nation we shall be as was the Cold War itself, for this war is for the soul of America." By invoking "the soul of America" and then pitting the political Right against liberalism—that is, "homosexual rights," "radical feminists," secularists—Buchanan's rhetoric effectively mobilized fears that the Other would usurp "a nation we still call God's country." A year later, in 1993, Octavia E. Butler published *Parable of the Sower*, a dystopian novel exploring what happens when we as Americans are locked in a divisive "cultural war" that unjustly affects the disenfranchised. In *Parable of the Talents*, the sequel to *Parable of the Sower*, a fascistic president, allied with white fundamentalist Christianity, rises to power with the slogan "Make America Great Again." While the correspondences with President Donald Trump's presidency seem uncanny, even prophetic, Michael Brandon McCormack, in his essay in this collection, reminds us that Butler thought of these novels as "cautionary tales." As such, they are "warnings of what *might* come to pass 'if this continues'—if we should fail to make radical sociopolitical interventions and fundamentally reimagine what it means to be human *in the here and now*" (see Chapter 15). Whether prophecy or caution, now is a time when we clearly need to take inspiration from Butler's narrative wisdom—from her prescient thoughts on the synergy between politics and religion in the United States, from the craft of her imagination, from her practical and spiritual insight about how we can shape the present and future.

This volume, *God Is Change: Religious Practices and Ideologies in the Works of Octavia Butler*, turns to Butler's work as a crucial resource in times of moral, political, and social crisis. Butler envisions spiritual community beyond the bifurcated, polarizing world we live in. The chapters herein explore Butler's religious imagination and place her fiction in new and provocative interpretive contexts to demonstrate and share the intellectual, spiritual vitality of her work. The collection proposes that Butler provides a lens of philosophical understanding and a blended epistemology of religion, healing, and liberation to reimagine and reshape the world: "At its best," Butler wrote, "science fiction stimulates imagination and creativity. It gets reader and writer off the beaten track, off the narrow, narrow footpath of what 'everyone' is saying, doing, thinking" ("Positive Obsession" 135). For readers who have felt railroaded and circumscribed by hegemonic cultural norms, Butler envisions alternative ways of knowing and believing, paths of fruitful contemplation "off the beaten track." However, just as the array of interpretive responses in this collection demonstrates, her fiction by no means prescribes those divergent routes; rather, it resists labeling and doctrine, undermines an ontology of complacency, and puts dialectical investigation into motion.

The concept of revolutionary change took shape in Butler's meditations, work, and writing, beginning with the publication of her first novel, *Patternmaster*. However, in the Parable series, Butler developed Earthseed, a religion created and promulgated by Lauren Olamina, the charismatic leader of a successful movement. Earthseed inspires much of the scholarship included in this volume, which gives new readings and interpretations of this religion in light of the biographical, political, and cross-cultural contexts of the essays. Earthseed, as a faith that will create and sustain a new way of life in the apocalyptic world that Butler's characters find themselves inhabiting, is predicated on the belief that God is change: "All that you touch / You change. / All that you Change / Changes you. / . . . / God is Change" (*Parable of the Sower* 3). Followers need to learn how to adapt and accept that change is the only constant in their world. The God of Earthseed is "inexorable, / Indifferent" to the fate of humanity, so disciples of Earthseed need to prepare and plan for disaster and change (*Parable of the Sower* 25). They can, however, transform the impact of change by adapting to it as they strive to reach the Destiny of Earthseed, which is to "take root among the stars" (*Parable of the Sower* 77). This threefold agenda comes together to form a way of life that allows adherents not only to survive but to thrive as well. In an interview Butler states:

> I had in mind how certain historical populations have used religion to focus a group toward long-term goals—such as building cathedrals or

the pyramids. I wanted Lauren to envision, but then also to focus the Earthseed group toward, the goal of changing human attitudes about the treatment of the Earth and each other. (Mehaffy and Keating 75)

In other words, although Butler strikes back against the cultural war Buchanan declared, her work demands that readers inhabit a truly intersectional space, reflecting her own subjectivity as a Black American woman and centering the potential for religion as a creative force rather than dogma. Butler's personal ambivalence around religion in fact provided productive impetus for her writing. From an early age Butler was inculcated into the Baptist faith; her grandfather was a practicing minister (like Lauren Olamina's father in *The Parable of the Sower*), and her mother believed that the church would provide her with a strong moral and ethical foundation. Yet, almost immediately, Butler began to question and critique the church and its teachings. As an adult, she became agnostic. While she turns away from religion as the cornerstone of her life, it does become a touchstone in her fictions. As McCormack notes, for Butler, religion becomes a "significant resource for reflecting upon the shifting terrain of social justice work in the future, and the role of religious institutions, beliefs, and practices in such struggle" (8).

Since Butler's death in 2006, critical work on her corpus has proliferated. Scholars have especially focused on the utopian and dystopian dimensions of her work, assessing the liberatory potential of her generic innovations along dimensions of race, gender, politics, science, and culture.[1] As Chuck Robinson has noted, adding his own deconstructive turn to Butler's conception of "minority," "Compelling readings of Butler exist from the perspectives of critical race theory, Afrofuturism, black feminism, queer theory, and most recently disability studies" (483). Butler's fictional worlds have also inspired claims about the transgressive power of erotics depicted therein, as, for example, in Nolan Belk's reading of the Xenogenesis trilogy. On another front, research on the Octavia E. Butler archive, made available at the Huntington Library near Pasadena, California in 2013, has brought Butler scholarship beyond the bounds of discrete, published works to inspire new perspectives on her writerly fascinations, most notably in the book-length, biocritical study by Gerry Canavan titled *Octavia E. Butler*. Scholars have drawn from the trove of archival materials to consider how drafts of the novel *Fledgling* elaborate on the themes of symbiosis and genetics (Sanchez-Taylor). Butler's research on nonhuman organisms showcases her contribution as a Black feminist philosopher of science and develops a queer take on biology (Bhang, Van Engen). Most significantly, Butler's work as a writer, editor, and mentor built "a home place" for Black writers (Alexander).

The overview above represents the proverbial tip of the iceberg, both in breadth and volume. And yet relatively few articles grapple directly with the subject of religion in Butler's oeuvre. Much of this smaller subset of scholarship weighs in on the emancipatory potential of Earthseed, putting Butler's fictional religion in dialogue with Black theological traditions, particularly Black Liberation theology and a Black feminist biblical perspective. For example, Clarence Tweedy points out that Earthseed shares with Black theology a mission to counter the forces of racial and economic oppression, even while the Parable novels, as he observes, implicitly raise the specter of "messianic doctrine," a form of demagoguery. McCormack celebrates Lauren Olamina as "an Afrofuturist (fifth wave) womanist theologian who only embraces notions of God that can be corroborated with her own experience and ultimately can be beneficial to her community" (19). Kimberly Ruffin interprets Earthseed as a persuasive syncretism of religion and science, premised on an "Afrofuturist black feminist biblical hermeneutics that strives to resolve conflict between scientific knowledge and religiosity" (91). In Butler's fiction, this salutary syncretism does the work of dismantling "the religious-secular binary" (Hammer), and in ways that reconcile spirituality with scientific knowledge (Teish). Donna Spalding Andréolle argues that, in fact, Earthseed, while it challenges Judeo-Christian values that license oppression, rests on premises of Christian fundamentalism, more specifically the "original Puritan Project," with its ideology of a manifest destiny. Meanwhile, Vincent Lloyd goes furthest when interrogating claims about Earthseed's emancipatory power, asserting that Earthseed reinforces a neoliberal cultural logic that in fact undercuts the possibility of real change by promoting the atomized self as change agent.

The emphasis in religion-focused scholarship, then, is on how Butler challenges, resignifies, and/or replicates forms of existing religious and cultural ideologies. Sometimes these forms are gestured to in very broad terms, as when James H. Thrall, comparing Earthseed to other "invented" religions in fictional works, comments that Lauren Olamina's *Books of the Living* (whose verses head each chapter in the Parable novels) "might be modeled on . . . marriages of scriptural principles with illustrative history, stories, or commentary in existing religious traditions" (513, 515). David Morris argues that Earthseed, which marries Lauren Olamina's religious mission with her "commitment to religious truth[,] . . . assembles a workable utopian program" in ways that parallel Pauline Christianity (274). Also more specifically, Sarah Wood focuses on how Butler challenges patriarchal, white-authored Christianity by drawing on traditions of West African religion (through the character of Anyanwu, in the Patternist series) and by "problematizing the

Biblical story of Genesis" (through the character of Lilith, in the Xenogenesis trilogy, 144).

The chapters in the present anthology build on this scholarship in two important ways. First, analysis included here heightens our appreciation for the range and depth of Butler's thinking about spirituality and religion providing such critical contexts as an exploration of Hindu theology and mythos (Nanda), Soto Zen Buddhism (Kocela), Black female theology (Stanley), the theistic philosophy of Emmanuel Levinas (Grover), Yoruban cultural and spiritual practice (Gibson, Brooks de Vita), biblical wisdom literature (Naylor Davis). Each chapter showcases how Butler's fiction mobilizes the resources of narrative to invite meditation on what it means to be human and live with grace.

Secondly, the chapters herein bring home how Butler's work offers resources for healing and community building: the community sustained and engendered by Earthseed dramatizes the power of ritual as a treatment for trauma (Osinski). Shelby L. Crosby's chapter, "Creating New Worlds: Earthseed as a Tool of Black Liberation," explores how Earthseed has been picked up and used by activists to advance liberation for people of color. Earthseed, as Brianna Thompson declares, "is a liberating religion that Lauren [Olamina] ministers through erotic pedagogy[,] . . . a loving, transformative force." In the absence of community, the ability to shape-shift and effect metaphysical migration, powerfully rendered in Butler's novel *Wild Seed*, brings "liberation and justice to black female bodily memory" (Whiteside). Butler's novels broadcast the voices of Black women speaking in the voice of reason and prophecy, an impetus for social transformation (Burns). "By mixing SF [science fiction] with religious themes, Butler's fiction encourages readers to question social values that mark marginalized bodies" (Hampton). Michael Brandon McCormack sums it up: "Octavia Butler offers a prophetic vision of the interplay between religion, violence, healing, and liberation that not only warns of potentially apocalyptic fates but also offers possibilities for more liberating futures." And, as Chuck Robinson suggests, reading Butler is, in and of itself, a sustaining religious practice.

The first part of this volume, "Spiritualities and Religious Constructs," explores the role of spirituality in Butler's canon and how the construction or creation of an alternate "religion" leads to different models of world building, transcendence, and even concepts of trade. Contributors wrestle with Butler's creation of a spiritual and religious ideology, questioning how religion is constructed, how believers function within their faith, and how the faith system of Earthseed works as both sacred text and wisdom utterances. Additionally, they recognize the philosophical heft of Butler's literary meditations on this theme, and they show how her critique of established religion complements her depiction of spiritual connection and practice. Moreover, chapters in this part interrogate the construction of a universal God that can be shaped and imagined by the characters and readers of Butler's fiction. Authors draw on other religious traditions, like Hinduism and Buddhism, to build a case for describing the construction of an alternate religious vision of a new world where God is change. By alternately addressing these themes, the selections complement each other concerning the concepts of community building and transcendence.

The first chapter of this part, Gregory Hampton's "Religious Science Fiction: Butler's Changing God," argues that Butler's creation of a religious philosophy in Earthseed creates a space that dismantles oppression, in particular, through her creation of Black female heroines who seek to end oppression through their relationship to change and acceptance of difference. Expanding the parameters of Butler's thinking about religion, Aparajita Nanda, in her chapter "Transreligious World Building: Hindu Evocations in Octavia Butler's *Lilith's Brood*," explores hybridity and identity through the Hindu principle of prana and how it is essential to Butler's alternate religion of creativity for human survival. Christopher Kocela considers Butler's religious ideology through the lens of Zen Buddhism, proposing that taken together *Parable of the Sower* and *Parable of the Talents* give us "a nondualistic understanding of the relationship between means and ends that emphasizes the need for collective action by celebrating diversity and challenging hierarchical and discriminatory thinking." Charlotte Naylor Davis, in her chapter that focuses on the *Books of the Living* (Earthseed's sacred text), argues how personal transformation and freedom are ways that can be best appreciated through analysis of their roots in biblical wisdom literature in Western culture. Mary Grover's contribution draws on the thinking of the philosophers Emmanuel Levinas and Seyla Benhabib to demonstrate that Butler's sense of ethics, while standing in opposition to twentieth-century American Christianity, rests on certain faith-based beliefs in universal dignity. The part concludes with Chuck Robinson's chapter, "*Parable of the Talents* as Genre Criticism and the Holy Spirit of Speculative Fiction," which considers the sacred community that Butler creates in the novel, demanding that the reader become an active participant in her religious philosophical community.

In the second part, "Trauma and Healing," contributors examine how Butler's Earthseed and work ethics help its members to confront their trauma, learn how to heal, and move beyond it. Considering how Butler develops trauma and restorative spaces in the Parable series, Butler's *Wild Seed*, and three of her short stories ("Crossover," "The Book of Martha," and "Speech Sounds"), these authors note that while Butler's worlds are marked by "inevitable violence," they are also grounded in the ideas of constant change and transformation (Outterson 434). Submissions in this part build on Sarah Outterson's claim to provide different ways in which traumatic space can be transformed into healing space.

In "'Only Actions': Ritual and the Embodied Processing of Trauma in *Parable of the Sower* and *Parable of the Talents*," Keegan Osinski opens Part II arguing that religious communities can provide safety and community for their followers through the process of ritual. Ritual, for Osinski, as modeled in the Parable series, is essential for followers to process and release trauma. In "Migration, Spirituality, and Restorative Spaces: Shape-Shifting to Heal in Octavia Butler's *Wild Seed*," Briana Whiteside contends that it is through migration and shape-shifting that Black women can combat oppression and heal from trauma. Like Whiteside, Ebony Gibson explores healing; however, for Gibson, healing is a function of the genetic trade that the Oankali offer in *Lilith's Brood*, which she interprets in light of Yoruba culture. Building on the biblical allusions referenced in the names of Mary and Martha, Jennifer L. Hayes applies a Black feminist reading to Butler's short stories "Crossover," "The Book of Martha," and "Speech Sounds." Hayes examines the mental and emotional trauma these heroines go through as they weigh their contributions to the ongoing vitality of their society through which they often seek a sense of restoration and healing. Closing out the part, Tarshia L. Stanley in "Shapers of God: Octavia E. Butler's *Parable of the Sower* and Womanist Theological Practice" explores the intersections of religion and politics and how Butler's religious ideology builds community. Stanley proposes that while not traditionally read as a Black liberation theological text, Earthseed builds not only on of the work of Howard Thurman and James Cone but also on groundbreaking womanist Black theologians to shape a new space to reimagine community and strategies of community building.

In the third part, "Black Liberation and Notions of Freedom," contributors explore various notions of freedom that Butler presents throughout her canon, particularly in her novels. Thinking through "the representations of the increasingly violent public discourse, policies, and practices of the far-right religious groups" in Butler's work, particularly the Parable series, contributors seek to understand the fear and violence inspired by Butler's God of change and how those oppressed by the violence can respond when oppressors take their liberties, when fear rules their lives.

Part III opens with Alexis Brooks de Vita's "Octavia Butler's Xenogenesis Trilogy, *Bloodchild*, and the Androgynous Third." Brooks posits that the acceptance of and partnership with an ooloi, the androgynous third, makes freedom and peace possible. Brianna Thompson, however, provides a very different interpretation of the ooloi, based on erotic pedagogy, which supports and nourishes its adherents through intimate connection. For Phyllis L. Burns in her chapter, "Black Women's Prophecy: O. E. Butler's Parables," freedom only comes when Black women are free; thus Butler intervenes in the perpetual silencing of Black women, constructing a social space that is free only after Black women have been released from the societal restrictions that hamper them. Michael Brandon McCormack recognizes that, while fictitious, the Parable novels' world mirrors our contemporary white nationalist discourse infected with the political/public theological rhetoric of "Make America Great Again." He places Butler in the domain of American prophecy, reading her work as a trenchant take on the "affects and effects" of religio-political oppression. Closing out the volume, Shelby L. Crosby's chapter, "Practicing the Future Together: Earthseed as a Tool for Black Liberation," explores how political activists have adopted Butler's religious ideology as a way to imagine a new world. Earthseed becomes a transformative political practice.

Whether through adapting to and becoming part of an alien race, surviving an apocalyptic United States, or attempting to build a race of superhumans that have extraordinary psychic abilities, Octavia Butler's worlds are demanding, often cruel, and designed to expose cultural and individual biases. This collection focuses on and explores Butler's religious imagination and its potential for healing and liberation. Contributors have focused primarily on the Parable and Xenogenesis series because these texts provide both the most directly theological forms (like the Parable novels' verses) and because their narratives map so distinctly onto Butler's larger project of exploring humanity's ability to endure change and thrive.

Throughout her corpus, Butler explores, critiques, and creates religious ideology. She uses religion as a tool for transformation and change crucial to the worlds she creates. In doing so, she reveals her pessimism, joy, fear, and hope for humanity. Butler proposes her version of religion in her literary texts as offerings rather than arguments with foregone conclusions. She provides readers with a space beyond today's polarization, a space of encounter, performance, and community. Readers can make what they will of this space. This collection continues the dialogue that Butler puts in motion when she offers ideas about religion rather than predetermined conclusions. This volume illuminates current religious and political conversations; moreover, it points to the importance of moving toward healing through religious and spiritual ideology rather than default reactionary political responses. *God Is Change* meditates on alternate religious possibilities that open different political and cultural futures. It is quite apparent, given the present political climate, that right-wing religious conservatives continue to wage Pat Buchanan's "cultural war." It is this war that Butler is intervening in and why *God Is Change* is so very necessary.

NOTE

1. See, for example, Pfaelzer, Thibodeau, Yoo, Zamalin, and, above all, essays in a dedicated issue of *Utopian Studies*, vol. 35, no. 2, 2008.

WORKS CITED

Alexander, Phoenix. "Octavia E. Butler and Black Women's Archives at the End of the World." *Science Fiction Studies*, vol. 46, no. 2, 2019, pp. 342–357.

Andréolle, Donna Spalding. "Utopias of Old, Solutions for the New Millennium: A Comparative Study of Christian Fundamentalism in M. K. Wren's *A Gift upon the Shore* and Octavia Butler's *Parable of the Sower*." *Utopian Studies*, vol. 12, no. 2, 2001, pp. 114–123.

Belk, Nolan. "The Certainty of the Flesh: Octavia Butler's Use of the Erotic in the *Xenogenesis* Trilogy." *Utopian Studies*, vol. 19, no. 3, 2008, pp. 369–389.

Bhang, Aimee. "Plasmodial Improprieties: Octavia E. Butler, Slime Molds, and Imagining a Femi-Queer Commons." *Queer Feminist Science Studies: A Reader*, edited by Cyd Cipolla et al. University of Washington Press, 2018, pp. 342–357.

Buchanan, Patrick. The U.S. Oratory Project. "Culture War Speech: Address to the Republican National Convention" (17 Aug. 1992). Voices of Democracy. https://voicesofdemocracy.umd.edu/buchanan-culture-war-speech-speech-text/. Accessed October 2019.

Butler, Octavia E. *Parable of the Sower*. Grand Central Publishing, 2000.

———. *Parable of the Talents*. Seven Stories, 1998.

———. "Positive Obsession." *Bloodchild and Other Stories*. 2nd ed., Seven Stories, 2005, pp. 123–136.

Canavan, Gerry. *Octavia E. Butler*. University of Illinois Press, 2016.

Hammer, Everett. "Determined Agency: A Postsecular Proposal for Religion and Literature—and Science." *Religion and Literature*, vol. 41, no. 3, 2009, pp. 91–98.

Lloyd, Vincent. "Post-Racial, Post-Apocalyptic Love: Octavia Butler as Political Theologian." *Political Theology*, vol. 17, no. 5, 2016, pp. 449–464.

McCormack, Michael Brandon. "'Your God Is a Racist, Sexist, Homophobic, and a Misogynist . . . Our God Is Change': Ishmael Reed, Octavia Butler and Afrofuturist Critiques of (Black) American Religion." *Black Theology*, vol. 14, no. 1, Apr. 2016, pp. 6–27.

Mehaffy, Marilyn, and AnaLouise Keating. "Radio Imagination: Octavia Butler on the Poetics of Narrative Embodiment." *MELUS*, vol. 26, no. 1, 2001, pp. 45–76.

Morris, David. "Octavia Butler's (R)evolutionary Movement for the Twenty-First Century." *Utopian Studies*, vol. 26, no. 2, 2015, pp. 270–288. *EBSCOhost*, search.ebscohost.com/login.aspx?direct=true&AuthType=ip,shib&db=mzh&AN=2016305944&site=ehost-live&scope=site.

Outterson, Sarah. "Diversity, Change, Violence: Octavia Butler's Pedagogical Philosophy." *Utopian Studies*, vol. 9, no. 3, 2008, pp. 433–456.

Pfaelzer, Jean. "Women Write the Future: Teaching Feminism and Utopianism in the Twenty-First Century." *Transformations: The Journal of Inclusive Scholarship and Pedagogy*, vol. 20, no. 2, 2009/2010, pp. 39–54.

Robinson, Chuck. "Minority and Becoming-Minor in Octavia Butler's *Fledgling*." *Science Fiction Studies*, vol. 42, no. 3, Nov. 2015, pp. 483–499.

Ruffin, K. "Parable of a 21st Century Religion: Octavia Butler's Afrofuturistic Bridge between Science and Religion." *Obsidian III*, vol. 6/7, 2005, pp. 87–104.

Sanchez-Taylor, Joy. "Fledgling, Symbiosis, and the Nature/Culture Divide." *Science Fiction Studies*, vol. 44, no. 3, 2017, pp. 486–505.

Teish, Luisah. "The Spirit in the Seed." *Strange Matings: Science Fiction, Feminism, African American Voices, and Octavia Butler*, edited by Rebecca J. Holden and Nisi Shawl, Aqueduct Press, 2013, pp. 96–104.

Thibodeau, Amanda. "Alien Bodies and a Queer Future: Sexual Revision in Octavia Butler's 'Bloodchild' and James Tiptree, Jr.'s 'With Delicate Mad Hands.'" *Science Fiction Studies*, vol. 39, no. 2, 2012, pp. 262–282.

Thrall, James. "Authoring the Sacred: Humanism and Invented Scripture in Octavia Butler, Kurt Vonnegut and Dan Simmons." *Implicit Religion*, vol. 17, 2014, pp. 509–531.

Tweedy, Clarence W., III. "The Anointed: Countering Dystopia with Faith in Octavia Butler's *Parable of the Sower* and *Parable of the Talents*." *Americana: The Journal of American Popular Culture, 1900 to Present*, vol. 13, no. 1, 2014, http://www.american popularculture.com/journal/articles/spring_2014/tweedy.htm.

Van Engen, Dagmar. "Metamorphosis, Transition, and Insect Biology in the Octavia E. Butler Archive." *Women's Studies*, vol. 47, no. 7, 2018, pp. 733–754.

Wood, Sarah. "Subversion through Inclusion: Octavia Butler's Interrogation of Religion in Xenogenesis and *Wild Seed*." *FEMSPEC: An Interdisciplinary Feminist Journal Dedicated to Critical and Creative Work in the Realms of Science Fiction, Fantasy, Magical Realism, Surrealism, Myth, Folklore, and Other Supernatural Genres*, vol. 6, no. 1, 2005, pp. 87–99.

Yoo, Jihun. "Transhumanist Impulse, Utopian Vision, and Reversing Dystopia in Margaret Atwood's *Oryx and Crake* and Octavia E. Butler's *Dawn*." *Modern Language Review*, vol. 114, no. 4, 2019, pp. 662–681.

Zamalin, Alex. "Octavia Butler and the Politics of Utopian Transcendence." *Black Utopia: The History of an Idea from Black Nationalism to Afrofuturism*, Columbia University Press, 2019, pp. 123–136.

Part I

Spiritualities and Religious Constructs

1

Religious Science Fiction

Butler's Changing God

GREGORY HAMPTON

> [Science fiction is] a realistic speculation about possible future
> events, based solidly on adequate knowledge of the real world, past
> and present, and on a thorough understanding of the nature and
> significance of the scientific method.
>
> —HEINLEIN, *Stranger in a Strange Land*, 21

> Science-fiction is the search for a definition of man and his status
> in the universe which will stand in our advanced but confused state
> of knowledge.
>
> —ALDISS, *Trillion Year Spree*, 8

> Science-fiction is relevant; it is important; it has something to
> do with the world; it gives meaning to life; and it enlightens the
> readers. And it has all these characteristics as no other form of
> literature has.
>
> —ASIMOV, *Foundations*, xi

In defining the boundaries and utility of a genre, the above passages suggest
that three of the most dominant voices in the genre of science fiction (SF)
agree that it can be a device used to understand and reshape the real world.
Despite the elements of fantasy, time travel, and utopian societies, the genre
of SF is very much a literature that directly reflects the society that produces
it. "Derrida argues that all Literature addresses the nuclear condition: the
risk of absolute efficacy" (Luckhurst 103). Consequently, it is also a literature
that has the ability to critique and police the boundaries of the real world in
a fashion that is comparable to that of religion. Heinlein's observation about
realistic speculation based on the past and the present is reminiscent of biblical revelations. Aldiss's assertion that SF is necessarily an existential quest
coincides with what is generally understood as the function of religion, and

Asimov's declaration of SF's relevance to the real world reads like a Sunday school sermon. Indeed, SF is far from a juvenile literature designed for escaping reality. According to Freud, religion was an attempt to control the mental world by means of a world of the oldest and most compelling wishes of humankind (Walker 850). Religion is a tool intended to critique the real world in the unbounded laboratories of our imaginations. Discussions of utopian or heavenly societies do not negate discussions of an imperfect world with imperfect representations of humanity. Given these observations, the discussion examining relationships between religion and SF seems more than fitting as both seek to provide assistance in navigating our imperfect real world.

Adam Roberts's *The History of Science Fiction* asserts that science fiction would be better named "technology fiction," as the term "'science' is generally understood to be a discipline which seeks to understand and explain the cosmos in materialist (rather than spiritual or supernatural) terms" (4). Roberts continues his assertion by observing that SF is "a mode of doing science (or 'philosophy' more generally conceived) as well as a mode of doing fiction" (6). Ultimately, through terminology supplied by the German philosopher Martin Heidegger, Roberts arrives at the notion that SF is a process that thinks: "not only in the sense of rehearsing a great many concepts, possibilities, intellectual dramas and the like, but in the deeper sense of textually enframing the world by positing the world's alternatives" (12). Thus, by associating SF with what is traditionally understood as the pondering and explanation of the real world, Roberts argues "that the reemergence of SF is correlated to the Protestant Reformation" (ix). Consequently, *The History of Science Fiction* is largely founded on the notion that the borders of SF and religion have been blurred for a very long time. Roberts dates SF as far back as the ancient Greek novel and cites seventeenth-century examples of ancient science fiction, such as "Johannes Kepler's *Sominum* (1634), Francis Godwin's *The Man in the Moone* (1638) and Cyrano de Bergerac's *Voyage a la lune* (1655)" (ix). More importantly, Roberts makes note of that fact that religion and science (technology fiction) have been at odds since René Descartes.

During the late sixteenth and early seventeenth centuries, the balance of scientific enquiry shifted to Protestant countries, where the sort of speculation that could be perceived as contrary to biblical revelation could be undertaken with more (although not total) freedom. Descartes, for instance, settled in Holland in 1629, in part because his native French Catholic culture was proving to be hostile to his scientific inquiries. In Descartes's mind was the recent condemnation of Galileo's astronomical work by the Catholic Church, a shocking development for many scientific thinkers at the time. Indeed, there were more troubling developments than this, especially for the more imaginative minded (which is to say, science-fictional) thinkers (ix).

The speculative fiction of Octavia Butler often targets issues of religion and spirituality as a way to raise questions about how the body is valued in the real world as well as the spiritual world. As a writer known for her cautionary tales that question social ethics, religion seems an appropriate location from which to begin dismantling fundamental social values. In interviews, Butler has suggested that her slant toward religion has partially been a result of her grandfather being a Baptist minister and her mother raising her as a Baptist in order to install her moral conscience at an early age (Zimmer 1, Zindell 3). Religion is ultimately a mechanism that polices the borders of social value and disvalue. In her narratives Butler employs the integration of postmodern slave narrative forms with feminist creation stories to question the political and spiritual value of marginalized bodies. By outlining practical behavior that advocates the end of oppression rooted in hierarchies of identity via clear paths of spirituality, the fiction of Butler expands the parameters of the genres she writes across. Butler's use of SF in conjunction with religious references allows her to rewrite history and the future with plausible fantasy and faith-based mythology. By mixing SF with religious themes, Butler's fiction encourages readers to question social values that mark marginalized bodies. This is made evident through Butler's harsh critique of patriarchy, capitalism, and any form of oppression that appears to be based on the rejection of change or a universal notion of God.

In this chapter I assert that the employment of religion and religious themes in the fiction of Octavia E. Butler makes her fiction both assessable and plausible as a source of social commentary and advice to an increasingly marginalized and especially African American audience. I contend that Butler's consistent employment of black bodies and spiritual references in her fiction appeals to a marginalized populous that identifies with archetypes on the borders of the secular and the religious. Butler provides a lens of philosophical understanding, a blended epistemology of religion, healing, and liberation to reimagine and reshape the world. The humanitarian and universal elements of Butler's religious and cultural references allow her audience to identify with archetypes that are appealing and familiar. As the "Black Church has historically demonstrated its institutional genius in its ability to shape itself according to the needs of its congregation" (Toth 213), it is not surprising that the malleable and eclectic spiritual institutions imagined in Butler's fiction would appeal to readers culturally linked to institutions that embrace the marginalized. Through close readings of *Parable of the Sower* and "The Book of Martha," I consider the value of religious and spiritual references as persuasive devices used to bridge a mystical gap between religion, SF, and the real world. Because of the probable source and employment of religion, SF and folklore in our society are a mixture that yields speculative fiction that is paramount to a mythology that is commonly accepted as truth by the populous as a means of survival.

Among Butler's many approaches to religious themes, two of her most contemporary narratives, *Parable of the Sower* (1993) and "The Book of Martha" (found in the second edition of *Bloodchild and Other Stories* [2005]), speak directly to the policing of social values via the employment of religion. In *Parable of the Sower*, Lauren Olamina leads a community of individuals up the Pacific Coast while writing and teaching a religion based on the acceptance of change and difference as God. And in "The Book of Martha," God allows Martha Bes to develop a functional utopia for humanity by augmenting the experience of individual dreams. Butler consistently develops female characters who seek the end of all oppression by understanding the movement of change and its relationship to difference and the spiritual. In *Patternmaster* (1976), Amber avoids the feudal patriarchy of the Pattern, leads Teray through an Arthurian quest, and declines a place of security and power as one of Teray's wives. In "Near of Kin" (1979), readers are persuaded to reevaluate the social taboo of incest by identifying with a nameless protagonist and her uncle/father. In *Dawn* (1987), Lilith is forced to become the spiritual leader and matriarch of a congregation that represents the only hope of survival for humanity. Religion and religious values are interrogated in all of Butler's fiction directly or indirectly because they necessarily influence the way a society defines, loves, hates, and reproduces bodies.

The female protagonists employed by Butler support the generally accepted notion that women have historically been closer to concepts of God and religion both literally and metaphorically. "By now it is so taken for granted that women are more religious than men that every competent quantitative study of religiousness routinely includes sex as a control variable" (Stark 495). The bodies of both Lauren and Martha are crucial to the existence of God in their respective narratives. For Lauren, God has no shape and every shape, as "God is Change." For Martha, her body allows God to take the form(s) as it is the image of Martha and humanity that God uses as a model and referent point. Martha's God is only limited through the existence of her bodily experience. In speaking with her God, it is both her mind and body that allow an encounter to occur. Without the human body, God has no form or shape to be perceived—just a voice giving directions. Martha has agency and the ability to shape God. "You see what your life has prepared you to see. . . . What you see is up to you, Martha. Everything is up to you" ("Book of Martha" 191). The body of God shifts, but it is Martha's body that is the more interesting as she is a woman with a familiar biblical narrative attached to her name. Butler's choice in naming her protagonist was not coincidence. Martha, the sister of Mary and Lazarus, is the perfect candidate to assist Butler's God in reconstructing the world. The Martha of Luke 10.38–423 is not easily distracted and is both a devoted and diligent worker defined by the household and the confines of Victorian gender roles. Butler writes most of the Victorian out of her Martha by replacing the four cardinal virtues of purity, piety, domesticity, and submissiveness with independence, inquisitiveness, bravery, and a sense of self-sacrifice that can only be described as biblical.

Women substantially outnumber men in conventional and nonconventional religious groups. Folklore and canonical literary tradition have long classified religion as "women's work" (Stark 496). Because of the female reproductive system and monthly menstrual cycles often associated with the moon and the power of "Mother nature," women have been imaged as having a closer link to God than their male counterparts (Walker 680). The examples of this phenomenon are numerous and widespread: Nathaniel Hawthorne's Hester in *The Scarlet Letter* can frolic about in woods that men can only fear; Mary Magdalene is said to have been closer to Jesus Christ than many of his male disciples; and the Hebrew protagonist Lilith (the first wife of Adam) has the power to speak the unspeakable name of God and defy the most sacred laws of man. Butler's writing of women necessarily engages the murky discourse of the "body" that has been a popular topic in the academy for more than a decade now. Locating the discussion of the female body in the church and religion further complicates the concept of the body as well as begins an excavation of how God is imagined concerning gender.

With the collapse of traditional patriarchy and the evolution of modern patrism, the changing status of women in society has been reflected in, among other things, the religious conceptualization of God and the social division of labor within the church between the (primarily male) priestly leadership and the (primarily female) lay membership. The old patriarchal God of traditional fundamentalism gave way initially to a more "democratic" vision of God as friend and confidant. "[Insofar as] Christianity is committed to the idea of a personal God, it has been difficult to imagine how this concept of personality could be degendered to give expression to equality between men and women" (Turner 35).

Butler's fiction successfully "(de)genders" God and, in doing so, creates a "democratic" image of God that may not be a symbol of social equality but is definitely gender friendly. Both Lauren and Martha confront gods that can be molded and shaped by the people (primarily women) who worship them. By investing her fiction in such religious themes, Butler's fiction begs the investigation of the already blurred borders of religious belief and SF.

Ingo Morth makes the claim, in "Elements of Religious Meaning in Science Fiction," that religion and SF are comparable not only by means of the formal aspects of utopia and transcendence but also by the transgressions of boundaries of knowledge, experience, and behavior. Morth suggests that SF establishes a fantasy world that literally transgresses the boundaries of everyday existence in the true sense of the word, constructing a world of different structures of meaning based on the future or an alternative environment into which the reader enters (Morth 88, 89). I would like to go a step further than Morth by suggesting the relationship of religion and science fiction, as deployed in the works of Butler, challenges the boundaries of everyday existence but does not completely transgress how religion and fantasy affect the value of bodies in the real world. Morth makes an insightful observation that, when faced with the loss of closed concepts of the world in modern times, many writers fall back on earlier interpretations of the world that are no longer controversial and easily accessible within the general stock of knowledge (Morth 91). This insight is especially poignant in the case of Butler's fiction because it consistently seeks to persuade an audience of color to reevaluate the society's method of marking bodies via gender, race, class, and so on.

The African American has historically used religion and places of worship as a device of guidance and survival. In defense of her views on religion, Butler says,

> Religion kept some of my relatives alive, because it was all they had. If they hadn't had some hope of heaven, some companionship in Jesus, they probably would have committed suicide, their lives were so hellish. But they could go to church and have that exuberance together, and that was good, the community of it. When they were in pain they had God to fall back on. I think that's what religion does for the majority of the people. (Zindell 3)

As a producer of cautionary speculative fiction speaking to an audience that has not been traditionally targeted by the genre of SF, Butler's employment of religion seems to be a stroke of genius. Until the arrival on the SF scene of African American writers like Samuel Delany and Butler, religion was easily considered to be more valid by most audiences than fantasy novels about white and metallic futures. What I would like to suggest with the term *valid* is that an audience is more likely to embrace the stories of the Bible as more "legitimate" tools to navigate the real world than stories found in "illegitimate" SF novels despite the fact that the sources of mythology in both text and genre have a very similar foundation, our collective imagination.

According to Donna Spalding Andréolle, *Parable of the Sower* is a feminist narrative of self-awakening and self-fulfillment that blurs the boundaries of SF and religion by "combining it [SF] with specific religious overtones, to describe the ascent to divine status of a young, half African American, half Mexican American woman" (119). The presence of an Old Testament God in "The Book of Martha" further signifies a familial bond, in that Martha is commanded by a shape-shifting God to avoid another apocalyptic flood by engaging in eugenic experiments that will lead to the genesis of a better humanity. Folklore, SF, and spirituality are shown to possess elements of one another and possibly to be located at the origins of each other. Butler's speculative fiction seamlessly weaves together (1) what we think we know, (2) what we don't know, and (3) what we don't want to know about ourselves. Where Martha is given the power of God, according to Andréolle,

> Lauren is a new Christ, the sower of the new seeds of Christianity, after the Armageddon which destroys the wicked civilization that has abandoned the founding beliefs of the nation. Yet *Parable of the Sower* is more than just an allegory of Christ's life transposed into imaginary, dystopian near future. (120)

Andréolle's acknowledgment of the possibility of Butler's fiction being more than allegory suggests that the fantasy world Morth claims the reader enters via SF might not be so far away from the world in which the reader already exists. Butler's fiction has consistently suggested that she not only kept a watchful eye on world news and popular culture but also analyzed it for dissemination into her startlingly speculative narratives. A society's daily response to religious beliefs—along with folklore, superstition, and supposed scientific fact—suggests that the Western imagination is unclear on the relationship between Plato's realms of the real and ideal or the material and the spiritual. Andréolle's analysis of *Parable of the Sower* asserts that "Butler is not calling the Christian worldview into question but rather, is reflecting on the validity of Judeo Christian values as the necessary ideological foundation of social order in the American imagination" (116).

In Butler's fiction, the spiritual beliefs of a character directly influence that character's ability to survive life-threatening situations throughout the narrative as religion defines the boundaries of the body. In *Parable of the Sower* this is true for the main character, Lauren Olamina, as her spiritual belief system acts as the key to not only her salvation but the salvation of all those who choose to follow her on her migration up the West Coast. Lauren's pilgrimage up the coast acts as a bodily ritual that assists her in outlining the praxis of her beliefs and the symbolic order of the Earthseed religion. The bodies of Lauren and her followers play an essential role in the formation of their religion. To call Lauren's group "motley" would be appropriate on several levels as they represent distinct difference in their varying race, class, gender, and sexual characteristics.

> Most feminist analyses of the construction of bodies attend primarily to social factors, such as gender, race, and class, but do not question how the body functions also as a map for the symbolic order. (Torjensen 946)

I would like to agree with Torjensen's observation and suggest that the bodies found in Lauren's group represent the acceptance of ambiguity that is at the foundation of the Earthseed religion. The foundation of Lauren's religious beliefs deviates from those of her African American father and his church but still have their beginnings in a Black church. Historically, Black churches have been an extremely valuable resource for Black communities in the United States since the antebellum period. The Black church was in many respects an example of Black nationalism in that they were built, financed, and controlled by African Americans. The Black church is and always has been a valuable resource for individuals and groups whose entrance into traditional social institutions of the larger (white) society has been denied (Frazier 1971).

In Butler's narratives, the church is a social construct designed to help maintain social order. This social order is often enforced by the employment of fear. In her discussion of how fear is used in Butler's fiction, Claire Curtis observes that

> Butler uses the fear of Noah and Martha to raise questions for the reader about the meaning of subordination and the qualities of secure living. If fear is not universal, then peace is not possible. Fear, for Hobbes, is built on the universal emancipator: equal vulnerability in the face of death. So, we are all naturally equal; we all fear; we are all driven to act by the same basic set of motivations. Butler is a theorist of fear. ("Theorizing Fear" 416)

Lauren acknowledges the influence of her father's church in her community despite her fear of the unknown and her evolving individual beliefs. Lauren admits that her father's church and its beliefs have not been her own for at least three years, but because of her fear of being defined as an outsider to her father's church, Lauren allows herself to be baptized and initiated into a church she has no faith in (*Parable* 6). Lauren's father and his church act as the glue that holds their deteriorating Robledo community together, at least temporarily. Reverend Olamina is the heart of the neighborhood in that it is through his faith and focus that the organization and sanity of the community is maintained. The loss of Reverend Olamina is foreshadowed by his wife's question, "What are we supposed to do if you die?" (*Parable* 69). Lauren's shift away from her father's church is a critique of the system of faith practiced by his church.

Reverend Olamina's faith is dependent on an Old Testament God that is inflexible and utterly mysterious. For Lauren, the God of the Old Testament is juvenile and mythical. She compares the Christian God to the Greek god Zeus—"a super-powered man, playing with his toys the way my youngest brothers play with toy soldiers" (14). Lauren questions both the function and practicality of her father's God.

Lauren and those who are to be the survivors of her community will need a church with a God that is not only flexible but malleable. Unlike her view of her father's Zeus-like God, Lauren's notion of God as change is both predictable and tangible. Change can be seen and accounted for in everyday life and death; change can be prepared for; change has no emotion or care to sway away from the objective. When Reverend Olamina does disappear from the Robledo community and the change that Lauren has prepared for finally arrives, the new mobile church, Earthseed, replaces the old, and the hope of survival is restored. What this replacement says to the audience of Butler's fiction is important on several levels. Lauren's new religion appears to be infinitely malleable and exclusionary only to those who do not value life and survival.

Earthseed is a set of social values that seems to borrow its best aspects from several religions across the globe, including many from her own father's church in Robledo. In this volume, Christopher Kocela's chapter, "God Is Change, Impermanence Is Buddha Nature: Religious Syncretism in Butler's Earthseed and Dōgen's Zen," supports my assertion by arguing that Lauren's insistence that "God is Change" reflects one of the best-known and unique features of Eihei Dōgen's Zen. Additionally, several parallels can be drawn between process theology and the framework of Lauren's fictional religion.

One of the main concepts of process theology is that the universe is characterized by process and change carried out by the agents of free will. Self-determination characterizes everything in the universe, not just human beings. God cannot totally control any series of events or any individual, but God influences the universal free will by offering possibilities. To say it another way, God has a will in everything, but not everything that occurs is God's will (Cobb and Griffin 9). While there are indeed similarities between the two religious doctrines, there are far too many distinctions to identify in this brief meditation. Process theology may be one of many sources visited by Butler in her creation of Lauren Olamina's very inclusive religion, Earthseed.

While clearly inclusive, Olamina's religion seems to embrace even those who might be rejected by more traditional religions and churches. Lauren's church is especially appealing to a marginalized audience because it seeks difference and is subject to change with the demands of its congregation. In addition, the demands that Lauren's church places on its congregation seem far from taxing.

> Once or twice
> each week
> A gathering of Earthseed
> is a good and necessary thing.
> It vents emotion, then quiets the mind.
> It focuses attention,
> strengthens purpose, and unifies people. (*Parable* 192)

In other words, besides attendance at the weekly gathering and understanding that the nature of God is change, preparing for God, learning from God (all synonymous with understanding one's self), there isn't a great deal of material sacrifice involved in being a member of the Earthseed religion. There are no monetary taxes, no commandments etched in stone to follow and enforce, no rejection of individuals based on different sexualities, races, genders, ages, or classes. Earthseed sounds like a utopian religion except for the very important fact that it exists because it acknowledges the impossibility of perfection and permanence. According to Claire Curtis's article "Rehabilitating Utopia: Feminist Science Fiction and Finding the Ideal," *Parable of the Sower* is an example of contemporary utopian fiction because it "recognizes the danger of perfection and in this sense differs from early more rationalist attempts to posit the best imaginable world," or in this case religion. "This is the key to the contemporary utopia: the fact that it incorporates into its own 'perfection' an acknowledgement that such perfection is simply unrealizable, but also ultimately dystopian" (Curtis 148). Lauren's church tries to systematize her observations and assumptions and act on them. With her bible, *Earthseed: The Books of the Living*, Lauren creates a manual of praxis, instead of mere faith and theory.

Butler's practice of critiquing the praxis of religion is manifest in "The Book of Martha," as Martha is asked to participate in the work of God. The marginalized audience identifies and perhaps believes in the plausibility of the "The Book of Martha" because Martha is utterly a representative of the ordinary person of color. She, like most of Butler's characters, sits on several fences regarding identity. She obviously has faith in God yet has not lived the life of a saint. She is an educated writer yet not a member of the upper-class elite because of her profession. Martha is not a traditional heroine, yet she undertakes the Herculean task of saving the world. Martha is chosen by God and Butler "for all that you [Martha] are and all that you are not" ("Book of Martha" 194). Because Martha is written as a female Job or Noah, a vessel of God, readers who associate themselves with the church are more prone to personally identify with the fictional character of Martha. In other words, the religious references found in Martha's narrative make her experience less SF or fantasy oriented and more socially allegorical.

The fiction of Butler has always involved discussions of gods and the worshippers of gods. And these discussions have always addressed the struggles of the powerful and the powerless. It began with the shape-shifting and body wearing of Anyanwu and Doro of the Patternist series and continued with the Oankali of the Xenogenesis series, all the way to the Change of the Parable series. Each representation of God interacted with those who accepted them as God until the worshipers began to see the flaws of God via the reflections of themselves. Eventually the powerless began to understand that it was they who created and shaped the Doro, the Anyanwu, the Oankali, and Change. In each of Butler's series, the powerless began to see that power is always relative and always within whoever or whatever has the initiative to seek it. Consequently, the worshippers of God usually have the potential to share the power of God.

Martha's conversation with God does not seem to deviate from Butler's long-standing narrative pattern. Martha's God needs her assistance to make humanity better. "You will help humankind to survive its greedy, murderous, wasteful adolescence. Help it to find less destructive, more peaceful, sustainable ways to live" ("Book of Martha" 192). Like the gods before, Martha's God needs the help of its creations. Like Doro, or the Oankali, the God in Martha's story is inexplicably dependent on the assistance of a worshipper who can hardly conceive of its image let alone its power. It is not coincidental that the same scenario plays out on numerous occasions in the Old Testament section of the Christian Bible. In many respects God resembles an adolescent with great potential for creation and destruction but who is ultimately the creation of parents who can never really understand what or how they have been allowed to come into existence.

"I have a great deal of work for you," he said at last. "As I tell you about it, I want you to keep three people in mind: Jonah, Job, and Noah. Remember them. Be guided by their stories." ("Book of Martha" 191)

Martha's God mentions the three well-known biblical characters who readily and hesitantly sacrificed their bodies in the service of what they believed to be the God Almighty. Somehow a God that needs from its creations is a God that is easier to believe in and to worship. Humanity seems to need to be needed even by the god(s) of humanity, which suggests a paternal/maternal love between gods and mortals. Consequently, Butler's fiction seems to employ this understanding with extreme proficiency.

Like the Oankali, Martha's God gives her an advantage over the average mortal: "You'll arrange it so that people treat one another better and treat their environment more sensibly. You'll give them a better chance to survive than they've given themselves. I'll lend you the power, and you'll do this" ("Book of Martha" 193). Martha's God lends her the power to do what she thought was impossible for all but God. The Christian God gives Moses the power to part the Red Sea, Doro gives Mary the power to create the pattern, the Oankali give Lilith the physical strength and virility of a goddess, and Change chooses Lauren as the recipient of foresight and wisdom beyond her walled Robledo community. Both King James and Butler translate and write of such a caring and compassionate God, considering the fact that they are also written as omnipotent, omniscient, and indifferent. The contradictory characteristics of God produced in religion and fiction and mythology appear to be due to the fact that God reflects those who worship gods. Ludwig Feuerbach's *The Essence of Christianity* (1841) was the first book to argue that God, or the gods, represented man's ideal and unrealized potential. In the fiction of Butler, gods are reflections of characteristics or potential, not fully realized by the followers of the many faces of socially constructed notion of a god. Despite the fact that Martha's encounter supports these assertions about the construction of God as a reflection of humanity, "she had come to like this seductive, child-like, very dangerous being" ("Book of Martha" 213).

Martha reminds us that the relationship between fantasy literature and religious myth was first brought to light by Freud's analysis of "The Extraordinary" (1919) and the psychological development of individual unconsciousness. Carl Jung then expands on Freud's personal unconscious to develop an analysis of the collective unconsciousness and its archetypes. Jung considered the fantastic to be a further expression of a comprehensive mythology of humankind (Morth 88). In other words, religion has the same origins as SF: the collective unconscious of human society. Both social constructs, religion and SF, attempt to explain, predict, and to speculate the happenings of the real world by stimulating the imaginations of real people.

According to the psychoanalyst Carl Jung, the part of the imagination or psyche that processes religion and folklore is the collective unconscious. Jung's collective unconsciousness is a sort of storage bend of human experience that all people are supposedly born with. This common reservoir of knowledge is the thing that Jung says influences all human experience and behavior. Religion, folklore, fantasy, and literature all act as evidence that common pieces of knowledge are shared among humankind. The contents of collective unconsciousness are called archetypes or the unlearned tendency to experience things in a certain way. Butler writes characters that identify with her reading audience as familiar archetypes or spiritual instincts. Jesus, Moses, Job, Paul, and Noah, for example, are all identifiable characters who demonstrate archetypes that a Black Christian audience can understand and associate with their real lives.

In his autobiography *Memories, Dreams, Reflections*, Carl Jung demonstrates through a telling of his own personal mythology how his understanding of the psyche and the psychology of religion come into being. According to Duane Bidwell's article "Carl Jung's *Memories, Dreams, Reflections*: A Critique Informed by Postmodernism," Jung uses images from forty-two of his own dreams along with those of thirteen clinical cases to develop his theories of the collective unconsciousness, the existence of archetypes (patterns of meaning that shape a person's life), and the ego or the supreme archetype (Bidwell 15). This is all to suggest that the construction of the self, God, and religion seem to be inextricable according to Jung.

Other scholars have also contemplated the relationship of myth, reality, religion, and the real world and found that mythology is a response to the mysteries of reality. W.E.B. Du Bois, for example, is quoted by Don Hufford in an article entitled "The Religious Thought of W.E.B. Du Bois," as saying,

> Religion is a theory of the ultimate constitution of the world, more particularly in its moral aspects. . . . The church, on the other hand, is the organization which writes down and from time to time rewrites the exact religious belief which is prevalent and which carries out celebrations and methods of worship. (Hufford 74)

Du Bois's quote, taken from *The Crisis* (October 1933), speaks directly to what Butler's character Lauren, from *Parable of the Sower*, does throughout her trek up the West Coast toward Canada. *Earthseed: The Books of the Living* becomes an instructional manual on how to practice what seems to be an inclusive theology based on the acceptance of difference and the inevitability of change. In a very literal sense, Lauren becomes a traveling evangelist spreading her brand of salvation like the Christian archetypes Paul or Jesus. As a sort of "jack-leg" preacher, Lauren easily identifies with African American Christian readers associating a fictional account with the historical fact of migrating Black bodies up the East Coast as well as the midwestern United States. Lauren's pilgrimage mimics a familiar historical narrative reminiscent of the migration of marginalized people due to religious persecution.

> For any fictional narration to attain the level of cultural myth, it must possess three features: assemble common beliefs of culture which are grounded in historical experience; give central focus to a historically representative figure of the community; be capable of evolving with the culture. (Slotkin, "Fatal Environment" 435)

> The utopian/dystopian narrative of survival and reconstruction, as epitomized in *A Gift Upon the Shore* and *Parable of the Sower*, illustrates the American cultural myth of progress and the powerful eschatological vision of the Puritan American self. (Andréolle 115)

The historical experiences of African Americans are peppered throughout all of Butler's fiction. Butler's writing easily taps into the eschatological vision of the African American self because it necessarily considers the physical and spiritual condition of dark bodies in the past, present, and future. The African American soul is not in the jeopardy it was in before the arrival of African American SF writers. Butler's fiction does not require the death of marginalized bodies in her fiction as did more traditionally white-dominated moments in the genre. Both *Parable* and "Martha" are narratives that assemble common beliefs that are grounded in a historically marginalized struggle for survival. Lauren and Martha represent common women in their respective communities who are identifiable with a contemporary reading audience. All of Butler's fiction is capable of evolving with contemporary American culture because it is necessarily a product of American experience.

As utopian/dystopian narratives of survival and reconstruction, both the *Parable* novel and the short story "The Book of Martha" speak to a broad audience by virtue of universal points of appeal. However, the African American reader is uniquely targeted by Butler's fiction via images, scenarios, and cultural experiences that are common to an African American experience that is shared more lucidly by marginalized people. The employment of religious and or spiritual archetypes functions as a device of validation and transformation of cautionary tales to realistic speculation that might be heeded given the right circumstance. Consequently, Butler's employment of religious themes supports the reevaluation of an entire genre by marginalized audiences previously uninterested in SF.

NOTE

Chapter 1 "Religious Science Fiction: Butler's Changing God" is reprinted from Chapter 5 of *Changing Bodies in the Fiction of Octavia Butler: Slaves, Aliens, and Vampires* by Gregory Jerome Hampton (Lexington Books, 2010). Used by permission of Rowman & Littlefield.

WORKS CITED

Aldiss, Brian W. *Trillion Year Spree: The History of Science Fiction*. Avon Books, 1986.

Andréolle, Donna Spalding. "Utopias of Old, Solutions for the New Millennium: A Comparative Study of Christian Fundamentalism in M. K. Wren's *A Gift Upon the Shore* and Octavia Butler's *Parable of the Sower*." *Utopian Studies*, vol. 12, no. 2, 2001, pp. 114–123.

Asimov, Isaac. *Foundations*. Doubleday. 1951.

———. *Nebula Award Stories 8*. Panther Books, 1973, preface.

Bidwell, Duane R. "Carl Jung's Memories, Dreams, Reflections: A Critique Informed by Postmodernism." *Pastoral Psychology*, vol. 49, no. 1, 2000, pp. 13–20.

Butler, Octavia E. *Bloodchild and Other Stories*. Seven Stories Press, 2005.

———. *Parable of the Sower*. 1993. Grand Central, 2000.

Cobb, John B., Jr., and David R. Griffin. *Process Theology: An Introductory Exposition*. Westminster Press, 1976.

Curtis, Claire P. "Rehabilitating Utopia: Feminist Science Fiction and Finding the Ideal." *Contemporary Justice Review*, vol. 8, no. 2, June 2005, pp. 147–152.

———. "Theorizing Fear: Octavia Butler and the Realist Utopia." *Utopian Studies*, vol. 19, no. 3, 2008, pp. 411–431.

Frazier, E. Franklin. *The Negro Church in America*. Schocken Books, 1974.

Heinlein, Robert A. "Science Fiction: Its Nature, Faults and Virtues." *The Science Fiction Novel: Imagination and Social Criticism*, edited by B. Davernport, Advent Publishers, 1969, pp. 21–30.

———. *Stranger in a Strange Land*. Putnam Press, 1961.

Hufford, Don. "The Religions Thought of W.E.B. Du Bois." *Journal of Religious Thought*, 1997, vol. 53/54, no. 1/2, 1997, pp. 73, 22.

Luckhurst, Roger. *Science Fiction: Cultural History of Literature*. Polity Press, 2005.

Morth, Ingo. "Elements of Religious Meaning in Science Fiction Literature." *Social Compass*, vol. 34, no. 1, 1987, pp. 87–122.

Roberts, Adam. *The History of Science Fiction*. Palgrave Macmillan Press, 2005.

———. "Remembering Toni Morrison." *Fresh Air*. NPR, 9 Aug. 2019, www.npr.org/podcasts/344098539/fresh-air._

Stark, Rodney. "Physiology and Faith: Addressing the 'Universal' Gender Difference in Religious Commitment." *Journal of the Scientific Study of Religion*, vol. 41 no. 3, 2002, pp. 495–507.

Torjensen, Karen Jo. "Genders, Book Review, Bodies, Religion: Adjunct Proceedings of the XVIIth Congress for the History of Religions." Edited by Sylvia Marcos. ALER Publications, 2000. Found in *Journal of the American Academy of Religion*, vol. 69, no. 4, 2001, pp. 945–948.

Toth, John F. "Power and Paradox in an African American Congregation." *Review of Religious Research*, vol. 40, no. 3, 1999, pp. 213–229.

Turner, Bryan S. "The Body in Western Society: Social Theory and its Perspective." *Religion and the Body*, edited by Sarah Coakley, Cambridge University Press, 2000, pp. 15–41.

Walker, Alice. *In Search of Our Mothers' Gardens*. Harcourt Brace Jovanovich, Publishers, 1983.

Zimmer, Marion. "Interview with Octavia Butler." *Marion Zimmer Bradley's Fantasy Magazine*, July 2005, www.adherents.com/people/pb/Octavia_Butler.html.

Zindell, David. "Octavia Butler: Persistence." *Locus Magazine*, June 2000, www.locusmag.com/2000/issues/06/Butler.html.

2

Transreligious World Building

Hindu Evocations in Octavia Butler's Lilith's Brood

APARAJITA NANDA

Ten years after her death, Octavia Butler's books continue to transcend the boundaries of genre, solidifying her place in the canon of African American literature. Hailed as the preeminent African American science fiction writer, she won multiple Hugo and Nebula Awards and was the first science fiction author to earn a MacArthur Fellowship (a.k.a., the "Genius Grant"). Literary critics have focused especially on how Butler's themes of power and control speak to issues of race, gender, and sexuality in groundbreaking ways that reconfigure representations of bondage and freedom from servitude in a science fiction world. Relatively less critical attention has been directed toward her exploration of religion. In *Conversations with Octavia Butler*, a set of interviews compiled by Consuela Francis, Butler, despite her professed atheism and aversion to religion as an instrument of hate and persecution, reveals a qualified respect for religion as a source of inspiration.

> "I've met science fiction people," she says. "Oh, well, [they say], we're going to outgrow [religion]. I don't believe that for one moment. It seems that religion has kept us focused and helped us to do any number of very difficult things, from building pyramids and cathedrals to holding together countries, in some instances. . . . I'm not saying it's a force for *good*—it's just a force. So why not use it to get you to the stars." (182–183)

In Butler's literature, religion is more than a set of beliefs about the universe with a corresponding moral code. Her depiction is far more progressive and radical. She advocates for change—where God is chaos, and ethos is change. Critics have argued that Christianity forms the basis of Butler's Earthseed religion in the *Parable of the Sower* and *Parable of the Talents*. Donna Spalding Andréolle calls "Earthseed . . . a sort of new-found Christianity based on the principle 'God is Change'" (114). Lauren Olamina, the charismatic founder of Earthseed in these novels, writes, "We do not worship God" (*Parable of the Sower* 17). The new religion asks its followers, instead, to "perceive and attend," to "learn from," to "shape God," "adapt," and "endure" (*Parable of the Sower* 17). These functional words abolish a passive, reverential worship of God. For Butler, God is dynamic and functional. I propose that in her writing, Butler actively works out a philosophy in which spirituality meets religion, a *practicing world view* that creates, accommodates, and embraces the principle of radical change. This practical approach to religion, where religion is defined as a way of active life, characterizes Hinduism. Furthermore, I suggest that in order to appreciate how this is so, one must read her work in light of Hindu mythological deities—Brahma, Vishnu, Maheshwar, Kali, and Durga—and her use of certain terms from Sanskrit, the ancient language of Hinduism. It is through these elements that we can glimpse the active, progressive presence of Hinduism dwelling within and among the more obvious Christian-derived religious picture in Butler's novels. As distinct from a faith-based inertia that merely submits itself to divine authority, Butler's imaginative project of change, which runs from Earthseed to and through *Lilith's Brood*, calls for apocalyptic destruction and the promise of change in its aftermath.

Though religion and science fiction may seem to be unlikely partners, the limitless possibilities offered by science fiction often provide fertile ground for exploring theological questions. As Steven Hrotic asserts in *Religion in Science Fiction*, one of the intriguing paradoxes of the science fiction genre is the symbiotic relationship it has enjoyed with religion since the 1920s. Before World War II, science fiction often used religion as a superstructure, but it never engaged with theological issues. Today, religious science fiction exists as a subgenre that delves into and explores notions of world ending, typical of apocalyptic and postapocalyptic science fiction, opening up myriad religious questionings. For instance, Walter Miller's *Canticle for Leibowitz* (1959) examines the role of Catholicism in a futuristic, postapocalyptic world. In Octavia Butler's own postapocalyptic world, change becomes the impetus behind Olamina's Earthseed religion. Earthseed recognizes that change is possibly the only constant in life: it is "the only lasting truth," as Lauren puts it in *Earthseed: The Books of the Living*, where "God is Change," adaptability and persistence are key, and where the "Self must create / Its own reasons for being" for "to shape God, [is to] shape Self" (*Parable of the Sower* 3, 258).

This new religion recognizes the human predicament and offers practical solutions based on the imperative of change; like Hinduism, this change recognizes the need for movement and regeneration brought forth by destruction and chaos. This reincarnative need is repetitive, but not erratic.

Butler's religious imagination is an all-inclusive one. Gregory Hampton observes that "[Butler] not only kept a watchful eye on world news . . . [but shaped] Earthseed [as] a set of social values that seems to borrow its best aspects from several religions across the globe" (89, 91). Critics have documented Butler's wide-ranging interests in religious thought and practice explored across cultures (Allen). Knowing she studied world religions does enable us to say with documentary evidence that the influence of other religions formed an integral part of her authorial intentions. Given her preoccupation with African myths and folklore and interest in Nubian culture, one may safely assume that Butler was motivated by the religions of the East in general (Keenan). We can already perceive the impact of Hinduism on Lauren Olamina's thoughts, when she encourages action rather than simple faith in divinity. Reading her work in light of Hindu religious thought and practice shows how her imaginative project breaks free of the confines of oppressive Christian beliefs and practice. Butler's religious imagination enthusiastically adopts certain traits of Hinduism—its philosophy of cyclical change from chaos to cosmos, ritualistic rites that demand a forfeiture of individual ego to embrace hybridity, the avatars or combinative nonhuman animal entities, a coalitional community connected by the life-force that flows through all living beings—as part of the Oankali world view in *Lilith's Brood*. While this paper does not claim that Butler directly imported Hinduism into her works, it forefronts the influence of Hinduism on her writing to offer a new critical framework in Butlerian studies that challenges the readings of *Lilith's Brood* that label the Oankali as colonial oppressors. In fact, such a schema allows us to appreciate the depth and scope of Butler's religious imagination as illuminated by an alternate belief system that provides not only a blended epistemology but also a new transnational lens to reshape the world.

Critiques of Earthseed (as merely a New Age version of Christianity) often forestall an understanding of Butler's thinking about and through change as the foundation of a world view and accompanying spiritual practice. *Lilith's Brood* needs to be reconsidered for the centrality it gives to change, a central precept in Hindu religion and myth, even while suggesting feminist revisions to locate kinds of change that bring about coalitional relationships. The Xenogenesis trilogy, republished as *Lilith's Brood* (consisting of *Dawn*, *Adulthood Rites*, and *Imago*), presents a war-fueled apocalypse in which humanity has nearly brought about its own demise and the ruin of its worldly environment. The Oankali, a nomadic, gene-trading alien species, rescue the few surviving humans with the intention of interbreeding with them to create a superior breed of human-Oankali hybrids in an environmentally viable milieu. Lilith Iyapo, an African American woman kept in an Oankali-induced coma for centuries, is awakened and instructed to convince the humans to join the Oankali agenda and happily procreate with them. From the Oankali point of view, the result of this process would be the annihilation of the pure human species and the creation of the hybrid human-Oankali entities Akin and Jodahs, protagonists of the last two books of the trilogy.

Lilith's Brood, written during the era of Ronald Reagan's arms race with the Soviet Union, was Butler's answer to what she calls the "self-annihilating mindset" of humans. In the panel discussion Science Future and Science Fiction held at UCLA in 2002, Butler spoke about dangers inherent in blind technological advancement that refuses to weigh the ethical repercussions of such an agenda. She pointed out that we need wisdom to do the right thing with the new tools that science offers us. In fact, even more than wisdom, we need "breaks" from technological progress and overt mechanization in the effort "to change human beings"; these "breaks," she clarified, reside in religion. Sustaining these breaks, she argued, will not be easy, but humanity needs them to survive and grow out of their hierarchical, destructive desire latent in Reagan's speech of a "winnable war," an attempt at what I term a *nuclear colonization*.

Butler's trilogy begins with colonial evocations, for, after all, the Oankali are gene traders whose civilizing mission is their attempt at genetically mutating humans. The scientific knowledge they lay claim to and the environmental concerns they address seek to justify their plan. Humans, they claim, need to be purged of the "Human Contradiction"—a combination of intelligence and hierarchical thinking—and they should accept a genetic elimination of the violent trait to produce a sustainable, creolized third identity: a human-Oankali construct in an ecologically sustainable zone (*Lilith's Brood* 442). The humans face a difficult choice: either comply with the Oankali agenda or face extinction. Some of the humans submit to the aliens; others resist, driven by the hope of conceiving and bearing human children.

The injustice of the Oankali agenda has been argued, given their enforced reproductive restrictions on the humans, as well as their tendency to treat them as experimental animals in service to a eugenic agenda. On the other hand, the Oankali insist on trading genes, a fair trade as compared to the alternative of taking or seizing them; they aim at crossing boundaries and borders for mutual benefit, so all species become a part of the Oankali belief of embracement. They preach a religion that is organic and call for a collective environmental affiliation and citizenship, which includes the religious, the secular, the social, and the political. In all, a deep sense of ambiguity shrouds the Oankali and their venture (J. Miller, Slonczewski).

However holistic this philosophy may seem, Oankali philosophy insists on destruction for new life to be born. In the process of genetic mutation, justified by the Oankali claim of eliminating the human gene of hierarchy and violence to combine with a symbiotic merging with other species, new species are formed. In this way, there is a destruction of identity as it is rooted in biology; rebirth thus entails a kind of sacrificial abolition of a being and a way of being. This process offers a striking reflection of Hinduism and its embrace of cyclical change, from destruction to regeneration, as the sustenance of the universe. In addition, multiplication of life in Hinduism is only possible when destruction of a static past is imminent; the reincarnative births in Hinduism occur only through the destruction that happens at the end of each life cycle. This evokes the regenerative process in *Lilith's Brood*—Butler's proposition of an *ecotone*, a new planetary environment where humans can adapt to a mutually beneficial life with other species, embracing diversity as a form of subsistence. Once again, the deep connection of nature with religion alludes to Hindu philosophy and its approach to ecology in the *Brhadaranyaka Upanishad* 6.3.6. I suggest that Butler's all-embracing sustainable zone is an imaginative play on Hindu tantric and yogic traditions that teach how to unite with the entire universe, which in itself is a manifestation of divine energy. Hinduism offers a powerful ideological counter to the link between colonialism and Christianity, a counter that focuses predominantly on mixing and change. I propose that Butler evokes this dynamic, however subtly, in *Lilith's Brood*—in a way that opens the novel up to new transnational and transreligious interpretations.

Constructing Hinduism

Hinduism, which dates to the second millennium B.C.E., is not a system of religious doctrines; it is a way of life, of "faiths and cumulative traditions" (Smith 26). Religion, as Timothy Fitzgerald insists, is a Western term with a Western history. Thus, approaching Hinduism with preconceived, nineteenth-century Protestant Christian ideas of "a single text, a single savior figure, a monotheistic god, prompting moral behavior," Sharada Sugirtharajah argues, is erroneous (74). European scholars acknowledged the religious diversity of Hinduism but saw it as sign of weakness. Richard King, commenting on the Orientalist debate as established by Edward Said, points out that labeling Hinduism as "mystical, irrational, uncivilized and feminine" was a deliberate ploy by the British, who colonized India for almost 250 years in order to control and dominate the native population (3). There was a colonial endeavor to construct a Hindu self-understanding that deliberately prioritized Sanskrit texts and Brahmanic teachings over indigenous folk texts to essentialize Hinduism (Oddie). The purpose was to alienate any indigenous contributions to Hinduism and idolatrous practices of worship in everyday Hindu life, thereby molding it into an elitist religion exclusive to the British-controlled Brahman priests.

Rituals and the Brahmanic interpretation of rituals played a very important role in Hinduism. In Hinduism, the three paths (*marga*) to follow in life are the paths of ritual and sacrifice (*karma-marga*), the path of knowledge (*jnana-marga*), and the way of devotional participation (*bhakti-marga*). Hindu life-cycle rituals (*samskara*) include initiation rites, marriage vows, ancestral worship, and rituals to be performed for the deceased. As Axel Michaels states, "Hindu India is special in that ritual surpasses belief and that surviving in such a socio-religious environment is only possible through participation in a great number of rituals" (2). *Mimamsa* in Sanskrit means "reflection" or "critical investigation." One of the six systems or views (*darshan*) of Hindu philosophy, Mimamsa aims to provide rules for interpreting the Vedas and the observance of Vedic rituals. As Mimamsa deals with the earlier part of the Vedas, known as Karmakanda (episode of action), it is also referred to as Purva Mimamsa (prior study) or Karma-Mimamsa (study of action).

My own reading of Hinduism, in response to the above, is syncretic. I recognize the Brahmanic texts—the Vedas, the *Vedanta*, and the Bhagavad Gita (Sanatana Dharma)—along with the ritualistic rites that form essential parts of Hinduism. However, I also advocate for recognition of the agency of folk religions, oral traditions, rituals, and contributions of women, thereby acknowledging the polythetic nature of Hinduism created by these overlapping areas. I propose that Hinduism combines the voices of authority and control found in Brahmanic texts and ritualistic rites *with* the indigenous folklore tradition that expressed the "social, political and psychological needs of the [masses], needs that were often distorted by the priestly elites that usually managed and controlled the religions" (Lorenzen 27). That Hinduism recognizes both traditions is represented in the way Sanskrit in postcolonial India transitions from a Brahmanic exclusivity to a domestic language used by women in everyday worship (*pujas*) and chanting (mantras) at home. As Brahman men forsook their Sanskrit calling and devoted time to what Laurie L. Patton dubs "minefields of technology," Sanskrit became a "*stri dharma*—the duty of women" (87).

This expansive sense of religion that we find in Hinduism opens alternate spaces in which Butler queries and challenges dogmatic adherence to patriarchal

Christianity. Butler wrestles with religion as an authoritarian doctrine of oppression, and her works, inspired by the scope of her religious imagination, transcend historicity, to take us beyond the Foucauldian critique of progressive energy recaptured by regressive discourse. She conflates her critique of Christianity with her espousal of a Hindu-inspired outlook that resonates through her tropes to create a spiritual philosophy and practice, a lens to revisualize and reconfigure a world view.

Butlerian World Building

Butler's world view is an extension of the real world, and she seeks to provide/suggest future directions for human survival in the present terms of Hinduism, where once orthodox Christianity had fueled colonial endeavors. The aesthetic appeal of these fictional spaces is combined with the social function of science fiction that calls for a sense of social and civic responsibility. Religion often plays a crucial role in civic society; as Jacques Derrida observes, religion is responsibility, or it is nothing at all. It is through language that all religious tenets are conveyed to the societal elite and the masses. As the primary tool of communication, language has an important role in Butler's alternate world building as she creates a "hybridized" language—English interpolated/interpellated with Sanskrit, the language of communication in Hinduism—to accommodate that vision.

Butler's use of Sanskrit words, some in mutated forms, in her characters' names establishes the importance of this Hindu language within the Butlerian matrix. Both Akin and Jodahs are called "Eka" and "Oeka," which in Sanskrit means "alone"—even "lonely" (*Lilith's Brood* 450, 547). Both Akin and Jodahs are defined by isolation, and their narratives are ruled by a want of bonding with the other. Akin, denied a connection with his Oankali sibling, establishes a cultural liaison with his human others. Jodahs, with his human mates, moves this discourse to a level of sexual intimacy that transforms it into a treatise of intense dependence on the other. Both Akin and Jodahs encourage a coalitional relationship among humans, animals, and plants, emphasizing the interconnectivity of all living beings and a demand to embrace difference. Additionally, the naming of the alien Oankali is complex and combines the creators, preservers, and destroyers of the Earth. The word *Oankali* can be split into the Sanskrit *Oan*, which represents the gods of the Hindu trinity, and *Kali*, the name of a Hindu goddess, a destructive incarnation of Shakti (strength) and Durga. The trinity comprises Brahma (the creator), Vishnu (the preserver), and Maheshwar (the destroyer) and the cyclical mode of creation, preservation, and destruction that defines the continuity of the world.

The role of Lilith, Butler's stern yet caring mother-protagonist, combines a complex Hindu deific stance with the everyday role of Hindu women. Lilith is at once the destructive incarnation of Kali and the preservative one of Durga. Lilith, the mother, always has her progeny's welfare in mind and uses all her linguistic skills to try to convince her human wards to join the Oankali fold. Unlike Kali, Lilith does not partake in violent acts, but she does use violence to stop sexual attacks by humans, revealing the necessity of violence, what Sarah Outterson calls "violence transmuted, not overcome" (441). This recurrent trope of violence is a necessity in Butler's world, a world that recalls but does not necessarily conform to the colonial endeavor of the civilizing mission that in the name of pedagogy justified violent interventions and the annexation of indigenous people's lives. In Lilith's more caring incarnation, she reminds one of Parvati, a gentler version of Durga, as she nurses and cares for her human wards, waiting for them to "learn and run" from the Oankali. Being human, Lilith is conversant with the language of communication (English), but it is her desire to learn the Oankali tongue that prompts her to ask Nikanj for writing implements. Given her status as the primary Oankali agent to convince the humans to join the Oankali fold, Lilith's desire to learn the Oankali language introduces possibilities of Lilith being a mediator of languages, too. As a cultural facilitator, Lilith recalls the role women played in postcolonial India to familiarize Sanskrit in everyday life in their domestic sphere of beliefs and rituals.

As in Hinduism, the performance of rites is essential to attaining adulthood in Oankali culture as already indicated by the title of the trilogy's second book, *Adulthood Rites*. Akin, Lilith's construct child, fails to bond with Tiikuchahk, his Oankali sibling, a failure that forever denies Akin the rituals he must perform to come of age. The title of the novel *Adulthood Rites* invites the reading of the narrative as a rite of passage. In view of Akin's in-between position, which is both destiny and innovation, his role transcends doctrine, incorporating mutability into the discourse. We gain a fascinating insight into Akin's mind when his bonding with Tiikuchahk fails, as the text wistfully notes:

> No lie could be told successfully in this intimate form of communication. The only way to avoid unpleasant truths was to avoid communication— to say nothing. But Tiikuchahk already knew. It repelled him and yet drew him in such an incomprehensible, uncomfortable way that he did not like to be near [Tiikuchahk] at all. (*Lilith's Brood* 436)

A successful performance of certain sexual ritualistic rites would have qualified Akin for the "intimate form of communication" with his sibling. The closeness of this very domestic situation between siblings that demands truth and only truth is for Akin now a fake, "uncomfortable" space that constantly reminds him of a lost cause, a failure to perform a crucial ritualistic rite of passage. For Akin, there is no escape though, as he is permanently trapped in what he calls an "incomprehensible" situation: simultaneously attracted and repelled by his sibling. Significantly, for this context, truth or *satyam* forms the core value of Hindu religious and spiritual practice. *Satyam*, or true being is a three-syllabled word, *sa*, *ti*, and *yam*. The *Briihadaranyaka Upanishad* (5.5.1) points out that *sat*, Purusha or Brahman, and *yam*, Prakriti or movement are essential to attain *moksha*, or liberation. However, *ti*, "untrue," refers to mortality and beingness. In my reading, though *ti* is flanked by truth, the protector and guardian of life, it threatens the attainment of this rite of passage. This passage suggests a reading of rites, as possibly Butler does, as something that transcends doctrine, incorporating mutability.

The same sense of frustration and fascination defines Akin's relationship with the resister humans as we move from Akin's intimate sphere, what I call domestic, to the public arena. Akin's abduction by some human resisters exposes him to human brutality, but his forced stay in the resister camps also builds bonds of affection. Despite being lost in this dilemma of intense animosity and ardent attraction, Akin ultimately sympathizes with the humans who have been denied reproductive rights. Akin, at this point, possesses what John Zavos, in a colonial milieu, calls a "supra-local identit[y]" (67). In precolonial India, Hindus often expanded their views through interaction and communication with people of other religions, for example, Muslims. Hindus often became very vocal spokespeople for the community and inhabited public spaces to articulate their religious beliefs. In time, they became a significant force that had a huge impact on the communal identity (Zavos 61, 62). Zavos asserts that their "supra-local identities" were born of interaction, not religious impositions. These interactive spaces often opened new possibilities for the "representation of religion as a facet of social and political life" that forged new group identities (Zavos 58). Akin inhabits similar spaces of "complex alliances . . . progressive, regressive and oppressive," as he intercedes between the Oankali and humans (57–58). He becomes a spokesperson for the humans, his belief born from an interactive space of social communication and political astuteness.

Even in his prenatal state, Akin is a relational identity, evoking the Hindu avatar, for after all he is both human and Oankali by birth. He looks human but has Oankali epistemological traits. As Butler introduces Akin in the body of a human, she combines human bodily functions with Oankali intellectual characteristics. Akin's tongue fulfills human functions, but even as Lilith nurses him, "he tasted her flesh as well as her milk . . . [and] focused all his attention on probing [her flesh]" (*Lilith's Brood* 256). The tongue delivers knowledge of cell structures and DNA. As an Oankali tool of empathy, it also channels the pain he causes others. The tongue can also act as a lethal weapon. Akin's knowledge is deeply embedded in what the Oankali call a "certainty of the flesh," a transference of knowledge through the interconnectedness of living beings, be they human, animal, or hybridized aliens. The multiple functions of the tongue remind one of Lilith's hybridized language, one that fulfills the simultaneous need of her go-between role as overseer and nurturer.

In Akin, Butler challenges "the oppositions between body and mind, nature and culture" (Alaimo 53). This merging of both nature and culture is what Maris Sormus calls the "natural cultural," an "intra-active becoming of the natural and the cultural, confirming the new materialist idea that there is no solid ground on which to stand but a dynamic world" (43). Born and bred an Oankali, Akin blurs alien-like qualities with human ones, as his consciousness becomes a site of struggle between his Oankali and human concerns. Initially he is shocked at the "mix of intense emotions (fright and anger)," but then a chance remembrance dawns on him. He remembers Lilith's anger, one that "had always frightened him, and yet here it was inside him" (321). As he strives to understand this human emotion, he remembers his mother's advice: if faced with a choice, he should "go the Oankali way. Embrace difference" (329). This incident opens up unique connective possibilities: as Akin embraces "difference," he utilizes his Oankali traits to understand his human "Other." Despite being part Oankali, Akin reverses the marks of colonialism that are embedded in the way the Other is defined, in the colonial categorizing and classifying of knowledge about the colonized being under their direct control. Akin's deeply networked communication with the Akjai, pure-breed Oankali, allows all the Oankali participants to act as knowledge producers as the discourse dismantles the segregated, exclusive Brahmanic knowledge bank encouraged by the colonizers.

Akin's mind is a space of combinative qualities both human and Oankali. To maintain peace, keeping with his nonviolent Oankali traits, Akin lies to Tino's parents that the killer of Tino, a human who had strayed over to the Oankali camp, is dead. The overwhelming pain Akin experiences upon witnessing human suffering generates the wish to alleviate it and forces him to question why humans choose death over the Oankali option of genetic healing. Ultimately, he realizes that the Oankali choice of genetic healing does not merely alleviate suffering for the humans but comes at the cost of denying humans their right to reproduction. As a result, Akin's musings lead him to question the Oankalis' restrictive clause that denies humans reproductive rights. This understanding, in turn, helps him to realize how vital the right to reproduce is for humans. As he tells Dehkiaht, his ooloi (a subadult Oankali), "Let them fail. Let them have the freedom to do that, at least" (*Lilith's Brood* 456).

As Akin decides to become the spokesperson for humans, he embodies what the Oankali political process calls a "melding of entities." He understands that "he was Oankali enough to be listened to by other Oankali and Human enough to know that resister Humans were being treated with cruelty and condescension" (*Lilith's Brood* 396). By virtue of his hybridity, Akin can communicate what he feels *organically* (through interbody neural connections) to all the residents of the Oankali shuttle, through the Akjai, a pure-breed Oankali. What Akin and the humans suffered at Phoenix, the resister settlement, and what Akin learned there about humankind reflexively *become* the *experience* of everyone on the Oankali shuttle. Akin's own experience of knowing his "Other" is passed on through knowledge he acquired by way of social interaction during his sojourn in the human resister camps. This intrabody communication recalls the communicative powers of "supra-local identities" discussed earlier. The way Akin communicates with the Oankali community through the Akjai and how the Akjai "broadcasts [Akin's] bewilderment" portrays intraspecies communication at its best, one that succeeds in convincing the Oankali community to give the humans another chance to breed on Mars.

The last novel of the trilogy, *Imago*, offers a compelling turn to the concept of the "supra-local" identity. It focuses on Jodahs, Lilith's genderless progeny, the first ooloi child born of the Oankali-human interbreeding. Jodahs incarnates the Hindu *advaita* philosophy of nondualism, in which the dichotomy of the Self and the Other is "transcended" into an awareness that is "centerless [and] without dichotomies" (Milne 176). However, there is a primary difference. Whereas *advaita-vada*, the philosophy of nonduality, prioritizes the *atma*, or soul, Jodahs expresses the advaita nondualism through the discourse of the body. Jodahs marks a milestone in the human-Oankali birth process: the genetic mix able to reproduce itself without any intervention from the traditional ooloi. Unlike Akin, who was an Oankali-human construct, Jodahs is a subadult Oankali born of Oankali and human genetic mixing. Whereas Akin's mixed birth makes him a skilled orator who is adept at communicating his beliefs when he needs to, Jodahs does not need language to convince humans. With Jodahs we move into a physical zone that prioritizes politics of the body. The narrative looks ahead at a reconciliation between the humans and the aliens, as the humans willingly participate with

Jodahs, drawn by its talents of physical shape changing and subtle bodily seductions.

Yet shattering boundaries has its dangers. That this transgression can cause harm haunts Jodahs, as it understands that it is "a flawed ooloi . . . [a] flawed genetic engineer—one who could destroy with a touch" (*Lilith's Brood* 524, 542). Jodahs is frighteningly dependent on others—it even takes on "the sex of the parent [it] had felt most drawn to" (*Lilith's Brood* 538). Once it enters the realm of sexual maturity, its body changes according to its desire for its mate. This shape changing of Jodahs's is an ongoing process that later becomes an absolute need for the participant. Patricia Melzer points out that Jodahs and its sibling Aaor's physical transformations are representations of Butler's version of *imago dei*, where "God is a trickster and changer, molds and is molded by others. For Butler, adaptability and persuasion are next to godliness" (94). In fact, Melzer clarifies that "Butler's un-human figures supersede conventional definitions as she incorporates elements of fantasy and mythology" to create new entities (70).

I would like to extend Melzer's definition to claim that Butlerian hybrids like Jodahs, replete in their adaptive and persuasive qualities, resemble the avatars, reincarnations of God in animal and/or human form, in Hindu mythology. Indeed, combinative identities are prevalent in Hindu mythology in the *Puranas*, as the god Vishnu reincarnates himself into animal form (*Srimad Bhagavata*). Every divine reincarnation happens in animal form: a fish, a tortoise, a boar, or *narashimha* (half man, half beast). God's reincarnation as an animal elevates the latter to a status of divine empowerment, endorsing the sacredness of Nature. Vandana Shiva, the noted environmentalist, highlights the message of these Vedic stories: "They prepare us for the worst and create hope for another period. . . . The stories are about caution, about boundaries, about the sacred, and above all about hope, because they tell us all these things have happened before" (Prime 131). Two interesting points can be gleaned from the quote: the redrawing of the human-animal boundary and the prophetic projection of things to come. In the world view that Butler proposes in Lauren Olamina's flexible articles of faith, "God is Change." In the *Parable of the Sower*, Lauren writes, "Why is the universe? / To shape God. / Why is God? / To shape the universe" (78). One can read the ancient advaita-vada (nondualistic philosophy) of Hinduism in Butler's close identification of God with the universe or the universe as a manifestation of God. Pantheism also accepts the worship of all gods. Some nineteenth-century theologians thought pantheism was "so exact a representation of the ideas of the Vedanta, that [one] might have suspected its founder to have borrowed the fundamental principles of his system from the Hindus" (Goldstucker 32).

Advaita-vada underscores Butler's conceptualization of the posthuman body as a conduit of ever-changing possibilities, one marked by chaos or violence in its claim to epistemology. From the outset of the second book, *Adulthood Rites*, Butler challenges the humanist claim to absolute knowledge as she introduces the relational self that draws on knowledge of the human and the animal, which moves through Akin and seeks completion in Jodahs. In *Imago*, Jodahs begins "to study [its mother's] flesh in a way [it] never had before" (*Lilith's Brood* 539). Jodahs clearly distinguishes that "humans thought this sort of thing was a matter of authority" (*Lilith's Brood* 545). "Constructs and Oankali," it adds, "knew it was a matter of physiology," thereby overturning human claims that knowledge comes to us exclusively through the mind and intellect (*Lilith's Brood* 545). On the other end of the spectrum, *Imago* ends with a sense of tender moments shared not only with Jodahs's human mates but also with the natural habitat, as it plants the seeds in a "spot near the river" (*Lilith's Brood* 746). As Jodahs brings it out of its body and plants it in the "rich soil of the riverbank," there begins a burgeoning of "independent life" (*Lilith's Brood* 746). Butler transcends the human-animal divide by connecting the birth of the "animal-oriented" posthuman species to the environment—one that can be read as a nod to the deep ecological connection of Hinduism, which reminds one of Butler's critique of Christianity.

Butler, in my opinion, ultimately proposes the Hindu concept of prana, a Sanskrit word often referred to as "life-force" or "life energy," as an antidote to human pride. Prana flows through humans, animals, and plants, emanating from and going back to its essential source in godhood as represented in the Bhagavad Gita and the Vedas. In Hinduism, man needs to reject the *aham*—the egotistical principle that produces the notion of the personal ego—to relate to the universe and cultivate an environmental citizenship. This connection with others is what informs Butler's Oankali and their seeking to transform a war-torn earth into a sustainable community. Maybe this was Butler's "test" of our embrace of transformative destruction. Because the environmental concerns of aliens are superior to those of humans, the aliens attempt to help humans deal with what is termed the "Human Contradiction," a predisposition toward arrogance that emanates from the human ego (*Lilith's Brood* 442). The trilogy's ethical underpinnings initiate a rethinking of humans and the relationship of humanity to its environment. Apart from offering a critique of the environmental crisis humanity is facing today, Butler provides a compelling vision of how to move ahead. The answer resides in the "interconnection" of all species and a collective environmental citizenship, an interconnection evident already in the Hindu principles and names informing Butler's fictional world.

In *Lilith's Brood*, Butler seeks to destabilize the voice of power, its claim to absolute knowledge and its tendency to divide by classification. Indeed, institutionalized religion attempts to endorse fixed, doctrinal renderings through the deliberate ordering and channeling of human life. At a glance, Butler woos chaos in her religion of change. Yet Butler's religion is not one of a reverence for chaos. Rather, it proposes a syncretic world view that draws ideas from global religions to reanimate her doctrine of change, which stands against dominance and oppression. The holy trinity of Hinduism—the creator, Brahma; the preserver, Vishnu; and the destructor, Maheshwar—symbolize the cycle of regeneration from destruction. Moreover, Butler's interpretation of religion in *Lilith's Brood* composes that of the Oankali, who define a cause as they create nature and delineate a purpose in their new religion. It includes ritualistic rites and asks for an adherence to a moral code of nonhierarchical behavior. The ambiguity at the heart of the Oankali agenda manifests itself in their religion, which promotes a relational, hybrid identity, one that dismantles anthropocentrism to acknowledge a deep connection with all living beings. These "amborgs," to use Joan Gordon's term, remind one of the Hindu avatars. Clearly the play on Sanskrit terminology and the ritualistic rites essential to Hinduism. *Lilith's Brood* indicates the subtle yet potent influence of Hinduism on Butler's alternate transreligious world building, her conceptual framework that proffers a more nuanced understanding of and critical engagement with religious belief and practice.

WORKS CITED

Alaimo, Stacy. *Bodily Natures: Science, Environment, and the Material Self.* Indiana University Press, 2010.

Allen, Marlene D. "Octavia Butler's 'Parable' Novels and the 'Boomerang' of African American History." *Callaloo*, vol. 32, no. 4, 2009, pp. 1353–1365.

Andréolle, Donna Spalding. "Utopias of Old, Solutions for the New Millennium: A Comparative Study of Christian Fundamentalism in M. K. Wren's *A Gift Upon the Shore* and Octavia Butler's *Parable of the Sower.*" *Utopian Studies*, vol. 12, no. 2, 2001, pp. 114–123.

Butler, Octavia. *Lilith's Brood.* Grand Central Publishing, 2000.

———. *Parable of the Sower.* Grand Central Publishing, 1993.

———. "Science Future and Science Fiction," *Bodies: A Digital Companion*, 3 Oct. 2008, http://scalar.usc.edu/works/bodies/octavia-butler-science-future-science-fiction.

Derrida, Jacques. *Acts of Religion.* Routledge, 2002.

Fitzgerald, Timothy. "A Critique of 'Religion' as a Cross-Cultural Category." *Method and Theory in the Study of Religion*, vol. 9, no. 2, 1997, pp. 91–110.

Francis, Consuela. *Conversations with Octavia Butler.* University Press of Mississippi, 2010.

Goldstucker, Theodore. *Literary Remains of the Late Professor Theodore Goldstucker.* W. H. Allen, 1879.

Gordan, Joan. "Gazing across the Abyss: The Amborg Gaze in Sheri S. Tepper's 'Six Moon Dance.'" *Science Fiction Studies*, vol. 35, no. 2, July 2008, pp. 189–206.

Hampton, Gregory. *Changing Bodies in the Fiction of Octavia Butler: Slaves, Aliens, and Vampires.* Lexington Books, 2010.

Hrotic, Steven. *Religion in Science Fiction: The Evolution of an Idea and the Extinction of a Genre.* Bloomsbury Academic, 2014.

Kenan, Randall. "An Interview with Octavia E. Butler." *Callaloo*, vol. 14, no. 2, 1991, pp. 495–504.

King, Richard. *Orientalism and Religion: Postcolonial Theory, India and "the Mystic East."* Routledge, 1999.

Lorenzen, David. "Hindus and Others." *Rethinking Religion in India: The Colonial Construction of Hinduism*, edited by Esther Bloch, Marianne Keppens, and Rajaram Hegde, Routledge, 2010, pp. 25–40.

Melzer, Patricia. "Metaphors of Transgression in the Work of Octavia E. Butler." *Alien Constructions*. University of Texas Press, 2006.

Michaels, Axel. *Homo Ritualis: Hindu Ritual and Its Significance for Ritual Theory.* Oxford University Press, 2016.

Miller, Jim. "Post-Apocalyptic Hoping: Octavia Butler's Dystopian/Utopian Vision." *Science Fiction Studies*, vol. 25, no. 2, 1998, pp. 336–360.

Miller, Walter. *Canticle for Leibowitz.* Lippincott, 1959.

Milne, Joseph. "Advaita Vedanta and Typologies of Multiplicity and Unity: An Interpretation of Nondual Knowledge." *International Journal of Hindu Studies*, vol. 1, no. 1, 1997, pp. 165–188.

Oddie, Geoffrey A. "Constructing Hinduism: The Impact of the Protestant Missionary Movement on Hindu Self-Understanding." *Christians and Missionaries in India: Cross-cultural Communication since 1500*, edited by R. E. Frykenberg, Routledge Curzon, and Wm. B. Eerdmans Publishing, 2003, pp. 155–182.

Outterson, Sarah. "Diversity, Change, Violence: Octavia Butler's Pedagogical Philosophy." *Utopian Studies*, vol. 19 no. 3, 2008, pp. 433–456.

Patton, Laurie L. "Women, the Freedom Movement, and Sanskrit: Notes on Religion and Colonialism from Ethnographic Present." *Rethinking Religion in India: The Colonial Construction of Hinduism*, edited by Esther Bloch, Marianne Keppens, and Rajaram Hegde, Routledge, 2010, pp. 79–91.

Prime, Ranchor. *Vedic Ecology: Practical Wisdom for Surviving the 21st Century.* Mandal, Airlift, 2003.

Slonczewski, Joan. "Octavia Butler's Xenogenesis Trilogy: A Biologist's Response." Presented at SFRA, Cleveland, June 30, 2000.

Smith, Wilfred. *The Meaning and End of Religion.* First Fortress Press, 1962.

Sormus, Maris. "Natural Cultural Hybridity and Becoming: Andrus Kivirähk's *The Man Who Spoke Snakish* in a Material Ecocritical Perspective." *European New Nature Writing*, vol. 6, no. 1, 2015, pp. 43–57.

Sugirtharajah, Sharada. "Colonialism and Religion." *Rethinking Religion in India: The Colonial Construction of Hinduism*, edited by Esther Bloch, Marianne Keppens, and Rajaram Hegde, Routledge, 2010, pp. 69–78.

Swami Krishananda. *Brihadaranyaka Upanishad*. Divine Life Society, 2019.

Swami Tapasyananda. *Srimad Bhagavata*. Sri Ramakrishna Math Chennai, 2019.

Zavos, John. "Representing Religion in Colonial India." *Rethinking Religion in India: The Colonial Construction of Hinduism*, edited by Esther Bloch, Marianne Keppens, and Rajaram Hegde, Routledge, 2010, pp. 56–68.

3

God Is Change, Impermanence Is Buddha Nature

Religious Syncretism in Butler's Earthseed and Dōgen's Zen

CHRISTOPHER KOCELA

Octavia Butler acknowledged the influence of Buddhism on her conception of the Earthseed religion in *Parable of the Sower* and *Parable of the Talents* ("Conversation" 336); moreover, both novels contain explicitly Buddhist imagery and terminology. Nevertheless, scholars have tended to ignore the Buddhist resonances of Butler's Parable novels, preferring to read Earthseed as, for example, an alternative form of Christianity (Jos 410), a representation of feminist utopian desire (Melzer 36–37), a reflection on process theology (Hampton 91), an example of African American womanist theology (Jones 117), and a science-based belief system that replaces traditional African American forms of spirituality (Allen 1362). By contrast, I will argue that Earthseed represents a syncretic religion constructed by its founder, Lauren Olamina, using a hermeneutic strategy known in Buddhist tradition as "skillful means" (in Sanskrit, *upāya*). Adapting her pedagogical strategies to suit the capacities of diverse audiences, Olamina offers a central spiritual teaching, "God is Change," that self-reflexively comments on the ability of Earthseed to survive and grow as a religious response to social, political, and environmental crises. In this regard Olamina's teaching bears a striking resemblance to that of Eihei Dōgen, founder of the Soto Zen school in medieval Japan, who challenged his followers to see that "impermanence is itself Buddha nature" (Dōgen 243). While all branches of Buddhism posit change or impermanence as an essential feature of existence (a point noted repeatedly in *Parable of the Sower* 26, 261), Dōgen's innovation, like Olamina's, was intended to inspire faith in the capacity for personal and communal adaptability, liberation, and healing. By comparing these teachings as provocative examples of skillful means, my aim will not be to show that Lauren's religion is modeled directly on Dōgen's but to suggest that Dōgen's Zen Buddhist understanding of impermanence offers an ethical touchstone for reexamining Butler's depiction of religion as a vehicle for promoting community and diversity, for challenging hierarchical thinking, and for reshaping social reality through critical analysis and compassionate action.

Scholars of comparative religion frequently identify Buddhism as a fundamentally syncretic religion. That is, although each of the major world religions has, over time, reconstructed itself through the adoption of cultural values and beliefs other than those out of which it originated, Buddhism is unique in having manifested almost no opposition to this evolutionary process since its inception, instead formally accepting syncretism as a legitimate means of spreading its influence and practice (Harrison 97–98). The basis for this formal acceptance of syncretism is the doctrine of skillful means whereby Buddhist teachings are not presented as metaphysical or moral truths but simply as the expedients most appropriate to helping particular audiences reach the enlightenment that the Buddha attained. Perhaps the most famous illustration of skillful means is the "parable of the burning house" in the third chapter of the Lotus Sutra. In this parable a father stands in the yard of his burning home while his three children remain playing inside, oblivious to the danger that threatens them. In order to lure them to safety, he promises each child a ride on a carriage pulled by a goat, a deer, and an ox, respectively; but once free of the fire, the children discover three identical carriages far greater than those they had been promised, each pulled by a magnificent white ox. Although it might appear that the father, who represents the Buddha, deceives the children in order to save them, his actions are justified by his compassion for them and by his skillful ability to discern the best means of rescuing each one in turn. In Mahayana Buddhism, use of skillful means becomes the highest spiritual practice of the bodhisattva, who pledges not to achieve enlightenment or to leave the "burning house" of samsara, the suffering world, until all sentient beings have first been saved. According to Catherine Cornille, Buddhism's formal receptivity to syncretism is a direct result of its "doctrinal humility" whereby "the Buddhist tradition has on the whole maintained a strong sense of the provisionality and conventionality of teachings or doctrines as skillful means" (55).

Yet although the doctrine of skillful means has been used to explain Buddhism's receptivity to interreligious dialogue and cultural diversity, it has also served the dubious ethical purpose of establishing hierarchies of teachings among various Buddhist sects and traditions. The Lotus Sutra itself, for example, is often understood as a polemical text that portrays its own representation of the Buddha's teachings as the "white ox carriage" relative to the inferior, though still useful, sutras that preceded it. As Hee-Jin Kim observes, such ethically problematic uses of skillful means are a consequence of overinvestment in the dualistic relationship between means and ends: so long as one portrays ends (enlightenment) as transcendent to means (teaching or practice), one submits to a teleological view that supports discriminatory and hierarchical thinking (30–31). To counteract this tendency, key figures in Buddhist history have sought to reframe the doctrine of skillful means so as to counteract its potentially dualistic representation of the relationship between means and ends, or practice and enlightenment. One such figure is Eihei Dōgen (1200–1253), founder of the Soto Zen sect at a time of deep social and political unrest in Kamakura-era Japan. In "Buddha Nature," a fascicle of his *Shobo Genzo*, or *Treasury of the True Dharma Eye*, Dōgen skillfully exploits an ambiguity in the Japanese language to retranslate a teaching from the Mahaparinirvana Sutra, "All sentient beings without exception have Buddha nature" to read "All sentient beings are the Buddha nature" (Stambaugh 6). Aimed at an audience that regarded Buddha nature as a possession or characteristic that, if nurtured, could lead to enlightenment in the future, Dōgen's retranslation collapses this conventional distinction between Buddha nature and impermanent beings such that "impermanence is itself Buddha nature" (Dōgen 243). For Dōgen, one purpose of this teaching was to encourage practice and spiritual faith by making clear that enlightenment is not a future attainment but a manifestation of one's spiritual practice in the present moment—a practice that, contrary to the politics of his time, he endorsed for men and women alike (Shields 69–71). For scholars of Buddhism, this teaching has come to exemplify a model of skillful means that uses language to perform rather than merely describe the religious attitude it endorses. Affirming the nondualism of means and ends, Dōgen extended the sphere of salvation to include not only human beings but nonhuman animals, plants, and the land itself (Leighton 30).

In the remainder of this chapter, I argue that Butler's Parable novels portray the Buddhist doctrine of skillful means as a hermeneutical framework for evaluating the ethics and syncretic adaptability of Lauren Olamina's Earthseed religion. *Parable of the Sower* begins with Olamina's description of a recurring dream in which she attempts to escape her burning house by flying (4)—an image to which she returns repeatedly in her subsequent diary entries. For example, when frustrated by her father's refusal to acknowledge the possibility that their Robledo neighborhood will one day need to be abandoned, she likens his attitude to "ignoring a fire in the living room because we're all in the kitchen" (63). As several critics have noted (Nilges 1341, Thaler 82), images of burning houses anticipate Olamina's formulation of the Earthseed Destiny, which consists in abandoning an environmentally damaged Earth for colonization of other planets. I suggest, however, that by evoking the parable of the burning house from the Lotus Sutra, this pattern of imagery also invites comparison of Olamina's spiritual leadership with that of the bodhisattva who uses skillful means to save all beings from the suffering world of samsara. As Gerry Canavan makes clear in his discussion of Butler's unpublished manuscripts, Butler was deeply interested in the figure of the bodhisattva and her commitment not to achieve liberation ahead of the needs of her community. One version of *Parable of the Trickster*, the intended third book in Butler's Parable series, was named "Bodhisattva" at a late point in its development and focused on a community of people struggling with their ability to use reincarnation as a means of perfecting human civilization (Canavan 156–157). In the context of the published Parable novels, the significance of the bodhisattva ideal resides in its capacity to illuminate the skillfulness and compassion with which Olamina uses her religious teachings to lead her followers to action and, eventually, salvation. It is therefore important that her central teaching, "God is Change," recalls Dōgen's view that impermanence is Buddha nature. As I will argue, Olamina's teaching, like Dōgen's, initially encourages a nondualistic understanding of the relationship between means and ends that emphasizes the need for collective action by celebrating diversity and challenging hierarchical and discriminatory thinking. In this regard, my analysis complements that of Aparajita Nanda, who, in her chapter "Transreligious World Building," in this volume, explores Butler's construction of hybrid identities in *Lilith's Brood* through reference to Hindu philosophy and folklore. In *Parable of the Sower*, the key impetus for Olamina's nondualistic teaching is the radical form of compassion enabled by her hyperempathy syndrome—a byproduct of her mother's drug addiction that forces her to experience the suffering and pleasure of those around her. But as Olamina becomes more and more convinced of the necessity of an otherworldly Destiny, her use of skillful means becomes increasingly dualistic, hierarchical, and ethically problematic. Particularly in *Parable of the Talents*, the changed nature of her religious leadership manifests in her heightened anthropocentrism and reduced concern for those peripheral to the Earthseed movement.

My analysis focuses on two scenes, one each from *Parable of the Sower* and *Parable of the Talents*, in which Olamina's teachings are explicitly compared by her interlocutors with Buddhist principles and values. I choose these scenes not only because they occur at crucial moments in Olamina's development as a spiritual leader but also because they portray Buddhism as a living, and at times persecuted, religion in the diegetic world of these characters (*Sower* 22, *Talents* 23, 84). That Californians of the near future should be familiar with Buddhist doctrines is not surprising given the state's historical association with the growth of Western Buddhism and Dōgen's Soto Zen in particular (Mitchell 121–122). Given this history, comparisons of Earthseed to Buddhism within Butler's novels call attention to important differences between Olamina's view of religious syncretism and that exemplified in the construction and spread of Buddhism.

"All Religions Change"

Late in *Parable of the Sower*, Olamina explains the fundamental principles of her Earthseed religion to Bankole, a former doctor she has befriended on her journey north across California following the destruction of her Robledo neighborhood. Although Olamina has already converted several members of her traveling group to the Earthseed faith and has become practiced at teaching its values, Bankole is the first person she has met on the road who is educated enough to question Earthseed's principles relative to its religious and philosophical sources. After observing that "Buddhism doesn't make a god of the concept of change, but the impermanence of everything is a basic Buddhist principle" (261), Bankole goes on to critique the long-term efficacy of Olamina's teaching:

> "I mean it's too . . . straightforward. If you get people to accept it, they'll make it more complicated, more open to interpretation, more mystical, and more comforting."
> "Not around me they won't!" I said.
> "With you or without you, they will. All religions change. Think about the big ones. What do you think Christ would be these days? A Methodist? A Catholic? And the Buddha—do you think he'd be a Buddhist now? What kind of Buddhism would he practice?" He smiled. "After all, if 'God is Change,' surely Earthseed can change, and if it lasts, it will." (262; ellipses in original)

Bankole clearly aims to reveal inconsistencies and contradictions in Olamina's teachings on change. On one level, he implies that her deification of change runs counter to the more sanguine acceptance of impermanence as an impersonal force in Buddhism. In Mathias Nilges's reading of the Parable novels, such a criticism proves trenchant: "God is Change," in Nilges's view, registers the fundamental trauma of the post-Fordist period, signifying a nostalgic desire to resist change and return to paternalistic structures of the past (1338). On a second level, Bankole presents the history of Buddhism and Christianity as evidence of his claim, sharply rebutted by Olamina, that her teachings will inevitably become more complicated over time in reaching diverse audiences. Here again the implication is that, despite preaching the universality of change, Olamina is in fact resistant to change in ways that will limit the spread and effectiveness of Earthseed. But while it may appear that Olamina exposes herself to this criticism by refusing to countenance new interpretations ("Not around me they won't!"), neither Olamina's equation of impermanence with God nor her stated refusal to complicate her teaching for the needs of future communities constitutes an infelicitous or unethical turn in her teaching when considered in light of the doctrine of skillful means that is central to Buddhism. As John Schroeder makes clear, "'skillful means' arises from the idea that wisdom is embodied in how one responds to others rather than an abstract conception of the world" (3). While Bankole attempts to involve Olamina in logical contradictions, her response crystallizes the compassionate and skillful nature of her teaching to this point in the novel.

Throughout *Parable of the Sower*, Olamina is open about the fact that her equation of God with change is not an effort to provide metaphysical proofs or paternalistic security but is, instead, a rhetorical gesture rooted in a desire to prevent the suffering of others. In an early diary entry, Olamina lists the various scientific and religious sources that have influenced her thinking about God and change before concluding: "But this thing (This idea? Philosophy? New religion?) won't let me alone, won't let me forget it. . . . Maybe it's like my sharing: One more weirdness; one more crazy, deep-rooted delusion that I'm stuck with. I am stuck with it. And in time, I'll have to do something about it" (26). By this point in the narrative, she has already described her delusional ability to "share" the pain and pleasure of others via "hyperempathy syndrome" (10–11); she has also made clear that, delusional or not, this syndrome feels very real to her and guides her behavior in significant ways, making her extremely reticent to cause pain to anyone. By comparing her religious thinking to her experience of sharing at the outset of the narrative, Olamina suggests that what is important about her view of God as change is not its philosophical or metaphysical truth, but its capacity to provoke action and to make her "do something about it." In this regard Olamina reads as a fully human representation of the most famous bodhisattva in Mahayana Buddhism, Avalokiteśvara, whose name means "regarder of the cries of the world" and who is capable of taking whatever form necessary to best respond to the suffering of others. Particularly once Olamina's Robledo neighborhood is burned down and she begins traveling northward dressed as a man, her repeated experiences of hyperempathy and her explanation of this condition to others around her strengthen the compassionate, bodhisattva-like orientation of her teaching.

Several critics have observed that Olamina's hyperempathy syndrome facilitates her investment in community building by helping to break down perceived boundaries between self and other that reify social prejudice and discrimination (Lacey 390, Miller 357, Phillips 306). Esther L. Jones interprets Butler's Parable novels through the lens of disability theory and argues that, although Olamina is capable of passing as unimpaired to her traveling companions, her exposure of herself as a "sharer" strengthens their community because it "universalizes the notion that interdependence is required for their survival" (123). Angela Warfield argues that Olamina's hyperempathy leads her to construct a Derridean vision of utopia not as a future goal but as a "no-place," which is "predicated on the ability to recognize that each moment of time is inextricably bound to others; all moments are moments of becoming—potentialities—that may appear dangerous, interesting, exciting, depressing, or wonderful, but affirmation calls us to see them as conditions of possibility" (66–67). In light of the Buddhist view of skillful means, the most important aspect of Olamina's hyperempathy as a vehicle for teaching communal interdependence is that it helps prevent the dichotomizing of means and ends, which can lead to hierarchical and discriminatory views. Traveling north to an uncertain destination through a landscape in which the suffering of others always threatens to immobilize and incapacitate her, Olamina teaches "God is Change" because it is the most rhetorically effective way to remind herself and others that the present moment is the only moment in which action is possible. She admits as much when questioned by her first Earthseed convert, Travis:

> "Why personify change by calling it God? Since change is just an idea, why not call it that? Just say change is important."
>
> "Because after a while, it won't be important!" I told him. "People forget ideas. They're more likely to remember God—especially when they're scared or desperate."
>
> . . .
>
> "Your God doesn't care about you at all," Travis said.
>
> "All the more reason to care about myself and others. All the more reason to create Earthseed communities and shape God together." (221)

Olamina's teaching here closely mirrors the nondualistic form of skillful means employed by Dōgen through his teaching that "impermanence is itself

Buddha nature." Recall that Dōgen's statement, by self-reflexively collapsing the difference between sentient beings and Buddha nature, linguistically performs the practice it calls for by charging all impermanent beings to take up the practice of manifesting the Buddha nature they already are. Similarly, Olamina's insistence that God is Change rather than a caring or compassionate being who promises security and comfort in the future performs the practice it calls for, which is to "shape God" in ways that manifest compassion for others in the present moment.

Given the similarity between Olamina's and Dōgen's use of skillful means, Bankole's view that there is a fundamental difference between Buddhism and Earthseed on the issue of change does not withstand scrutiny. When Olamina insists that she will deny her followers the right to render her teachings more complex or mystifying, this does not indicate a rejection of change per se but only of Bankole's narrow, teleological view of change as a linear progression toward diversity rather than an affirmation of diversity in the present moment. From Olamina's perspective, the role of the religious leader is not to encourage reinterpretation of one's teachings for the sake of unknown future communities but to remain responsive to the needs of those in the present. Thus when Acorn, the first Earthseed community, is established, Olamina conducts ceremonies for the dead using a variety of religious texts, including "Earthseed verses, the Bible, The Book of Common Prayer, the Bhagavad-Gita, John Donne" (*Talents* 58). Where Bankole portrays religious syncretism as a condition for the survival of a religion across history, Olamina sees religious syncretism as a survival strategy for the religious community itself: "Embrace diversity / Or be destroyed" (*Sower* 196).

Yet although Olamina resists the temptation to subordinate the needs of the present community to an unknown future when speaking to Bankole, she will not always be able to do so. One of the most conspicuous features of *Parable of the Talents* is its gradual effacement of Olamina's hyperempathy as an influence on her religious teaching. While Olamina becomes increasingly focused on leaving the "burning house" of Earth for the colonization of other planets, her second encounter with a character knowledgeable about Buddhism illuminates the changed value of her teaching as skillful means.

"Is This Buddhist?"

Following the destruction of the Acorn community and the enslavement of its surviving members at the hands of the Crusaders, an underground wing of President Jarrett's "Christian America" fundamentalists, Olamina decides that she can no longer devote herself to building physical communities but must, instead, create a religious movement capable of realizing the Earthseed Destiny. To that end she adopts a strategy suggested by a new traveling companion, Len, who tells her: "You need to do what Jarret does. . . . Focus on what people want and tell them how your system will help them get it. Tell folksy stories that illustrate your points and promise the moon and stars—literally in your case" (*Talents* 322). The last scene in which Olamina actively teaches another character about Earthseed occurs twenty pages from the end of *Parable of the Talents* and reveals Len's strategy at work. In the home of Joel and Irma Elford, a wealthy middle-aged couple living in the suburbs of Portland, Oregon, Olamina composes a poem designed to appeal to Irma's interest in environmental conservation. Reading it, Irma responds:

> "Is this Buddhist? No, I see that it isn't. I very nearly became a Buddhist when I was younger." She's 37. "Very simple little verses. Very direct. But some of them are lovely."
> "I want to be understood," I said. "I want to make it easy for people to understand." (343–344)

Irma's comparison of Earthseed to Buddhism recalls Olamina's dialogue with Bankole nearly eight years earlier in the timeline of the novels, throwing into stark relief how much her teaching has changed since then. While her insistence on simplicity was once motivated by openness to the present needs of her community, now she targets prospective converts by tailoring her presentation of Earthseed to their individual interests and goals, hoping they will use their skills, education, and finances toward fulfillment of the future Destiny. As Ellen Peel argues, this new strategy of "belief bridging" reveals just how rhetorically persuasive Olamina can be (61), but it also causes the reader to feel that "something may be wrong with the ways in which Lauren seeks to convince people" (69). In the Buddhist framework evoked by Irma, what is wrong with Olamina's new teaching method is that, while clearly skillful in its deployment of messages attractive to a broad range of audiences, it has become thoroughly dualistic by rendering all means subordinate to one end. Olamina's "positive obsession" (*Talents* 157) with the Destiny as the single path to salvation for Earthseed followers throws into doubt the compassionate motivation that should always underlie the use of skillful means. As Schroeder makes clear regarding the Buddha's teaching: "to say the Buddha established a definitive soteriological path constricts his teachings into a fixed remedy and drains them of compassion" (4). In *Parable of the Talents* the limits to Olamina's compassion become especially evident, despite the paean to nature that she writes for Irma, in her increasingly anthropocentric and hierarchical attitude toward the environment and those unable or unwilling to leave it.

Scholars are divided over the ethics of Olamina's teaching concerning ecology and the environment. According to Peter G. Stillman, Earthseed blurs the human/animal divide by insisting that human beings "cannot stand outside the evolutionary process and assert their independence from it" (29); similarly, David Morris sees Earthseed as ecologically progressive via its "desire to abandon mastery, to allow the amoral forces of the universe to help change a group of thoughtful and purposeful humans" (279). By contrast, Ingrid Thaler argues that "as much as Earthseed principles reflect on the interaction between human and 'nature,' they are ultimately anthropocentric" (89). By offering a static account of Earthseed and its principles, however, all of these readings overlook the important fact that Earthseed's ecological stance changes over the course of the Parable novels in keeping with Olamina's experience of hyperempathy and her use of skillful means. Early in *Parable of the Sower*, Olamina resists shooting the rodents and birds that eat her family's crops because doing so makes her suffer a "strange ghost blow" (37); shortly afterward she describes in detail her ability to share the pain and death of a dog she is forced to kill (44–45). Olamina's ability to share the pain of nonhuman animals seems to influence her view that God is not an anthropomorphic father figure but a rhetorical means of building community across a broad range of human, animal, and mineral forms: "Whether you're a human being, an insect, a microbe, or a stone, this verse is true: All that you touch, / You Change. All that you Change, / Changes you. / The only lasting truth / Is Change. God is Change" (*Sower* 79). Here again Olamina's teaching closely resembles that of Dōgen, whose equation of impermanence with Buddha nature breaks down dualistic distinctions between sentient and insentient beings: "Grass, trees, and forests are impermanent; they are buddha nature. Humans, things, body, and mind are impermanent; they are buddha nature. Land, mountains, and rivers are impermanent, as they are buddha nature" (Dōgen 244). Dōgen's advocacy of compassion toward all aspects of the environment has proven important to deep ecology and its efforts to challenge the "otherness" of nature in Western thought (Leighton 122–123). Yet although Olamina appears to share Dōgen's compassionate regard for nature early on, she never again describes her hyperempathy for nonhuman animals; moreover, her conception of the Earthseed destiny clearly privileges the needs of human beings over all other animal and plant species, some of which will be carried to new host planets only if they are deemed "good for us—for Earthseed—in the long run" (*Talents* 83). As Olamina comes to regard the Destiny as the only legitimate purpose of Earthseed, her teaching, though still rhetorically flexible in addressing different human audiences, becomes more and more dualistic in its characterization of the relationship between human and nonhuman others.

From a Zen Buddhist perspective, perhaps the most ironic feature of Olamina's teaching in *Parable of the Talents* is her repeated description of the Destiny as a form of "species adulthood" for human beings (*Talents* 144, 163, 293, 321). As Kosho Uchiyama explains, Dōgen uses the Japanese word *dainin* to mean both "bodhisattva" and "true adult": "A bodhisattva is one who sees the world through adult eyes and whose actions are the actions of a true adult" (127). To be an adult in Dōgen's sense means practicing a bodhisattva's respect for all components of universal life (Uchiyama 134). For Olamina, by contrast, adulthood comes to represent the primacy of human beings over all other animal and plant species through a survival-of-the-fittest logic: "The human species is a kind of animal, of course. But we can do something no other animal species has ever had the option to do. . . . We can grow up. We can leave the nest" (*Talents* 321–322). Olamina's use of natural imagery to buttress a teleological narrative of human evolution toward "species adulthood" and even "species immortality" (*Talents* 144, 293) represents the final stage in her efforts to garner support for the Earthseed Destiny. Viewed through the lens of skillful means, this teaching is ethically problematic because it serves dualistic and discriminatory ends, not only elevating humans above all other species but reserving the Destiny for a select group of Earthseed members. This anthropocentric and discriminatory turn in Olamina's teaching reflects what Mary Grover, elsewhere in this volume, describes as the ethical cost of transcendence in Butler's Xenogenesis trilogy. Perhaps it is not surprising, then, that Olamina's first diary entry in *Parable of the Talents* recounts a dream in which she has lost her hyperempathy (17). Where *Parable of the Sower* begins with a dream about a burning house that recalls the compassionate use of skillful means in the Lotus Sutra, *Parable of the Talents* opens by foreshadowing the lack of compassion that will come to characterize Olamina's teaching once the Earthseed Destiny becomes her primary goal.

Perusing Olamina's nature poetry late in *Parable of the Talents*, Irma is thus correct to recognize that it is not Buddhist—or at least not Buddhist in the best ethical tradition of compassionate skillful means. To the extent that references to Buddhism in the Parable novels reflect the syncretic openness and humility of Earthseed as a religion, Irma's comment signifies the diminishment of Earthseed's receptivity to the change it presents as its central doctrine. While Olamina's teaching originates in a syncretic assemblage and reconstruction of ideas pulled from a variety of philosophical, religious, and scientific discourses, Earthseed evolves into a religion that is only provisionally syncretic in that it resists incorporating other cultural and spiritual values once its key articles of faith are established. Obviously such resistance to syncretism does not bode well for the Earthseed colonists whose survival, via the Destiny, will depend on adapting to whatever circumstances they encounter in their foreign worlds. Viewed together, Butler's Parable novels portray religion as a social construct capable of forging new communities through compassion, tolerance, and respect for diversity amid political and environmental upheaval. Butler's novels also reveal that, despite its healing and world-building potential, religion is especially vulnerable to hierarchical and anthropocentric views when made to serve as the lone vehicle on a single path to salvation.

WORKS CITED

Allen, Marlene D. "Octavia Butler's *Parable* Novels and the 'Boomerang' of African American History." *Callaloo,* vol. 32, no. 4, Fall 2009, pp. 1353–1365. *Project Muse,* doi:10.1353/cal.0.0541.

Butler, Octavia E. "A Conversation with Octavia E. Butler." Butler, *Parable of the Sower,* pp. 333–341.

———. *Parable of the Sower.* Grand Central Publishing, 2000.

———. *Parable of the Talents.* Seven Stories, 1998.

Canavan, Jerry. *Octavia E. Butler.* University of Illinois Press, 2016.

Cornille, Catherine. *The Im-possibility of Interreligious Dialogue.* Herder, 2008.

Dōgen, Eihei. "Buddha Nature." *Treasury of the True Dharma Eye: Zen Master Dōgen's Shobo Genzo,* edited by Kazuaki Tanahashi. Shambhala, 2010, pp. 234–259.

Hampton, Gregory Jerome. *Changing Bodies in the Fiction of Octavia Butler: Slaves, Aliens, and Vampires.* Lexington, 2010.

Harrison, William H. *In Praise of Mixed Religion: The Syncretism Solution in a Multi-faith World.* McGill-Queen's University Press, 2014.

Jones, Esther L. *Medicine and Ethics in Black Women's Speculative Fiction.* Palgrave Macmillan, 2015.

Jos, Philip H. "Fear and the Spiritual Realism of Octavia Butler's Earthseed." *Utopian Studies: Journal of the Society for Utopian Studies,* vol. 23, no. 2, 2012, pp. 408–429. *EBSCOhost,* search.ebscohost.com/login.aspx?direct=true&AuthType=ip,shib&db=mzh&AN=2013700938&site=ehost-live&scope=site.

Kim, Hee-Jin. *Dōgen on Meditation and Thinking: A Reflection on His View of Zen.* State University of New York Press, 2007.

Lacey, Lauren J. "Octavia E. Butler on Coping with Power in *Parable of the Sower, Parable of the Talents,* and *Fledgling.*" *Critique: Studies in Contemporary Fiction,* vol. 49, no. 4, Summer 2008, pp. 279–294. doi:10.3200/crit.49.4.379-394.

Leighton, Taigen Dan. *Visions of Awakening Space and Time: Dōgen and the Lotus Sutra.* Oxford University Press, 2007.

The Lotus Sutra: A Contemporary Translation of a Buddhist Classic. Translated by Gene Reeves, Wisdom, 2008.

Melzer, Patricia. "'All That You Touch You Change': Utopian Desire and the Concept of Change in Octavia Butler's *Parable of the Sower* and *Parable of the Talents*." *FEMSPEC*, vol. 3, no. 2, 2002, pp. 31–52. *EBSCOhost*, earch.ebscohost.com/login.aspx?direct=true&AuthType=ip,shib&db=mzh&AN=2002401921&site=ehost-live&scope=site.

Mitchell, Scott A. *Buddhism in America: Global Religion, Local Contexts*. Bloomsbury, 2016.

Morris, David. "Octavia Butler's (R)evolutionary Movement for the Twenty-First Century." *Utopian Studies*, vol. 26, no. 2, 2015, pp. 270–288. *EBSCOhost*, search.ebscohost.com/login.aspx?direct=true&AuthType=ip,shib&db=mzh&AN=2016305944&site=ehost-live&scope=site.

Nilges, Mathias. "'We Need the Stars': Change, Community, and the Absent Father in Octavia Butler's *Parable of the Sower* and *Parable of the Talents*." *Callaloo*, vol. 32, no. 4, Fall 2009, pp. 1332–1352. *Project Muse*, doi:10.1343/cal.0.0553.

Peel, Ellen. "'God Is Change': Persuasion and Pragmatic Utopianism in Octavia E. Butler's *Earthseed* Novels." *Afro-Future Females: Black Writers Chart Science Fiction's Newest New-Wave Trajectory*, edited by Marleen S. Barr, Ohio State University Press, 2008, pp. 52–74.

Phillips, Jerry. "The Intuition of the Future: Utopia and Catastrophe in Octavia Butler's *Parable of the Sower*." *Novel: A Forum on Fiction*, vol. 35, no. 2–3, 2002, pp. 299–311. *EBSCOhost*, search.ebscohost.com/login.aspx?direct=true&AuthType=ip,shib&db=mzh&AN=2003000199&site=ehost-live&scope=site.

Schroeder, John W. *Skillful Means: The Heart of Buddhist Compassion*. University of Hawaii Press, 2001.

Shields, James Mark. *Critical Buddhism: Engaging with Modern Japanese Buddhist Thought*. Ashgate, 2011.

Stambaugh, Joan. *Impermanence Is Buddha-Nature: Dōgen's Understanding of Temporality*. University of Hawaii Press, 1990.

Stillman, Peter G. "Dystopian Critiques, Utopian Possibilities, and Human Purposes in Octavia Butler's Parables." *Utopian Studies: Journal of the Society for Utopian Studies*, vol. 14, no. 1, 2003, pp. 15–35. *EBSCOhost*, search.ebscohost.com/login.aspx?direct=true&AuthType=ip,shib&db=mzh&AN=2003871421&site=ehost-live&scope=site.

Stone, Jacqueline I. *Original Enlightenment and the Transformation of Medieval Japanese Buddhism*. University of Hawaii Press, 1999.

Thaler, Ingrid. *Black Atlantic Speculative Fictions: Octavia E. Butler, Jewelle Gomez, and Nalo Hopkinson*. Routledge, 2010.

Uchiyama, Kosho. *Opening the Hand of Thought: Foundations of Zen Buddhist Practice*. Translated and edited by Tom Wright, Jisho Warner, and Shohaku Okumura, Wisdom, 2004.

Warfield, Angela. "Reassessing the Utopian Novel: Octavia Butler, Jacques Derrida, and the Impossible Future of Utopia." *Obsidian III*, vol. 6–7, no. 2–1, 2005, pp. 61–71. *EBSCOhost*, search.ebscohost.com/login.aspx?direct=true&AuthType=ip,shib&db=mzh&AN=2007297551&site=ehost-live&scope=site.

4

Butler's Invention of Scripture in Light of Hebrew Wisdom Literature

CHARLOTTE NAYLOR DAVIS

n the *Parable of the Sower* and the *Parable of the Talents* (hereafter *Sower* and *Talents*) Octavia Butler creates a world in a near future, which we experience through the eyes of a woman trying to build her own new world. Lauren Olamina is both surviving and creating as she moves through the wreckage of a culture she was born into. What she creates comes in two forms—the community of Earthseed and the *Books of the Living*. In this chapter, it is the internal text, the *Books of the Living*, with which I am concerned. They stand as an interesting artifact, solid and fully formed, and yet they are the texts of a teaching focused on the tenet "God is Change"—a tenet that seems to fight against being made solid in the form of sacred or authoritative text.

Though scholars have written about the *Books of the Living* previously, they are frequently analysed as "sacred text" or "scripture" without discussing what exactly that is.[1] For sacred text is not a genre in itself—rather, the term *sacred text* is a descriptor of the function of a text, not its content. Books about holy things are not sacred, or all theology would be sacred; texts read in sacred places are not sacred, or all hymnody and liturgy would be sacred. What then are the *Books of the Living*, and how should we define them if they are indeed the sacred text of Earthseed? It is undeniable that they are religious in content. As Christopher Kocela shows in his chapter in this volume, the response to the apocalyptic situation within the book is to rethink religion but still use it, creating something in which we can see strands from Christian and Buddhist frameworks. My chapter builds on Kocela's assertion that the Parables repre- sent "religion as both socially interventionist and transcendently utopian" to ask how the *Books of the Living* can be thought of as sacred in such a landscape. In this chapter, therefore, I utilize the understanding and tools of the study of Hebrew scripture, and particularly wisdom literature, to help us understand what Olamina is doing as she creates the sayings of Earthseed and how we can understand their genre and function as sacred texts while maintaining that "God is Change."

In Thrall's "Authoring the Sacred: Humanism and Invented Scripture in Octavia Butler, Kurt Vonnegut and Dan Simmons," he, like many religious scholars before him, raises the issue of what it is that makes the sacred "sacred." He shows that all the scriptures "invented" (his term) by these authors are slightly different in genre, of different types and modes, and yet he says,

> Diverse as they are in setting and tone . . . each considers the possible outcomes of catastrophic, even apocalyptic crises, and comments realistically if despairingly on the nature of human failing that helped bring those crises about. Each, by way of contrast, endorses the power of language to advance human thriving, applying its invented scripture in an overarching endeavour to answer the question "how shall we live?" (510)

His discussion brings up key points that are at the center of biblical and sacred text research—that of the role of the author and the importance of the "literary quality of the aphorisms, verses or sayings" in the acknowledgment of something as "scripture" or "sacred." It is a crucial discussion in religious life: What makes text sacred? Who decides what is scripture? And I would say that in some ways we miss a crucial aspect of the texts when we refer to the writings in these books (and, say, the liturgy found in the MaddAddam trilogy by Margaret Atwood) as "invented" scripture. For, as any biblical scholar will tell you, all scripture is invented, authored and then authorized by someone. It is its function that makes it scripture, not its content.

In a number of articles, however, scholars posit that Olamina's religion stands against the rigid religion she grew up with. Indeed, Olamina contrasts herself with Job a number of times, and we certainly see the negative effects of a reductive reading of the Bible in the actions of "Christian America" and President Jarret's followers. It is my contention, however, that the *Books of the Living* can be seen as Olamina writing scripture because of their similarities with some biblical texts, not because of the differences. As we proceed, I modify my language to that of wisdom—for I would propose these texts are read as *wisdom literature*, which may or may not become sacred depending on the way it is used.

I would like to turn then to the Hebrew Bible and wisdom literature for some insights. The Hebrew Bible is not one sacred text but a collection of texts written down over approximately four to six hundred years but definitely forged and learned over far longer. It is not one genre: it contains some "history" (such as history is in the ancient Near East) and some erotic poetry (oh yes, Song of Solomon is not all an allegory, with apologies to the Victorian commentators). It contains stories written in exile, songs of lament given to help people in the darkest of times, and songs of war and worship, with substantial terror thrown in casually; it contains myths that predate writing but have been molded by a community in such a way as to fit their new world view; and most importantly it contains wisdom as we are about to define. First, I shall address the genre of the *Books of the Living* and then look at the function of the text within the Parables' own narrative and world.

Genre

As I have stated, I am concerned with genre because it is genre and function that make something sacred for people, not merely content. Both Thrall and Philip Jos search to find parallels between more reflective or liberal types of Christian theology, citing process theologians or Bonhoeffer; however, I do not think one can necessarily make these connections, especially as Olamina's ideas brook no personal savior: "My God doesn't love me or hate me or watch over me or know me at all, and I feel no love for or loyalty to my God. My God just is" (*Sower* 25). One cannot read Christian theology and omit the aspect of the personal nature of Jesus Christ, even in the most liberal readings. I therefore would like to leave ideas of Christian theological content behind. I posit that what we pick up on when reading the sayings of the *Books of the Living* is the nature of wisdom literature within the Hebrew Bible that has been embedded in Western culture.

Wisdom literature in the Christian Old Testament consists classically of three books—Job, Ecclesiastes (more properly Qoheleth), and Proverbs; if we add the books within the Hebrew Bible we also read Ben Sira and the Wisdom of Solomon. These books are of different modes (Proverbs is a book of sayings, Job a teaching narrative) but are classed together because of their linked themes. To give James Crenshaw's definition used by most wisdom scholars as a starting point for discussion:

> Formally, Wisdom consists of proverbial sentence, or instruction, debate, intellectual reflection; thematically, wisdom comprises self-evident intuitions about mastering life for human betterment, gropings after

life's secrets with regard to innocent suffering, grappling with finitude, and a quest for truth concealed in the created order and manifested in a feminine persona. When a marriage between form and content exists, there is wisdom literature. (Crenshaw 11)

Crenshaw's description does not talk about theological consistency but consistency in approach to the world in which the author is living: a searching and questioning, a need to form an understanding about how to exist in this world with its suffering and hardship and "finitude." Ernest Lucas suggests, in an article about other wisdom literature (Qumran and ancient Near East), that what can be found in wisdom literature is "a common approach to reality. This is 'humanistic' in that is it concerned with what is good for men and women. It is also 'experiential' in what the authors say is rooted in careful observation of life, especially the consequences of particular patterns of behaviour" (80).

It is this observation of life and patterns that strikes me as similar to the wisdom literature of the ancient Near East. The books of Proverbs and Ecclesiastes are both full of utterances that can be taken out of the sacred realm and seen as simple observations of the human condition. Proverbs contains much that debunks the idea of political stability and sayings that are basic "common-sense teaching":

> Be careful to know your own sheep and give attention to your
>   flocks, for possessions do not last forever nor will a crown
>   endure to endless generations. (Proverbs 27:23–24, New
>   Revised Standard Version)

He who sends a fool on an errand cuts off his own feet (Proverbs 26:6).

Olamina's texts have similar extremes of statement, equally as pithy:

> Embrace diversity
> Unite—
> Or be divided,
> Robbed
> Ruled
> Killed
> By those who see you as prey.
> Embrace diversity
> Or be destroyed (*Sower* 196)

A tree Cannot grow in its parent's shadow (*Sower* 82)

One of the other similarities that is striking between the *Books of the Living* sayings and particularly the book of Proverbs is the inconsistency in subject matter between the sayings. In the book of Proverbs particularly, we see sayings next to one another that do not connect in tone or subject. The Earthseed sayings are similar. When gathered together, they may be statements of cosmology/theology: "All that you touch you change, All that you change Changes you, the only lasting truth is change, God is Change" (*Sower* 3). Or they may include a saying about the nature of humanity: for example, her long section on repeating what we have heard, which seems more a political teaching than anything else (*Talents* 206). John Collins, writing on proverbial wisdom, queries the form of these sorts of text, particularly how they can be world building in the light of such inconsistency. He draws two conclusions: the first, that proverbial wisdom is trying to establish lasting, valid, and positive truths within the authors' own sphere (Lucas 5). Concerning the proverb "a well-fed person will disdain honey," he shows that, though it is about honey and food, "it also suggests a pattern which can be illustrated without any reference to food or honey. Whoever has plenty of anything is hard to please." Olamina's statement "In order to rise from its own ashes, a phoenix first must burn" (*Sower* 153) works similarly, coming directly from the experience of the destruction of her home but also applicable to any situation of destruction one encounters, real or metaphorical. Collins' second conclusion is that the lack of an attempt to establish consistency is part of the characteristics of a wisdom text—a text that is meant to be individual, usable wisdom, not one continuous stream or narrative. Rather, the proverbs are meant to be taken individually, ruminated on, and thoughtfully applied. Therefore, when subject matter is jarringly conflated or two statements seem to contradict one another, it is not necessary to make them fit together; each can be taken on its own merits and applied to different situations.

A much-cited example of this (and used by Lucas here) from Proverbs is 26:4–5:

> [4] Do not answer a fool according to his folly,
>   or you yourself will be just like him.
> [5] Answer a fool according to his folly,
>   or he will be wise in his own eyes.

Read together for the same situation these cannot work as life lessons. But they are only next to each other in such a way because of the way we now read and use the Bible. Held as a collection of wisdom utterances, there is no need for these two sayings to be applied to the same instance or be distinctly connected.

Olamina writes:

We are Earthseed
The life that perceives itself
Changing. (*Sower* 127)

And

Earthseed
Cast on new ground
Must first perceive
That it knows nothing. (*Sower* 178)

As a pair, the instructions are confusing, but that is not their function. If they work like wisdom literature, they stand alone, not to dictate behavior but to shed light on the situation one finds oneself in.

Before I move into the discussion about function, I would like to posit one more piece of evidence for the genre of the Earthseed sayings being wisdom literature, and that is the poetic nature of much of it and its use of parallelism and repetitive structures to expose truths. It reads neither like straightforward prose nor like conventional poetry; this collection of different types of material makes it more like wisdom literature, not less. Hebrew wisdom literature is rife with parallelism: Job, Ecclesiastes, and Proverbs all use such patterns to move the hearers' thinking from one realm to another. An example of simple parallelism in Proverbs would be as follows:

A wise child makes a glad father,
But a foolish child is a mother's grief. (Proverbs 10:1)

The parallel of wise and foolish is mirrored in father and mother, making the statement memorable and easy to understand. In the Earthseed sayings we read:

We give our dead to the orchards and the groves.
We give our dead to life. (*Talents* 58)

We also see longer sections in both the *Books of the Living* and wisdom literature that use the repetition of specific language to direct and shape the thinking of the hearer. It is worth noting here that the receiving communities of both Hebrew wisdom literature and Earthseed (in the world created by Butler) are mainly illiterate. Education in both settings is for the elite. Therefore, such patterns work well as memory aids and then shape the type of text that is applicable for the situation. More will be said about this below.

In Proverbs we read:

> [7] Whoever corrects a *scoffer* wins abuse;
>   whoever *rebukes* the wicked gets hurt.
> [8] A *scoffer* who is *rebuked* will only hate you;
>   the *wise*, when *rebuked*, will love you.
> [9] Give instruction to the *wise*, and they will become *wiser* still;
>   teach the righteous and they will gain in learning.
> [10] The fear of the LORD IS THE BEGINNING OF *wisdom*,
>   and the knowledge of the Holy One is insight.
> [11] For by me your days will be multiplied,
>   and years will be added to your life.
> [12] If you are *wise*, you are *wise* for yourself;
>   if you *scoff*, you alone will bear it. (Proverbs 9:7–12; italics mine)

The language of scoffing creates a textual "inclusio" and in doing so brings the reader back to the point of the passage—not only be wise, but don't be a "scoffer." The central section on wisdom is not as important as the beginning and end points—it is there to give a reason for needing wisdom, but if one only remembers the maxims, one will still be living in a way that benefits.

Repetition is similarly evident in Olamina's sayings:

> Beware
> *Ignorance*
> Protects itself.
> *Ignorance*
> promotes *suspicion*.
> *Suspicion*,
> Engenders *fear*.
> *Fear* quails,
> Irrational and *blind*,
> Or *fear* looms,
> Defiant and *closed*
> *Blind, closed*
> *Suspicious, afraid,*
> *Ignorance*

Protects itself,
And *protected,*
Ignorance grows (*Talents* 206; italics mine)

Here the repetition of language pulls the hearer through the statements, giving them a path of thought to follow that seems logical and consistent. It is not about evidence or argument; rather, the language and form are used to create space for rumination but also warning. The repetition of fear in the central section is used in parallel to ignorance in the first and third sections, to create a large picture of negative connotations. The final statement inverts the beginning statement "ignorance protects" and gives consequences of allowing the previous statements to be true. The hearer is pushed to action through one simple inversion of language.

Function

We come now, therefore, to the issue of the function of the text. As can be seen from the above discussion, the texts that contain proverbial wisdom, or more existential maxims, serve the hearers to give them guidance as well as teaching. However, the sayings in the *Books of the Living* also contain sections about civilization, religion, and the nature of our relationship to the idea that "God is Change." They are not all hopeful; neither do they give direct instructions for living. They embrace the fact that life is difficult and that the past can be hard to let go of. It is this sort of sentiment that I think puts the sayings in the category of wisdom literature rather than any other mode of sacred text.

Wisdom literature is unlike sections of law or history among the biblical literature, insofar as it does not "use force or intimidation to impose its point of view[; rather,] it does seek to persuade by engaging the reader in a vigorous process of reflection" (Gilbert 71). The reader is encouraged to relate to the subject matter or, in the case of Job, the protagonist in what Pierre Gilbert calls a "rhetorical trap," so as to be forced to confront the reality of trying to live fruitfully in the face of suffering. Thus far we have mainly focused on the book of Proverbs; we should turn to the function of the books of Job and Ecclesiastes next, as they both embrace and face such nihilism and search for the way forward.

Though all the biblical wisdom texts come from a world view that has Yahweh as an all-powerful God, they all serve as texts that struggle with the situation humans find themselves in. Job and Ecclesiastes powerfully challenge the reader to imagine that the things they hold dear mean nothing, or can and will be taken away—on what then, ask the texts, will you rely? This is partly due to Israel's history. Though the wisdom literature is mainly thought to be post-exilic (that is, written down after the exile, when the Hebrew people returned to Israel), the nation has lived in exile. The Babylonians destroyed the center of Hebrew worship (the temple in Jerusalem) and made the people of Israel exiles in Babylon. They had to leave their home and forge new ways of worship, thinking and living in a land that was hostile to them, and then work out not only how to live but also why they should keep going.

The similarities with the forming of Olamina's Earthseed thoughts are striking. In the world of *Sower* and *Talents*, Olamina is a woman in exile, cast out from her home to find a new place of safety. She is forced to confront a world of change, a world where the old rules and assurances have been torn down. She goes through a pattern of safety, exile, safety (Acorn), exile, and her idea that "God is Change" serves to help her navigate such upheaval. Similarly ancient Near Eastern wisdom literature texts give the hearer ways to think and adapt rather than didactic "truths."

In the Parables there are two main reactions to the uncertainty of the future and the terror of the past: Olamina and Earthseed's declaration of adaptability and hope among the stars (a human future), and Christian America's rigid hold to a "traditional" homogenous Christianity with hope in eternity. The latter has strictly delineated rules it believes will keep it safe; the former has tenets that speak of movement, diversity, and growth in the face of many dangers. Matthew Goff, writing on the genre of wisdom as applied to texts outside the Bible, comes up with a nuanced but important distinction in types of sacred writing that is helpful here: he encourages us to use the term *noetic* (of knowledge) for wisdom texts rather than *pedagogical* or *instructional*. He writes:

> With "noetic" I stress that wisdom texts foster in their intended addressees a desire to search for understanding of the world. The point is not just for the student to learn what he is being taught. . . . A composition can be legitimately considered a wisdom text, I suggest, if it seeks to instil a sense of noetic searching for knowledge in its intended addressees and if it participates extensively in sapiential discourse. (Goff 330)

Not only do I find the term *noetic* helpful in describing the function of the Earthseed texts; I find it useful in considering the notion that such adaptability and notions of God being change end up set down in a "text." Sacred texts are generally considered solid, immovable things—and such is the reaction to the Bible by not only characters within the text of the Parable series but also commentators on it. They place Olamina's type of religion, and religious text, in a different category to that of her father's (and in some ways rightly so); however, they forget to explain what a text does represent in a religious tradition that leaves all things to change and merely explain what it doesn't do. The noetic nature of the text fits perfectly with the contents of the text. "God is Change" is a maxim that pushes the hearer to contemplation, not obedience. Even some of Olamina's more rigid utterances (that Earthseed should meet every week, for example) are given in a spirit of noetic investigation rather than pedagogical instruction.

The function of a sacred text can be manifold, but one of the functions of sacred text is to help form identity. How do we know who is "us" and who is not? "We" are the people of this book. Jerry Phillips writes:

> As opposed to the fascistic, wider world where people seek only their "kind," Acorn is a community that embraces diversity, in terms of race, class, and sexual identity: its members are black, white, Asian, and Latino, rich and poor, gay and straight. However, Butler makes clear that Acorn is not so much "heaven on earth" as the modest attempt to realize that ideal. (308)

However, there is a need for in- and out-group boundaries. Marc has to leave when his constant challenging and preaching means he is incompatible with their brand of tolerance. Though "God is Change" is the ruling tenet behind many of the sayings of Earthseed, and with that comes the promotion of diversity and inclusion, one cannot ignore the "us" and "we" language that is used to differentiate those who are Earthseed from those who are not. The texts here give no solid rules as such; rather the text functions to help the group know itself. The Earthseed sayings, especially in the weekly gatherings at Acorn, give the group something to gather around (no matter how weakly they adhere to it or how questioning they are): to be in the group is to engage with Earthseed sayings. Change is allowed, challenge is allowed, but the text is where that challenge can sit and be centered. Without it the group have little to bond them, except maybe Olamina, and she does not wish to be that sort of leader. As Gregory Hampton discusses in his chapter in this volume, Butler's female protagonists stand against and wrestle with such top-down hierarchies, even as they are forced into such roles. The text therefore also functions in place of such an all-powerful/all-knowing leader—outsiders may ask, "What are you then? What are you following? What is Acorn?" And (as with Israelite law) the group members can answer that they are gathered around this object, this text, these ideas. This adaptability and inclusivity are facets of wisdom literature. Job and Ecclesiastes in particular allow for huge changes in the state of a person's existence. The texts then also function as something to push back against. They need not be "truth" or even "unchanging"; rather they function to allow change of mind, change of world view, change of concepts about existence and even God. Ideas of God conceived in exile need space to change and grow as they face the unknown.

An interesting quality of wisdom texts is that they do not declare themselves as rigid to any time or space. Job, for example, is a tale of when God and the adversary were together, and Job is an exemplum or character to be placed in your own experiences. Ecclesiastes talks about universal truths—money, family, government, hierarchy, nature—nothing specific. They are adaptable texts, and much of the meaning within them depends on the receiver of the text. Therefore, the texts themselves are not solid and immovable but rather susceptible to changes in the culture in which they are received and to its interpretative framework. Olamina's *Books of the Living* can be seen to work similarly. If they are simply described as sacred text, there is a clash between solid words from the divine that must be adhered to; however, if they are wisdom, they function as one point in a fluctuating reality. The text itself can represent change, because any reader brings themselves to the text and shapes it, and a hearer who engages with it in "noetic striving" shapes its outcome.

In conclusion then, I would like to mention the gift that Octavia Butler gives back to biblical scholarship with the creation of these texts—the observations/musings on the creation of the sacred. I started by pushing against the term *invented scripture* and looking for a better way to consider the nature of what we have in these books. Olamina says

> I've never felt it that it was anything other than real: discovery rather than invention, exploration rather than creation. I wish I could believe it was all supernatural and that I am getting messages from God. But then I don't believe in that kind of God. All I do is observe and take notes, trying to put things down in ways that are as powerful, as simple, as direct as I feel them. (*Sower* 78)

We do not have insight into the internal workings of the authors of Hebrew wisdom literature, but apart from parts of Proverbs, none of the authors claims to be writing from God or by direct inspiration as later high views of the Bible would have it. Rather we have texts that have become scripture because of how they function for the communities that received them. Butler gives us an interesting look into the way an author experiences these texts and actualizes them over time. When confronting Olamina in *Talents* (127), her brother levies the challenge: "You made Earthseed up. Or if you didn't make it up, you read it or heard about it somewhere." Olamina capitulates slightly, saying: "All the truths of Earthseed existed somewhere before I found them and put them together. They were in the patterns of history, in science, philosophy, religion, or literature. I didn't make any of them up." She tries to explain further that writing these is not the same as writing a novel: "By definition, a novel is fiction." For Olamina, the difference in her authorship is that "I believe it. I wouldn't teach people that things were true if I didn't believe them" (*Talents* 127). We see here the noetic striving of the author, which is passed on to the reader. This is something rarely examined in biblical studies as we do not have access to our authors. However, I think it goes some way to showing us how the process might look, how the author might strive, and for that I am thankful.

In wisdom text, the experience of the divine meeting the mundane is something to be wrestled with, struggled with, and ultimately come to terms with. There is hope laid out next to stark reality—the pain of Job's losses, the meaningless nature of Qoheleth's daily tasks, the finality of death—and we find similarities in the *Books of the Living*. None of the texts has content that speaks clearly, saying, "I am sacred," but they function within the receiving communities as such.

If sacred texts are solid diktats to be adhered to, the tenet "God is Change" is a strange one to set down in such writing. However, when we see the text as wisdom literature, we can not only rightly position the texts of Earthseed within the idea that "God is Change," but we can even use the idea that "God is Change" to understand their content, form, and function. Texts are constantly reinterpreted and applied. They are not the static elements that people imagine them, or hope for them, to be. This is even more true with sacred text, where the relationship between reader and text is unique and personal. When we construct text, we construct ideas and world views, but we also shape them. We can posit therefore that with sacred text we shape God by constructing texts about God. Olamina does this.

She teaches us: text is change.

NOTE

1. Marlene Allen, Phillip Jos, and James Thrall (see bibliography) all discuss the text as scripture without definition—Jos assumes that the entire text is "parable" but gives no justification for this genre other than Butler's own naming of the works themselves,

something that I would consider more of the hermeneutic set by Butler rather than the genre of the Earthseed sayings. Only K. Ruffin enters the discussion of genre and biblical text when she asserts the books are part of an "Afrofuturist black feminist biblical hermeneutic" which emphasises the importance of scribal literacy to the nature of the works here discussed (Ruffin 91).

WORKS CITED

Allen, Marlene D. "Octavia Butler's Parable Novels and the 'Boomerang' of African American History." *Callaloo*, vol. 32, no. 4, Winter 2009, pp. 1353–1365.

Berger, Peter L. *The Sacred Canopy*. Doubleday, 1967.

Black, Max. *Models and Metaphors*. Cornell University Press, 1962.

Butler, Octavia. *Parable of the Sower*. Grand Central Publishing, 1993.

———. *Parable of the Talents*. Grand Central Publishing, 1998.

Collins, John J. "Proverbial Wisdom and the Yahwist Vision." *Semeia*, vol. 17, 1980, pp. 1–17.

Crenshaw, James L. *Old Testament Wisdom: An Introduction*. Rev. ed., Westminster / John Knox Press, 1998.

Davis, Ellen D. *Proverbs, Ecclesiastes, and the Song of Songs*. Westminster / John Knox Press, 2000.

Firth, David G., and Lindsey Wilson, eds. *Interpreting Old Testament Wisdom Literature*. InterVarsity Press, 2016.

Forti, Tova. "Bee's Honey—from Realia to Metaphor in Biblical Wisdom Literature." *Vetus Testamentum LVI*, vol. 3, 2006, pp. 327–341.

Gilbert, Pierre. "Fighting Fire with Fire: Divine Nihilism in Ecclesiastes." *Direction 40*, vol. 1, 2011, pp. 65–79.

Goff, Matthew. "Qumran Wisdom Literature and the Problem of Genre." *Dead Sea Discoveries*, vol. 17, 2010, pp. 315–335.

Jos, Phillip H. "Fear and the Spiritual Realism of Octavia Butler's Earthseed." *Utopian Studies*, vol. 23, no. 2, 2012, pp. 408–429.

Lucas, Ernest. *Exploring the Old Testament, Vol. 3: Psalms and Wisdom Literature*. SPCK Publishing, 2003.

Phillips, Jerry. "The Intuition of the Future: Utopia and Catastrophe in Octavia Butlers 'Parable of the Sower.'" *NOVEL: A Forum on Fiction*, vol. 35, no. 2/3, *Contemporary African American Fiction and the Politics of Postmodernism*, Spring/Summer 2002, pp. 299–311.

Ruffin, K. "Parable of a 21st Century Religion: Octavia Butler's Afrofuturistic Bridge between Science and Religion." *Obsidian III*, vol. 6/7, 2005, pp. 87–104.

Thrall, James. "Authoring the Sacred: Humanism and Invented Scripture in Octavia Butler, Kurt Vonnegut and Dan Simmons." *Implicit Religion*, vol. 17, 2014, pp. 509–531.

5

Regarding the Other in Octavia Butler's Xenogenesis

Toward a Posthumanist Ethics

MARY M. GROVER

> I go from not paying any attention to how my characters should look to recognizing that it's very important how they look especially if they're not supposed to be human. I need to help my reader visualize them even though what my reader sees won't be what I had in mind.
>
> —OCTAVIA E. BUTLER

In a 1997 interview with Marilyn Mehaffy and AnaLouise Keating, Octavia Butler reflects on how the reader factors into the realization of her nonhuman characters. Above, the context is a discussion about the trilogy Xenogenesis, Butler's still radical vision of human-alien encounter. First published in 1987, Xenogenesis (*Dawn, Adulthood Rites, Imago*) introduces us to the Oankali, interstellar travelers who arrive on the scene after a global nuclear war has made the earth uninhabitable. The Oankali "rescue" the remnants of humankind, keeping them in stasis on their ship while terraforming the earth for colonization. Upon awakening, humans face a choice between genetic "trade" or sterilization. Those who opt for trade are assimilated into Oankali culture, joining families of five consisting of two male/female pairs—one set human and one set Oankali—all unified by an indeterminately sexed "ooloi." Ensuring family cohesion, ooloi's not only induce chemical dependency in their mates but also facilitate ecstatically erotic merging sessions among them. With such formidable powers of compulsion and seduction, the Oankali railroad humans into propagation of alien-human hybrids, "mixed" by ooloi (who possess a specialized organ for genetic engineering). Hybrid progeny, while seeming less alien to humans than their Oankali parents, nonetheless sport sensory tentacles that rustle, writhe, and penetrate skin to "taste" the biological essence of others. Butler's imagining of Oankali variations, however, goes beyond the tentacular archetype to include previous and emerging forms of this ever-evolving race, including the caterpillar-like Akjai, for example, which can communicate directly with the mother ship, or shape-shifting ooloi that seduce potential mates by incarnating their desire.

As Butler suggests, when it comes to the reader's experience of such characters, there is an unbridgeable distance between what she "had in mind" and what she "need[s] to help [her] reader visualize." Here, the space of storytelling is premised on a thoughtful outreach effort, "help" given by the storyteller. Butler's authorial stance toward her reader relinquishes power, minds the intersubjective gap. It is a commitment to a collaboration free from any sort of futile imposition of self or belief. This orientation, I would argue, *regards* ethical distance: "regards" meaning, simply, acknowledging and honoring the separation between embodied selves but also respecting how the Other steps into the space of our separation. In the case of fictional narratives, the writer-reader relationship, as Butler frames it above, endorses and emblematizes this truth about ethical encounter.

For Emmanuel Levinas, standing upon this truth of interpersonal distance and recognizing the ethical claims of the separate other is an act of faith, a belief that infinity wells up from the Other before me, demanding my recognition. In what follows, I aim to show that we can and should read Xenogenesis at the juncture between faith, philosophy, and story. In the Levinasian scheme of things, ethical accountability to the Other is not a choice but the first premise of being. The Other cannot be contained within a totality or system of our own creation. The revelation of the Other through receptive encounter stands in opposition to religion as dogma, which in Xenogenesis takes the form of evangelical Christianity, on the one hand, and the Oankali creed of biological determinism, on the other. In the drama of encounter between humans and Oankali, religion as dogma cracks open to allow for acknowledgment and discovery, a place where the impositions of doctrine and ego are shed in and through effortful encounter. In this chapter, I show how Akin, the first hybrid human-Oankali male, models this commitment. Because he cannot fully commune with either humans or Oankalis, his subjectivity is thus an experience of transcendent desire as Levinas describes it, a longing for the other that approaches without ever touching. Akin, Butler's ethical touchstone, is what happens when dogmatic commitment to an ideal (change, life, nonviolence) stumbles through way of practice into grace: grace as care for the other through regard, without the forcible intrusion of preemptive knowing, imposition of the ego, phagocytosis of romantic desire, or dictates of doctrine.

A humanistic poesy of interpersonal regard, however, as feminist critics have established in the case of Levinas, readily slides into masculinist biases, a postmodern death sentence for any sort of heart-stirring humanism that disregards the solipsism of its generalizations. While Levinas gives us a phenomenology that at its core envisions only two parties in the exchange, Xenogenesis presses issues of discursive ethics in its representation of consensus building among the Oankali, a process facilitated by a mind and body link of discussion among multiple parties. If we locate the potential for justice in consensus among participants in public discourse or, as Butler models for us, in discussion within and between communities, what constitutes fair participation? As Butler dramatizes and Seyla Benhabib argues, the terms of participation should be negotiable, open for reexamination. Moreover, personal narrative counts. In Xenogenesis, Butler is vitally concerned with how narrative is integral to a moral standpoint and thus with ethical encounter between *ungeneralizable* selves.[1] In stressing the moral force of storytelling, which has the power to transmit embodied experience, Butler is also very much in alignment with Benhabib, who proposes a "universalist feminist discursive ethics" that "retain[s] a principled universalist moral standpoint while acknowledging the role of contextual moral judgment in human affairs" (134). The embedded and embodied self is enmeshed in narratives: "The self is not a thing, a substrate, but the protagonist of a life's tale" (162).

Ultimately, Xenogenesis presumes an ethics of encounter rooted in faith that it is possible to share moments of reciprocal regard with the Other, despite the complex intrusions of power and dogma that veil or repress revelation of a self. This faith has been occluded in criticism of Butler's work that measures the value of Butler's writing along a scale of "progressive" versus "regressive," making evaluative arguments about how well her vision of gender, race, religion, and community dismantles oppressive structures of hierarchy and instead provides us with liberating alternatives.[2] Stepping outside the interpretive framework of ideological liberation versus oppression, I focus here on how Xenogenesis furthers respect for alterity, specifically by modeling ethical dialogue as an unscriptable process of learning, of discovery. At the same time, I demonstrate how Butler's posthumanist sense of ethics is leavened with an awareness that objectifying apprehension of the Other pretermits justice. For Butler, justice entails an awareness of how discursive injustices perpetuate objectification of the Other as unworthy of regard. The drama of encounter in Xenogensis centers on moments of regard that sideline, if only for brief and meaningful exchanges, biases.

Deaf Creeds

The Oankali view of humankind, tidily summed up as "the Human Contradiction," maintains that humans are genetically doomed on account of a fatal conflict between intelligence, on the one hand, and hierarchal behavior, on the other. Throughout the trilogy, they propound upon this doctrine: In *Dawn*, for example, the protagonist, Lilith, is schooled by her Oankali mentor Jdahya, who patiently explains humans' genetic flaw, likening it to a malignant cancer. In *Adulthood Rites*, Akin contemplates what he has been taught about this condition: "The Human Contradiction again. The Contradiction, it was more often called among Oankali. It was fascinating, seductive, and lethal. It had brought Humans to their final war" (432). Here, "the Contradiction," oft invoked by Akin's elders, acquires the status of a preexisting truth, having the explanatory force of religious doctrine. It is asserted to justify Oankali treatment of humans as mere instruments in their mission of trade. The Oankali accordingly preach a biological determinism that rationalizes the use of their genetic technology to subsume or else sterilize humans. With each new interspecies trade, the Oankali spread their gospel of change across the galaxy. The practice produces a litany of "begats," or "stories of the long, multispecies Oankali history" (65), a genetic scripture that lives within each Oankali individual. The doctrine of trade, through transubstantiation, effects radical transformation, giving rise to another new kind of species that emerges at the end of the trilogy.

Critics have trenchantly criticized the ethics of Oankali trade. In Amanda Boulter's reading, the encounter between Oankali and humans is "replete with historical echoes, in which the relationship between the Oankali and the humans evokes the power structures of human slavery, colonization and eugenics" (180). Christina Braid argues that the Oankali, despite their seeming aversion to physical violence, are in fact violently coercive. Even while the Oankali abandon themselves to interdependency with humans, they in fact exploit humans: "While not all humans are violent, part of the ambiguity in *Xenogenesis* rests in the implementation of Oankali justice, a force which seems to impress violence upon the Humans in the forms of cultural, genetic, and sexual repression" (58). Sarah Outterson, in her own compelling take on violence in Xenogenesis, argues that violence "also carries the idea of violation of boundaries, transgression of the lines defining personal identity and integrity" (434). As a change agent, violence is in fact intrinsic to learning and change in the face of encountering difference. Braid homes in on the nature and origin of this violence (however fruitful)—Oankali "intellectual chauvinism." In characterizing this lamentable bias, Braid notes the applicability of Levinasian thought: "The Oankali irresponsibility, which fails to respond to the Humans, represents an injustice described as 'reduction of the other by the same (self)'" (qtd. in Levinas 55).

I will go further and argue that the unfolding encounter between the Oankali and humans is in fact a dynamic study in how the Levinasian "same"—the solipsistic self—stifles ethical revelation of the Other. Levinas's concept of "objectifying cognition" illuminates the force and consequence of this habit as manifested in Xenogenesis, where we find both humans and Oankali implicated in violent ethical retrenchments. Objectifying cognition imposes a static form on the dynamic presence of the other, presumptive schemae for knowing. Acting as an intersubjective soundproof barrier, it mutes the voice of the separate other. Objectifying cognition is an instrumentalist stance wherein objects come into being purely as a function of one's purposes for them. As Stephen W. Potts remarks in the course of an interview with Butler, the Oankali "are the ultimate users, adapting not only the entire genome for [their] own purposes, but ultimately destroying the planet for all other life as well" (67). Oankali insistence on the "Human Contradiction" is a "thematization and conceptualization, which . . . are not at peace with the other, but suppression or possession of the other" (Levinas 46). Humans, likewise putting up barriers to intersubjective revelation and reciprocal regard, thematize the Oankali as "worms," "animals."

As mass-disseminated dogma, Christianity mirrors the Oankali creed of genetic determinism in its ethical deafness. Akin's encounter with a plastic, holographic-type image of Christ, excavated from the ruins of human civilization, transmits a critique of evangelical Christianity in consumer culture:

> Akin moved [the picture] slightly in his hand, watching the apparent movement of Christ, whose mouth opened and closed and whose arm moved up and down. The picture, though scratched, was hard and flat—made of a material Akin did not understand. He tasted it—then threw it hard away from him, disgusted, nauseated. (*Adulthood Rites* 380)

Plastic Christ disseminates patriarchy in its most toxic form—unquestioned male authority. Unlike Akin, who, significantly, will always be short, looking up to others even after his metamorphosis to adulthood, plastic Christ holds forth from on high.[3] Incapable of listening, plastic Christ proclaims. Without a participating audience, his preaching is literally and figuratively mechanical. Like Marcus, the ambitious young preacher who presumes the superiority of evangelical Christianity in Butler's *Parable of the Talents*, plastic Christ anticipates no pushback (whereas Marcus gets plenty [*Parable* 163–166]). Without a listener who is respected as separate and different, patriarchal religious authority is toxic, hard, flat. Meanwhile, the Oankali's implacable devotion to transformative fecundity steamrolls the feelings and objections that humans voice throughout the process. As a result, that human "voice" often takes the form of brutality, attacks on the Oankali and butchery of those humans who affiliate themselves with the monstrous "worms." Sarah Wood has explored how "Butler problematizes the standpoint and authority of white-authored Christianity" (87–88). I am suggesting that, in addition to this project, Butler problematizes "standpoint" and "authority" and instead places faith in compassionate regard.

Faith in Regard

Some have inferred a posthumanist ethical platform of sorts in the fruition of Oankali trade. Theodora Goss and John Paul Riquelme, for example, while acknowledging the likeness between the Oankali's ongoing trade mission and that which "accompanied the European establishment of empires" (448), argue that Xenogenesis reworks gothic tropes to dismantle hierarchy, undoing binaries to "create an inescapable network of mutuality" (449). Aparajita Nanda, while she elaborates on the Oankali's imperialistic exertion of power and cultural dominance, nonetheless finds "a future of regenerative hope" in the trilogy's conclusion with the emergence of a new, posthuman species (131). These well-qualified readings elaborate on the ethical "goods" that come of Butler's "vision of mutable bodies and social structures," which, as Peter Sands argues, "situates her within the utopian tradition of 'social dreaming,' which is one of contingency, perspectivism, and positionality, often in the service of a social dream or dream of action in the world held by the rhetor" (4).

I maintain that Butler's positive construction of ethical good is foundational, not contingent, and not to be located within the ambivalent utopia of hybrid community that emerges in the conclusion of the final novel in the trilogy. Nor is it limited to critique of ethically bankrupt creeds. Rather, an ethics of encounter manifests itself in the character of Akin. Kidnapped as a toddler by human "resisters," Akin is a mediating figure, strategically abandoned by the Oankali to live among humans and learn about them. If the resisters can see the Oankali only as loathsome worms, alien colonizers; if the Oankali can see humans only as genetic time bombs; if both parties, through objectifying cognition, do violence to the other, then Akin anchors the process of clash and merger in an ethics of openness and receptivity. We find him in a continual process of observing, wondering, asking questions, seeking to learn instead of confirm. Part Oankali, Akin is horrified by human violence and seeming disregard for life. At the same time, he is set apart from the Oankali in his sympathies for humans. As Nanda has observed in her take on the character, Akin is a *kin* and *akin*: kin to both humans and Oankali but at the same time *like*, not *of* (123). With this disposition, Akin rights a wrong, persuading the Oankali to restore human fertility and allow humankind to pursue its own destiny on a terraformed version of Mars.

Akin is motivated by what Levinas calls *metaphysical desire*, a longing for that which is necessarily beyond perception, ungraspable—the transcendent other. This desire underlies ethical connection premised on the truth of (faith in) the distance between self and other, which Akin must contend with, even while he longs to close the gap. When the sympathetic resister human Tate allows Akin to "taste her" through penetration with the sensory filaments in his tongue, knowledge of the Other remains beyond his grasp:

> Later he realized that he had actually tried to become her, to join with her as he might with his closest sibling. It was not possible. He was reaching for a union that the humans had denied him. It seemed to him that what he needed was just beyond his grasp, just beyond that final crossing he could not make, as with his mother. As with everyone. He could know so much and no more, feel so much and no more, join so close and no closer. (*Adulthood Rites* 388)

As distinguished from the objectifying act, "metaphysics approaches without touching" (Levinas 109). Akin's desire cannot possess but instead reaches after understanding. If religion can be construed as "the bond that is established between the same and the other without constituting a totality" (Levinas 40), Akin is a metaphysical priest. Committed by genetic and symbolic selection to an ethics of receptive regard, Akin is the only character in the novel said to listen "carefully" (367), the only character who never uses the word *listen* as a command. *Listen*, used as an imperative fourteen times in the trilogy by eight different characters, conveys urgency to be understood due to deafness on the part of a biased interlocutor. Akin, in contrast, models a regard for the Other that enables learning from the resisters through dialogue: "He made them his teachers" (*Adulthood Rites* 398). This orientation, which other characters slip in and out of, is Akin's being and purpose.

Butler's implicit critique of evangelical Christianity in the era of consumer culture (a nauseating blah-blah propounded by plastic Christ) is undergirded by faith in intersubjective regard as moral ground zero. We stand on this ground when Jdahya responds to Lilith's feeling of entrapment in the trade by offering what he believes to be very wrong—to take her life in order to free her. We also stand on this ground during encounters between Lilith and Tate, who maintain respect for one another even while Lilith throws in her lot with the Oankali, and Tate with the human resisters. In such exchanges, sympathetic connection encompasses difference, as when Gabe, a resister and former actor, performs *King Lear* for Akin, who is baffled and terrified at first but then likens the new experience of dramatic pathos to how the Oankali communicate: "It's like what we do. . . . It's like when we touch each other and talk with feelings and pressures" (402). Here, understanding proceeds through simile rather than metaphor. The revelation of the Other is something like (akin) rather than a presumed equivalency that rides roughshod over the Other with metaphorical abandon.

Posthumanist Regard

From the perspective of critical frameworks that emphasize the empirical and ethical necessity of giving resonance to marginalized voices, humanistic accounts of intersubjective ethics are themselves ethically suspect because they are so often implicated as masculinist, classed, heteronormative, racialized "truths." The Levinasian notion of radical alterity, in particular, deracinates selves from the singular history of their embodied pains and pleasures within unbalanced systems of power. "Justice," as Sonia Sikka asserts, "requires attention to specificity" (115), and "Levinas's indifference to the differences between faces results in a tendency not to do justice to faces that are specifically other" (115). And as William Large observes, "Even though Levinas never quite says so, one has the suspicion . . . that the ethical relation is a relationship between men" (70). Face-to-face interactions do not exist within an egalitarian power bubble but are imbricated in an ethics of discourse within communities, where conversations with multiple participants shape norms and determine collective action.

In Xenogenesis, Butler explores the necessary and consequential interrelation between intersubjective and communicative ethics, between intersubjective regard and political justice. A communicative ethics, as Benhabib characterizes it, "sets up a model of moral conversation among members of a modern ethical community for whom the theological and ontological bases of inequality among humans has been radically placed into question" (51). Benhabib proposes "steps" for creating "norms of universal respect and egalitarian reciprocity" that "can be formalized" (30).[4] Within Benhabib's framework, personal narrative becomes a crucially valid mode of participation in public discourse, since storytelling relays a singular, embodied experience. Like Benhabib, Butler proposes storytelling as a mode that promises inclusion for disenfranchised others; however, Butler goes on to show how intersubjective distance, especially in relation to storytelling, must be appropriately modulated in public discourse to ensure intersubjective regard.

The interrelation between these ethical domains plays out in Akin's advocacy for the resisters, a plot line that highlights how powerful storytelling promotes fairness in public discussions that decide the fate of individuals within a community. While the Oankali are adamant in their belief that humans won't survive the "Human Contradiction," Akin passionately believes that they should have their fertility restored and be given the freedom to shape their own destiny, for better or worse. The Oankali remain unmoved—until Akin imparts the story of his coming of age, which he first relays to a receptive, subadult ooloi, through direct sensory stimulation:

> Then, carefully, in the manner of a storyteller, [Akin] gave it the experience of his abduction, captivity, and conversion. All that he had felt, he made it feel. He did what he had not known he could do. He overwhelmed it so that for a time it was, itself, both captive and convert. He did to it what the abandonment of the Oankali had done to him in his infancy. He made the ooloi understand on an utterly personal level what he had suffered and come to believe. (*Adulthood Rites* 456)

Next, Akin's soulful Akjai mentor transmits the experience via the ship to the Oankali, who through the consensus-building process eventually agree to relocate humans to Mars (488). Akin, through the Akjai, speaks for the resisters, who are completely excluded from a conversation that will decisively determine whether humans will be allowed to continue as such. Here, the obvious flaws of the consensus-building process are brought into relief. Humans (and, we also learn, Oankali subadults), are directly affected by the outcome of consensus building, and yet they cannot participate in it. Consensus building among the Oankali, though it might seem to be utopian, is therefore a mode or style of discourse that blatantly perpetuates the exclusion of individuals whose inability to participate consequently denies their wishes and needs.

Akin's mediated participation in the search for consensus also dramatizes how justice hinges on empathetic response to a story, on the ability to share in the embodied experience of a separate other, the capacity to internalize their point of view. The Oankali mode of embodied story transmission ensures that the receiver will understand the Other's perspective "on an utterly personal level." Like Benhabib, Butler locates justice in inclusive public discourse that "does not deny our embodied and embedded identity, but aims at developing moral attitudes and encouraging political transformations that can yield a point of view acceptable to all" (Benhabib 212). A facility for telling and appreciating stories is thus integral to Benhabib's universalist discursive ethics, since moral judgment, as she maintains, "involves certain 'interpretive' and 'narrative' skills which, in turn, entail the capacity for exercising an 'enlarged mentality'" (177). The Oankali's genetically engineered ability to impart embodied experience can be understood as a commitment to the ethical necessity of such skills in public discourse.

At the same time, powerful storytelling foregrounds the challenge and peril of self-narration, for both tellers and listeners, pressing issues of "narrative ethics," in the sense that Adam Z. Newton has developed that concept: "the dialogic system of exchanges at work among tellers, listeners, and witnesses, and the intersubjective responsibilities and claims which follow from acts of storytelling" (18). A narrative ethics concerns itself with the price that narrative exacts on readers/listeners, with the risks that accompany narrating the self, or, as Newton says, "storying the self." Butler brings issues of narrative ethics beyond the dyad of teller and listener into the arena of public discourse. When radically disparate experiences are shared in this domain, what pitfalls accompany narrating the self, especially as a mode of public discourse? The stories of marginalized others often go untold, unheard, unacknowledged; on the other hand, Butler suggests that the force of suffering communicated through such stories can be too strong, mobilizing the defenses of listeners whose subject position is in fact fortified by the preclusion of the outsider's pain. The Oankali, when undergoing Akin's story via sensory transmission, are made so uncomfortable as to deny the validity of Akin's experience: "As soon as the experience ended, people began objecting to its intensity, objecting to being so overwhelmed, objecting to the idea that this could have been the experience of such a young child" (*Adulthood Rites* 456). For implicated listeners, opening up to the suffering of a marginalized other poses a special threat. Those who complacently thrive within a system must *admit* the trauma it has caused others.[5]

If we are to be so moved by stories that they influence our moral decision-making process, we must have a strong yet flexible sense of self to overcome the fear of emotional engulfment. In *Adulthood Rites*, the ability to balance self-cohesion with receptive empathy is in fact a coming-of-age achievement. Adult Oankali can achieve and tolerate "utter blending" when aiming to find "consensus on some controversial subject" (442). But Akin, a subadult who hasn't yet acquired "adult perception," must actively learn to manage the profound discomfort of "that incredible unity," which makes him feel "as though something were crawling down his throat and he [can] not manage a reflexive cough to bring it up" (443) With the Akjai's guidance, however, Akin is able hang on to his own sense of self while joining to others in a circuit of connection: "He was equally aware of them and their bodies and their sensations. But somehow, they were still themselves, and he was still himself" (444). Part human, part Oankali, Akin shows us that separate and self-contained beings can overcome empathy aversion.[6]

Lilith's position relative to the Oankali, on the other hand, foregrounds the threat of narrative penetration. Like her son Akin, she must strive to maintain self-integrity as she merges with the Other, mothering construct children and taking part in Oankali domestic life. Akin's access to Oankali linkage empowers him, giving him more knowledge of and control over a genetically engineered environment. But for Lilith, coming to accept queer union with the Oankali is capitulation rather than an empowering rite. Lilith never joins in consensus making, even while she merges with her ooloi mate Nikanj in various ways. It is unclear whether she can be given the ability to participate or is not given that ability because she does not count. In any case, she is not politically enfranchised by the Oankali. Lilith is literally penetrated by the ongoing story of Oankali trade partnerships when, without her knowledge, Nikanj impregnates her with a construct child. The ethics of this act are ambiguous. Nikanj believes that motherhood will rescue his mate from the shattering loss of her human lover Joseph, who has been murdered by resisters. "'You are ready to be a mother,' Nikanj tells her. 'You could never have said so'" (Dawn 242). Lilith later concedes that, in fact, she did want a child, but here, Nikanj's "comfort" sounds like rhetoric justifying sexual assault, that is, "You know you wanted it." Given the unequal power relations, narrative penetration—the ongoing story of trade relations—verges on rape.

Here, Butler's thematic treatment of narrative as penetration calls into question the humanistic solipsism intrinsic to a narrative ethics that does not include a sense of communicative ethics. The relationship between storyteller and listener/reader, in Newton's model of narrative ethics, which takes inspiration from the Levinasian poesy of intersubjective encounter, is figured as dyadic. But as Lilith and Nikanj's exchange shows, participants in this relationship are implicated in alliances and affiliations that determine the potential for reciprocity between them. Exclusions and power dynamics within larger communities are intrinsic to the most intimate exchanges between individuals. As Lilith and Nikanj engage in narrative trade with each other, the blatant exclusions of Oankali consensus making affect the balance of power between them. Nikanj's affiliation with the Oankali positions Lilith as a tool for trade even in this face-to-face dialogue, in which Nikanj's receptivity furthers the Oankali's instrumentalist designs on Lilith: "It wanted not only language, but culture, biology, her own life story. . . . Whatever she knew, it expected to learn" (63). Dyadic revelation of selves through story is freighted with the reductive values and demands of the groups to which those selves belong. For the partner who is not enfranchised by the dominant discourse, impregnation can bring self-alienation, birthing a new kind of subjectivity, a marginalized identity: in Xenogenesis, that new subjectivity is literalized, made incarnate as Akin, the legacy of Lilith's self-alienated self-compromise.

Resisting Narrative Penetration

The sequence of novels in the Xenogenesis trilogy has been read by many critics as a pathway to utopian promise, culminating in a liberating, flexible, communal way of being. Critics have also found revolutionary potential in the Oankalis' more fluid and provisional sense of gender, which emerges when an individual undergoes metamorphosis, within a network of relationships. With these values in view, the tag team of narrative voices that accompany us in the sequence of the novels could be read as a kind of posthumanist seduction—especially if you posit a white, heterosexual, male reader/viewer of science fiction, someone whose reading pleasures typically derive from identification with a tough, resourceful, virile male protagonist. Arguably, that protagonist is merely feminized and racialized in the figure of Lilith in *Dawn*, the first novel of the trilogy. But *Adulthood Rites* moves readers a step closer toward Oankali subjectivity, immersing them through third-person limited narrative into the thoughts and perceptions of Akin, whose Oankali nature (empathic, vegetarian, drawn to what is Other) is offset by his "male" nature. Having identified with an Oankali-human construct, readers of the third novel find themselves in league with Jodahs, the very first construct ooloi, at first unsure of its powers but then coming into them with godlike strength to heal—and seduce—in both male and female form. In *Imago*, this first-person narrator fully discloses to us its vulnerability, manipulations, and desires. Undergoing a coming-of-age identity crisis, the "I" presumes our sympathy and support as it gives us an embodied experience of the conflicts that ensue when it becomes ooloi during metamorphosis, instead of male or female as planned by the Oankali. Reading without resistance to this particular narrator, one might conclude, along with Nolan Belk, that "for Butler, the locus of hope is in the power of the erotic—the trust in the body's deep desires for propagation, love, and connection" (373). Posthumanist seduction completed.

In my early teens, I consumed the third novel in the series as a romance. Queer, turned on, craving romantic love, I eagerly gave myself over to the pleasures of seduction and conquest and blissful union to be had through ready identification with Jodahs. Many decades and a couple waves of feminism later, in the era of the "me-too" movement, it's hard to imagine that an informed teen would ingest the narrative as I once did: Jodahs habitually drugs resisters with "ooloi substance" to overcome them. Force is justified, seemingly, because resister humans just do not know what they are missing out on until they are penetrated. Unless we overlook, ignore, or condone the pleasure that Jodahs gains through violently coercive means, it is impossible to experience comfortable identification with this "I."[7]

But the first two novels in the sequence, it might well be argued, have braced us for this encounter: Our alliance with Lilith keys us to suspect an agenda that disregards human agency. Akin, meanwhile, shows empathetic receptivity to the story of people who commit vicious acts (humans), and yet while Akin is less defended than Lilith, we enter into the process by which he must "manage the terror" of self-dissolving closeness with the Other, keeping a grip on his autonomous self. In this way, the sequence of narrative relationships primes a reader to meet the "I" of *Imago*, Jodahs, with healthy resistance to its presumptuously penetrative demands for sympathy. Arranging this handoff, from Lilith to Akin to Jodahs, Butler builds a community of narrators, giving readers flexible agency of affiliation in their experience of encounter with the themes and experiences they activate for themselves in the course of reading the novels. Xenogenesis thereby enters us into the interrelation between intersubjective, narrative, and discursive ethics that its themes and plot lines explore: even while taking in one story according to the relational terms that its telling sets up, we come conditioned by other such encounters, stories imbricated in a power dynamics influenced by their protagonists' affiliations, however flexible or seemingly fixed. Because we take in a story from a perspective imbricated in an embodied experience of identity and affiliation, the encounter is all at once dyadic and inflected by inclusions and exclusions effected within larger communities.

Mehaffy and Keating argue that "the narrative embodiments of [Butler's] fiction advocate a therapeutic reclamation of [the] flesh as a primary site and signifier of knowledge and communication, both personal and collective, both material and narrated" (49). Butler's posthumanist ethics embraces this premise: in decision making that affects members of a polity, the significance of singular, embodied experience must be recognized. At the same time, Xenogenesis also dramatizes how fear of narrative engulfment and penetration need to be acknowledged and negotiated when storied selves claim their price of empathy. Even with these concerns, Xenogenesis, as I have argued, presumes an ethics of encounter anchored in faith that moments of reciprocal regard with the Other, despite the insidious incursion of power and dogma, are foundational to the struggle for justice—and the evanescing visitation of grace.[8]

NOTES

1. Benhabib's term.

2. At one end of the spectrum, for example, Patricia Melzer credits Butler for "counter[ing] the construction of dualisms by assuming multiple, contradictory notions of self that undermine the binary and by creating an alternative way to view difference" (68). And on the other end, Elana Gomel argues that Butler's work lacks merit because her characters are insufficiently posthuman (143).

3. There is a remarkable coincidence between Akin's perspective, given his relative shortness, and how Levinas attributes ethical height to the other.

4. These include, for example, "We ought to treat each other as concrete human beings whose capacity to express [a] standpoint we ought to enhance by creating, whenever possible, social practices embodying . . . the principle of egalitarian reciprocity" (48–49).

5. A current example is first-world resistance to the pain of refugees whose plight is a function of the unequal distribution of resources within a global economic system that benefits insiders and scapegoats outsiders.

6. Admittedly, the feat requires an infusion of endorphins to alleviate the pain, administered in this instance by the Akjai, which "stimulates the release of certain endorphins in [Akin]'s brain—in effect, causing him to drug himself into pleasurable relaxation and acceptance" (443). The assistance of endorphins here can be likened to the effect of familiar genre pleasures, which allow viewers to tolerate the suffering of others whose stories demand sympathetic response—generic elements like romance, sex, hope, or positive identification with characters (such as white saviors) who are more like enfranchised readers/viewers than marginalized others depicted in the narrative.

7. See especially the seduction scene in which Jodahs silences the "horse shouting" of a target by "looping one sensory arm around his neck, then moving the coil up to cover his mouth" (687).

8. For inspiration, feedback, and moral support, many thanks to Elizabeth, Adam Z. Newton, Aparajita Nanda, and Carmen Butcher.

WORKS CITED

Belk, Nolan. "The Certainty of the Flesh: Octavia Butler's Use of the Erotic in the *Xenogenesis* Trilogy." *Utopian Studies*, vol. 19, no. 3, 2008, pp. 369–389.

Benhabib, Seyla. *Situating the Self,* Kindle ed., Polity Press, 2007.

Boulter, Amanda. "Polymorphous Futures: Octavia E. Butler's *Xenogenesis* Trilogy." *American Bodies: Cultural Histories of the Physique*, edited by Tim Armstrong, New York University Press, 1996, pp. 170–185.

Braid, Christina. "Contemplating and Contesting Violence in Dystopia: Violence in Octavia Butler's *Xenogenesis* Trilogy." *Contemporary Justice Review*, vol. 9, no. 1, 2006, pp. 47–65.

Butler, Octavia E. *Parable of the Talents.* Warner Books, 1989.

———. *Xenogenesis.* Guild America Books, 1989.

Gomel, Elana. *Science Fiction, Alien Encounters, and the Ethics of Posthumanism.* Macmillan, 2014.

Goss, Theodora, and John Paul Riquelme. "From Superhuman to Posthuman: The Gothic Technological Imaginary in Mary Shelley's *Frankenstein* and Octavia Butler's *Xenogenesis*." *Modern Fiction Studies*, vol. 53, no. 3, 2007, pp. 434–459.

Large, William. *Levinas' Totality and Infinity*. Bloomsbury, 2015.

Levinas, Emmanuel. *Totality and Infinity*. Translated by Alphonso Lingis, Duquesne University Press, 2008.

Mehaffy, Marilyn, and AnaLouise Keating. "'Radio Imagination': Octavia Butler on the Poetics of Narrative Embodiment." *MELUS*, vol. 26, no. 1, 2001, pp. 45–76.

Melzer, Patricia. *Alien Constructions: Science Fiction and Feminist Thought*. University of Texas Press, 2006.

Nanda, Aparajita. "Power, Politics, and Domestic Desire in Octavia Butler's *Lilith's Brood*." *Callaloo*, vol. 36, no. 3, 2013, pp. 773–788.

Newton, Adam Z. *Narrative Ethics*. Harvard University Press, 1997.

Nilges, Mathias. "'We Need the Stars': Change, Community, and the Absent Father in Octavia Butler's *Parable of the Sower* and *Parable of the Talents*." *Callaloo*, vol. 32, no. 4, 2009, pp. 1332–1352.

Obourn, Megan. "Octavia Butler's Disabled Futures." *Contemporary Literature*, vol. 54, no. 1, 2013, pp. 109–138.

Outterson, Sarah. "Change, Violence: Octavia Butler's Pedagogical Philosophy." *Utopian Studies*, vol. 19, no. 3, 2008, pp. 433–456.

Sands, Peter. "Octavia Butler's Chiastic Cannibalistics." *Utopian Studies*, vol. 14, no. 1, 2003, pp. 1–14.

Sikka, Sonia. "The Delightful Other: Portraits of the Feminine in Kierkegaard, Nietzsche, and Levinas." *Feminist Interpretations of Emmanuel Levinas*, edited by Tina Chanter, Pennsylvania State University Press, 2001, pp. 96–118.

Wood, Sarah. "Subversion through Inclusion: Octavia Butler's Interrogation of Religion in *Xenogenesis* and *Wild Seed*." *FEMSPEC*, vol. 6, no. 1, 2005, pp. 87–99.

6

Parable of the Talents as Genre Criticism and the Holy Spirit of Speculative Fiction

CHUCK ROBINSON

In Octavia Butler's favorite plot, a crisis pulls a struggling community in opposing directions, to go *back* and repair or move *forward* and change. *Parable of the Sower* and *Parable of the Talents* explore this "fix versus fly" conflict through Lauren Olamina's construction of Earthseed, a religion characterized by a worshipful attention to change and spiritual commitment to interstellar exploration. Butler intended to follow Earthseed practitioners through different planetary adventures and adaptations (cf. Canavan 123–126), but the two extant Parables only chronicle Earthseed's development to the point that its community of believer-practitioners leave Earth. Like most of Butler's work, the Parables do noteworthy things with genre, abounding with references to genres as diverse as sermon, cookbook, and road map. Genre criticism, of a sort, even finds a place in *Sower* when Lauren rejects promising news of the corporation-managed city, Olivar, in terms of "the company-city subgenre" of science fiction and when she assumes her father's preaching duties to prevent a church meeting from becoming a certain genre of ceremony, "an impossible impromptu funeral" (123–124, 134).

Butler scholars, likewise, recognize the author's contributions to the genre(s) of speculative fiction. According to Kimberly J. Ruffin, Butler "extols an Afrofuturist black feminist biblical hermeneutics that strives to resolve conflict between scientific knowledge and religiosity" (91). Ruffin's argument harmonizes with Shelley Streeby's reading of an "archiving, constellating, and annotating" Butler as "an active agent in creating counter-histories and alternative futures by saving, organizing, connecting, and speculating on these disparate materials" (720). Hee-Jung Serenity Joo celebrates "Butler's peculiar deployment of science fiction devices onto [a] realist landscape" as "one instance of the power of science fiction in extrapolating, and warning against, the dangers of state and capitalist hegemonic rule" (295). Scholars like Ruffin, Streeby, and Joo are joined by several authors in the present volume. In the opening chapter, Gregory Hampton examines how Butler connects spirituality to the rejection of identitarian and hierarchical modes of social organization, a line of enquiry extended by Mary Grover in her reading of Butler's ethics of dyadic encounter. Both readings figure spirituality as a genre of resistance to coercion, adding important nuance to scholarly appreciation of Butler's applications genre. Beyond applying genre, though, Butler also comments on the thing itself. Much like Charlotte Naylor Davis draws attention to Earthseed as both narrative and text *within* a narrative in her chapter, I treat the Parables as both genre texts and texts about genre texts. Reading the Parables as Butler's authorial commentary on genre, I agree she positions speculative fiction (hereafter sf) as a vital source of critical cosmology by analogously positioning *Parable of the Talents* as a self-conscious commentary on the generic construction of its prequel, *Parable of the Sower*.

At all levels—formal, generic, and thematic—Butler's fiction rejects static forms of freedom and demographic justice in favor of continuous, transgressive escape from any and all forms (social or otherwise) that limit transformation.[1] Butler does not merely endeavor to reconcile particular genres, forms, or discourses (like science and religion, in Ruffin's analysis) in order for some impasse *between the two* to be overcome. Rather, the Parables recognize genre itself as necessary to the breakthroughs in human knowledge and belief that, in Ruffin's words, "secure the continuation of the human species" (89). Beginning where Joo's reading ends, with Butler's "extrapolat[ion of] . . . the dangers of state and capitalist hegemonic rule" (295), I move on to examine her extrapolation of the uses and disadvantages of extrapolation itself, as a genre of expression, by which Butler warns against the conservative inflection of the abnormalizing forces at play in literary, social, and religious performance.

Joanna Russ once invoked engagement with "religion as process, not as doctrine" as a particularly promising feature of sf (11). In the present volume, chapters by Christopher Kocela, Tarshia L. Stanley, and Keegan Osinski show that Earthseed and the Parable novels support this claim. If Earthseed is a next step in religion-as-process, which forms the basis of *Sower*, then *Talents* is the step after that, a parable in which speculative fiction itself becomes the new religion and wellspring of the human/holy spirit. It does so through a simultaneity of critical perspective, generic practice, and religious purpose.

Similar to Lauren Olamina learning to appreciate how conceiving of Earth-seed as a religion requires her to consider—and bend—generic expectations, in interviews Butler frequently spoke of both the traditional narrowness and the potential capaciousness of speculative fiction. Butler's Parable novels produce a vision of how speculative fiction itself can serve as a novum, in Darko Suvin's sense, of the human story. To fully appreciate this claim requires some awareness of the distinct but overlapping literary, rhetorical, and theological registers of genre theory.

In an issue of *New Literary History* devoted to genre, Thomas Pavel revisits two opposing "temptations" of genre theory: "to freeze generic features, reducing them to immutable formulas," and "to deny genres any conceptual stability" (201). These temptations are, arguably, the two extremes stemming from the long-standing disagreement as to whether "the genre's building blocks" (semantics) or "the structures into which they are arranged" (syntax) are the proper focus of study (Altman 10). The rhetorician Carolyn Miller famously sidesteps this debate, offering a "pragmatic . . . rather than syntactic or semantic" theory of genre "based in rhetorical practice and . . . organized around situated actions" (155). Miller suggests that a purely materialist explanation of social action (of which genre is but one example) is inadequate, since "before we can act, we must interpret the indeterminate material environment; we define, or 'determine,' a situation" (156). Founding a new process of interpretation—an endeavor to "define . . . a situation"—is much on young Lauren Olamina's mind during the last days of the Robledo community in *Sower*.[2] Beyond these grammatical and pragmatic dimensions of genre, Ann Astell and Susannah Monta emphasize the "givenness" of genre as a potentially theological feature that connects individual practitioners to a diachronic tradition in a way that is *supersocial*,[3] that is, about the "holy spirit" of a spatiotemporally transcendent community.

On the occasion of her baptism, Lauren examines the strangeness of the proceedings and Christianity in general, noting how, "to the adults, going outside to a real church was like stepping back into the good old days when there were churches all over the place" (*Sower* 8). The parents "thought a proper baptism was important enough to spend some money and take some risks" (13). Yet, in an instance of semantic aberrance, "ask seven people" about God, Lauren notes, "and you'll get seven different answers" (15). This insight leaves Lauren unsatisfied with the only syntax that could accommodate these "seven different answers," that "God" is "just another name for whatever makes you feel special and protected" (15). Upon the paradoxical death of Mrs. Sims, a devout Christian neighbor who commits the mortal sin of suicide, Lauren imagines herself "like Alicia Leal, the astronaut" who dies on a mission to Mars, as someone who believes "in something that I think my dying, denying, backward-looking people need" rather than "some kind of potential Job," like Mrs. Sims (25). She then lists some semantic elements that will eventually be organized by the syntax of Earthseed: change in general, thermodynamics, Darwin, Buddhism, Ecclesiastes (26). While she conveys confidence that her ruminations express "the literal truth," she also shows an acute lack of generic confidence: "This thing (This idea? Philosophy? New religion?) won't let me alone, won't let me forget it, won't let me go" (24, 26). All three levels of genre analysis can engage this moment without going much deeper into *Sower* (though other occasions for analysis abound throughout both novels).

An extensive engagement with the literary dimension of genre could elucidate Lauren's efforts to develop a new syntax (Earthseed) to shape the aberrant semantic elements of her reading (listed above) and also her social experience (decaying communities, arson cults, climate change). Turning to rhetorical genre—the iterable, heuristic, communicative action that binds a community together—would give new meaning to Lauren's efforts managing the divergence and repeatability of the fledgling religion. But I will restrict my attention to the theological register of genre, since through her endeavors to gather and lead adherents, Lauren comes to inhabit a gray area between the authorial, authoritative, and authoritarian. Claiming Earthseed as a religion that came to her, Lauren attempts to shed the arbitrariness of authorship but perhaps overshoots authoritative prophecy for authoritarian control of the message. Yet the theological "givenness" of genre is best illuminated by the critique of Lauren's authority that appears in *Parable of the Talents*, a critique pointing toward Butler's articulation of her "positive obsession" with speculative fiction. Through this critique, the Parable novels position sf itself as the redemptive, transgressive novum of our modern age.

Theologically inflected genre criticism can address both what Lauren and her community do with Earthseed and what Butler and her community do with the Parables. Astell and Monta distinguish three modes of connection between a genre and its individual practitioners in their meditation on the "theological and religious ramifications" of genre criticism, one of these having direct bearing on Lauren's work with Earthseed: that "between the reader's generic perceptions of a work and their enacted belief or suspension of disbelief as shaped by those perceptions" (97).[4] Lauren taps into the genre of religious/revealed truth specifically to "enact belief" and engage "suspension of disbelief" on the part of her coveted followers. Such would be a technical gloss of what Lauren means by her repeated assertions that she and her followers *need* the Destiny of Earthseed. This theological dimension of genre marks the decisive split between the given and the recognized, where a *given* presentation of Earthseed diverges from a *particular* response to it. (I would urge my reader to keep the repetition implied in both *re-cognition* and *re-sponse* firmly in mind.) This split, for Astell and Monta, is one place where something theological can happen in textual encounters, but in the case of Octavia Butler's fiction—especially *Parable of the Talents*—this is where sf takes up its most powerful and quasi-religious place.

More so than *Sower*, *Talents* makes its readers responsible for thinking for themselves, opening the theological register of genre criticism by estranging readers from Lauren Olamina's potential godhood or prophethood. The Parable novels are not texts of Earthseed. While they offer fragments of *Earthseed: The Books of the Living*, the whole message of Earthseed will forever be inaccessible to readers of the Parables. More, the expedition has already left Earth, and Lauren Olamina is dead by the time her estranged daughter, Asha Vere, publishes *Parable of the Talents.*[5] *Talents* develops the chief tension of *Sower*—between Earthseed as a given, already-achieved thing and Earthseed as readers come to know it—with even more complexity by unfolding *both* at the chronological tempo of Olamina's life *and* through the asynchronous editorial commentary of her estranged daughter, written sometime after Olamina's death in 2090. Asha continues the interspersal of Earthseed scripture from *Sower* and adds select excerpts from Bankole, Lauren's husband, and Marcos, Lauren's estranged brother, along with her own narrative. Rather than presenting Earthseed as the ultimate religious truth, critical recognition of Lauren through the form of the novels and the editorial interruptions of Asha Vere allows readers to adopt Pavel's sense of genre "as a set of good recipes, or good habits," refocusing on Earthseed's secular and socially situated *use* of the genre of religion as a "good recipe" for survival (202).

If Earthseed itself is the work, *Parable of the Sower* and *Parable of the Talents* are the works of criticism, accessible to outsiders, situating them to "figure out the nature of [the] . . . work" (Pavel 202). Lauren's singular voice might discourage reader dissent if one reads only *Sower*, but the inclusion of multiple points of view in *Talents* opens space to think critically about each perspective. From the prologue onward, Asha characterizes Lauren as a religious zealot. She quotes the "God is Change" verse, saying, "The words are harmless, I suppose, and metaphorically true. At least she began with some species of truth," closing a prologue that begins with the worry that "they'll make a god of her" (1). Other reflections are no kinder: Lauren "worked hard at seducing people," she accuses, and so Acorn grows "by birth, by adoption of orphans, and by conversion of needy adults" (63, 23). It could be argued that Asha's reference to Lauren as seducer invalidates her commentary, since one of Olamina's post-Acorn companions offers the same analysis after Lauren wins another convert, saying, "You seduce people. My God, you're always at it, aren't you?" (372). However perceptive Asha's criticisms are, she mostly knows her mother through her journals and the writings of others; she may have uncritically amplified Len's judgment, as a resentful "orphan" might. Still, however tendentious, Asha's interpretations of her mother recontextualize some of Lauren's own words. While Lauren will undoubtedly retain most readers' sympathies by virtue of all the horrors that befall the Acorn community, Asha still offers readers a fresh—if adversarial—perspective to evaluate Lauren's own commentary.

Amid a long entry in which Lauren reflects on the growth of Acorn and Earthseed, what could be taken for pragmatism can begin to sound like cynicism: "Here was real community. Here was at least a semblance of security. Here was the comfort of ritual and routine and the emotional satisfaction of belonging" (63). After a mother invokes God during a ceremony for the birth of her child, Lauren writes, "When she talks about God, she doesn't mean what I mean. I'm not sure that matters. . . . In the future, when her son says 'God,' I think he will mean what I mean" (65). This sounds self-aggrandizing after reading editorial material from Lauren's daughter, as do Lauren's musings about expansion as she thinks of partnerships with neighboring settlements: "As we absorb them, I also intend to either absorb some of the storekeeper, restaurant, or hotel clients that we'll have—or I want to open our own stores, restaurants, and hotels" (71). With the contrast provided by Asha's commentary and the tone of the excerpts from Bankole she provides, readers have at least some basis to consider how Lauren's vision of Acorn's future is not entirely new or absolutely benevolent; it rediscovers something like imperialism or feudalism—a reterritorialization by immanent domain.

Persisting in her portrayal of Lauren as imperialistic zealot, Asha compares her to a formidable counterpart: her estranged brother, Marcos. Asha offers an excerpt from his text, *Warrior*, that ends with Marcos's own mantra-worthy line: "What we have broken we can mend" (109). Just as Asha's comments motivate critical recognition of uncomfortable nuances in Lauren's words, familiarity with the pragmatic forward-looking habit of Earthseed reveals unhappy nuances in Asha's comparison of these "two would-be world-fixers" (110). While she describes her mother's efforts with palpable anger, she doesn't heap similar scorn on "Uncle Marc," despite the pungent resentment she attributes to him as "a man with a wound that would not heal until he could be certain that what had happened to him could not happen again to anyone, ever" (111). This may sound critical, but Asha lets him off the hook due to her clear sympathy with his *intentions*: "Uncle Marc wanted to make the Earth a better place. Uncle Marc knew that the stars could take care of themselves" (111). Here, she drops the oppositional analysis she has been applying to her mother up until literally two paragraphs before. Asha, like Marc, is devoted to "healing" on Earth—mending what is broken—rather than growing anew in some abnormal, unreal, impossible beyond of Earth. Yet, paradoxically, she refuses healing with her mother and advances Earthseed's objectives by authoring *Talents*. Readers of Butler—readers of both Parables—then, perceive, interpret, and determine this irony (as Miller would have it) as it emerges through the split between Earthseed as given (by Lauren to readers of *Earthseed: The Books of the Living*) and Earthseed as recognized by Parable readers.

As is foregrounded here by Asha's preference for Uncle Marc, any devotion—religious or otherwise—risks falling into a redundant conservativism, tempting one to vilify rather than engage deviations. With a fixed syntax and semantics of experience, a static social group knows it has *had the answer all along* and teaches its members how to *arrive back at that given answer.*[6] Even Lauren falls into this trap when Acorn becomes a kind of reconstitution of Robledo or when she spitefully allows Marcos to embarrass himself by preaching at an Earthseed gathering ("I couldn't let him begin to divide Earthseed," she confesses [152]). Readers of *Talents*, then, are presented with three major perspectives, each one questionable. Asha represents something like an agnostic, though questionable for her uncritical preference for an emotionally palatable belief. Marcos presents a God of permanence, sustaining coherent expectations of form and content, in which view any aberrance ought to be "returned to form." Such permanence is questionable as it leaves no room for transformative events. In *Sower*, Lauren decides that aberrance—in the shape of various crises facing Robledo—reveals genres of durable, mendable permanence as illusory. She comes to recognize a God of change in forms and contents like learning, outreach, travel, meaning making, and social transformation. In this scheme, aberrance can be questioned, engaged, shaped, and reshaped because the syntax of the genre is itself *abnormal*—it grows out of / beyond form rather than returning to it. And here is the trick: whereas questions might embarrass the agnostic and the devotee of permanence, the devotee of change encourages questions. Earthseed recognizes that it must eventually, inevitably break with its own form: Acorn must burn; Lauren must die; Earth must be left behind. Paradoxically, it retains expectation and recognition of change—the eruption of the new—as the only constant. Rather than teaching Earthseed, the Parables educate readers in these generic truths through the *example* of Earthseed. Butler's cherished "grow, learn, fly" formula involves Lauren, Asha, and Butler herself but also leaves them behind.

Genre itself is a fugitive thing: individual practitioners cannot indefinitely keep pace; a gap always opens—a space for a critical recognition that abuts theological reflection.

In his chapter on the Parables, Gerry Canavan documents Butler's effort to transform Lauren from an older, more ruthless character to a more "lovable" version "by making her more like herself" (131). A key piece of evidence, here, is "the opening epigraph of *Sower*" (131), an invocation of "persistent, positive obsession" (*Sower* 1) that points to two of Butler's essays on writing, "Positive Obsession" and "Furor Scribendi." Both essays champion persistence and in the afterword to "Furor," Butler concludes that persistence "applies to anything that is important, but difficult, important, but frightening. We're all capable of climbing so much higher than we usually permit ourselves to suppose" (143–144). Both Butler and Olamina use the general capaciousness of genre to unforgivingly push humanity toward transformation, transplantation, and fugitivity.

In the "Positive Obsession" essay, Butler ends with her ruminations on the "good" sf does for "Black people," pointing somewhat cryptically to the "obvious" answer: "At its best, science fiction simulates imagination and creativity. It gets reader and writer off the beaten track, off the narrow, narrow footpath of what 'everyone' is saying, doing, thinking—whoever 'everyone' happens to be this year" (135). Though Butler admits skepticism when asked if she "would . . . like to break down some of the walls between generic marketing categories" ("Oh, that's not possible," she answers) (Potts 72), elsewhere she recommends sf as "a more open genre than any other" (ConT 417).[7] Both Butler's skepticism and her championing of sf resonate with Suvin's classic theorization of the genre in *Metamorphoses of Science Fiction*.

Suvin confronts the consumer success of sf with its equally urgent "*historical potentialities*," arguing that sf, having a "potentially unlimited thematic field," cannot be defined by any particular semantic elements ostensibly common to the genre, like future settings or scientific breakthroughs (viii). Likewise, from her earliest interviews, Butler comments on the capaciousness of sf, which, she writes, "appealed to me more, even, than fantasy had because it required more thought, more research into things that fascinated me. . . . Science fiction and fantasy are so wide open that I never had to drop them to be able to pick up other things" (ConS 334–336).

Butler's most striking comments during the long period of the Parables' incubation and publication come from a 1980 interview in which she shares what are, perhaps, the first glimmers of Earthseed. Butler opines that it is not "wise" for sf to ignore religion, which "has played such a large part in the lives of human beings" (Harrison 9).[8] She wants humanity to outgrow a *kind* of religion, "the Big Policeman in the Sky," since such traditions really aren't "controlling people and helping to channel their energy away from destruction" (9). Such ruminations do much to underscore Earthseed as the Parables' Suvinian novum—the "cognitive innovation . . . a totalizing phenomenon or relationship deviating from the author's and implied reader's norm of reality" that is the core of speculative fiction (64).

For Suvin, sf unfolds "the space of a potent *estrangement*" and departs from the "locus and/or dramatis personae" of "'mimetic' . . . fiction" but in a way that will strike the reader as "*not impossible* within the cognitive (cosmological and anthropological) norms of the author's epoch" (viii). Suvin's sense of *cognition* "implies a creative"—and critical, he adds elsewhere—"approach toward a dynamic transformation rather than toward a static mirroring of the author's environment" (10). The novum as "totalizing phenomenon" in this understanding of sf deserves thorough emphasis. While things like the Paints, Lauren's "sharing" disorder, and the virtual reality films that make Asha Vere famous are indeed new curiosities of the world of the Parables, these are not the elements that found and totalize the deviation of Lauren's fictive United States from ours. Earthseed is the totalizing cognitive innovation, the novum, of the Parables, an element of this fictive world that bursts onto the scene, unbidden and unanticipated, to change *everything*. Butler does not ask us religiously and worshipfully to anticipate the arrival of something like Earthseed; rather she invites us to think critically and metacritically about how we *could* come to think that way and what we *would* accomplish as a community of such thinkers.

Critically, the Parables ask readers to consider the consequences of a fundamental change to the human relationship to genre, worship, social action, and the social construction of truth. Metacritically, Butler's imagination of a near-future sf narrative makes a parable of her genre-writing efforts, endeavoring as they do to engage sf in each of the literary, rhetorical, and theological dimensions of genre practice. That is, Butler wants to move beyond the literary conjuration of a sense of wonder and estrangement to reorient social consciousness and action. By reading Butler, one learns her genre of sf and, in Miller's sense of "rhetorical education," becomes newly capable of "understanding how to participate in the actions of a community" of humankind (Miller 165). The new horizon that Earthseed makes available to Lauren and her world is a parable of sf as cognitive innovation in our world. If a new kind of thought can be a novum, then sf, itself overflowing genre,[9] can be an instance of genre-as-novum. Reading the Parables as parables of genre suggests a science-fictional analysis of genre beyond the generic analysis of science fiction. Science fiction can be an engine of change, a way to novelistically, ritualistically, generically *worship* our will to go elsewhere, using this will to unseat resentful wishes that things *would have been* different or *would return to normal.*[10] The holy spirit of sf serves as an escape pod, since its practitioners are driven to move beyond current boundaries rather than idly reproducing them. And, in exactly this sense, Octavia Butler has been the Lauren Olamina of science fiction.

NOTES

1. Marlene D. Allen similarly positions Butler's rejection of solutions within existing forms (history, the U.S. nation form) as a kind of critical realism in "Octavia Butler's Parable Novels and the 'Boomerang' of African American History." In "Minority and Becoming-Minor in Octavia Butler's *Fledgling*," I similarly argue that Butler rejects the concept of the minority as a static, objective identity in favor of the fluidity of becoming.

2. Miller also articulates three potential sources of genre failure: lack of a common sense of what is happening, disagreement about the situation as a recurring or enduring one, or failure to see genre as relevant to action (165). Each of these failures occurs in *Sower*.

3. My term, intended as a counterpart of "supernatural."

4. Astell and Monta also examine the relationship of genre author and their text to the genre tradition and that of genre reader as textual critic to that same reader as self-critic. I used the term *mode* above; each of these relationships could be thought of as a mode, or inflection, of the general connection between some instance or moment of genre practice and the invisible community/providential history in which it takes part.

5. In the prologue to *Talents*, Asha refers directly to "writing and assembling this book," suggesting that she may be the author-editor of *Talents* (2). This is not unambiguously the case for *Sower*. There are no editorial interruptions in *Sower*, though it boasts the same formatting apparatus: Earthseed versus introducing books (header by year) and chapters.

6. Here, I draw inspiration from Patricia Roberts-Miller's theorization of demagoguery. Cf. *Demagoguery and Democracy* (The Experiment, 2017).

7. Back matter entitled "A Conversation with Octavia Butler" follows the Grand Central editions of both *Sower* and *Talents*. I use the abbreviations ConS and ConT to designate these texts in parenthetical references.

8. It is worth remembering that Russ's "Speculations: The Subjunctivity of Science Fiction," in which she discusses sf's attention to religion, was originally published in the December 1973 issue of *Extrapolation*. Further research might qualify whether and how Russ influenced Butler (they certainly shared Samuel Delany as a point of contact), but I only intend to point, however weakly, to the zeitgeist.

9. Veronica Hollinger has referred to sf as a *mode* rather than a genre, that is, "a method, a way of getting something done" or "a way of living in the world" (qtd. in LeMenager 222).

10. In a recent issue of the sociology journal *Contexts*, a special segment asks, "What can we learn from the intersection of science fiction and sociology?" (13). Daniel Hirschman, the editor of the segment, suggests five key points of intersection. Sf narratives serve as (1) Weberian ideal types, (2) "reservoir[s] of 'extreme counterfactuals,'" (3) a "supplement to history and anthropology" (since "when sociologists grapples with the big transformations of modernity, [they] often struggle to characterize how else things could have been"), (4) "inspiration for imagining a more just society" and "futures to avoid," and, finally, (5) as its own social field (13–14).

WORKS CITED

Allen, Marlene D. "Octavia Butler's Parable Novels and the 'Boomerang' of African American History." *Callaloo*, vol. 32, no. 4, 2009, p. 1353.

Altman, Rick. "A Semantic/Syntactic Approach to Film Genre." *Cinema*, vol. 23, no. 3, 1984, pp. 6–18.

Astell, Ann W., and Susannah Brietz Monta. "Genre and the Joining of Literature and Religion: A Question of Kinds." *Religion & Literature*, vol. 46, no. 2/3, 2014, pp. 95–110.

Butler, Octavia. "Furor Scribendi." *Bloodchild and Other Stories*, 2nd ed., Seven Stories, 2005, pp. 137–44.

———. *Parable of the Sower*. Grand Central Publishing, 2007.

———. *Parable of the Talents*. Grand Central Publishing, 2007.

———. "Positive Obsession." *Bloodchild and Other Stories*, 2nd ed., Seven Stories, 2005, pp. 123–136.

Canavan, Gerry. *Octavia E. Butler*. University of Illinois Press, 2016.

Harrison, Rosalie G. "Sci-Fi Vision: An Interview with Octavia Butler." *Conversations with Octavia Butler*, edited by Conseula Francis, University Press of Mississippi, 2010, pp. 3–9.

Hirschman, Daniel, et al. "Why Sociology Needs Science Fiction." *Contexts*, vol. 17, no. 3, 2018, pp. 12–21.

Joo, Hee-Jung Serenity. "Old and New Slavery, Old and New Racisms: Strategies of Science Fiction in Octavia Butler's Parables Series." *Extrapolation*, vol. 52, no. 3, 2011, pp. 279–299.

LeMenager, Stephanie. "Climate Change and the Struggle for Genre." *Anthropocene Reading: Literary History in Geologic Times*, edited by Tobias Menely and Jesse Oak Taylor, Pennsylvania State University Press, 2017, pp. 220–236.

Miller, Carolyn R. "Genre as Social Action." *Quarterly Journal of Speech*, vol. 70, 1984, pp. 151–167.

Pavel, Thomas. "Literary Genres as Norms and Good Habits." *New Literary History*, vol. 34, no. 2, 2003, pp. 201–210.

Potts, Stephen W. "'We Keep Playing the Same Record': A Conversation with Octavia Butler." *Conversations with Octavia Butler*, edited by Conseula Francis, University Press of Mississippi, 2010, pp. 65–73.

Roberts-Miller, Patricia. *Demagoguery and Democracy*. The Experiment, 2017.

Robinson, Chuck. "Minority and Becoming-Minor in Octavia Butler's Fledgling." *Science Fiction Studies*, vol. 42, no. 3, Nov. 2015, pp. 483–499.

Ruffin, Kimberly J. "Parable of a 21st Century Religion: Octavia Butler's Afrofuturistic Bridge between Science and Religion." *Obsidian III*, vol. 6–7, no. 1–2, 2005, pp. 87–104.

Russ, Joanna. "Speculations: The Subjunctivity of Science Fiction." *To Write like a Woman: Essays in Feminism and Science Fiction*, Indiana University Press, 1995, pp. 15–25.

Streeby, Shelley. "Radical Reproduction: Octavia E. Butler's HistoFuturist Archiving as Speculative Theory." *Women's Studies*, vol. 47, no. 7, 2018, pp. 719–732.

Suvin, Darko. *Metamorphoses of Science Fiction: On the Poetics and History of a Literary Genre*. Yale University Press, 1979.

Part II

Trauma and Healing

7

"Only Actions"

Ritual and the Embodied Processing of Trauma in
Parable of the Sower *and* Parable of the Talents

Keegan Osinski

The anthropologist Ronald Grimes, in correspondence with the psycho-analyst and ritual theorist Jeltje Gordon-Lennox, is quoted as saying, "If DIY rituals are really going to meet our needs, they have to be made up out of the familiar, not the exotic: metaphors that make sense to us, language that reflects the way we see the world, and symbols with which we have a history. Start with your own broken teacups, the stuff in your backyard, keepsakes in the backs of drawers" (Gordon-Lennox, "Rhyme and Reason" 81). For the members of Earthseed, the emerging religion developed by Octavia Butler's protagonist Lauren Olamina in her books *Parable of the Sower* and *Parable of the Talents*, the creation of rituals out of the "broken tea-cups" of their broken lives served as an important spiritual-religious response to the trauma they had experienced in the apocalyptic fallout of their context. The embodied effects of trauma require an embodied response, and rituals can provide the space and material practices to help process traumatic events held in the body. The rituals of Earthseed illustrate this need and religious response, as well as the inadequacy of old systems and rituals to address new conditions, as well as their unique traumas and the resultant necessity to develop proper ritual response to the given situation.

The Embodied Nature of Trauma

The last twenty years have been marked by a veritable explosion of research regarding trauma and the body in neurobiology, psychology, and a host of other fields and subfields. What has become clear as a result of all of this work is the material and embodied nature and effects of traumatic events—trauma is not, as it were, "all in one's head," an ethereal, intangible thought-memory or even simply a discrete neural path. Traumas and their effects lodge themselves in the physical bodies of survivors, disrupting normal bodily functions and manifesting in a variety of physical symptoms.

The neurologist Robert Scaer defines trauma as "anything that represents a threat to our survival as a human being . . . by impinging upon, or rupturing that intangible but very real perceptual boundary that separates our safe sense of self from the world around us" (6). When under stress in this moment of threat, the brain releases the hormone norepinephrine into the central nervous system, resulting in measurable somatic responses like sweating, pupil dilation, and muscle toning. These reactions prepare the body to fight or flee the danger or alternatively to freeze altogether (Scaer 13). The physical response to a trauma often also results in a mental dissociation from the moment, a breakdown of the facilities the brain uses to process stimuli. Marcia Mount Shoop therefore describes trauma as, "in an embodied sense, this incapacity to witness fully the event as it occurs" (50). Because of the body's heightened intensity of awareness, it is unable to process what is happening in real time, and so the traumatic event gets "stuck" in the body. The body, and the mind through the body, will then return to and repeat the event, attempting to process it again and again, returning the victim to the scene of the trauma as if it were really happening, over and over. In survivors of trauma who develop post-traumatic stress disorder (PTSD), the trauma can resurface in nightmares and flashbacks that immerse the survivor's body into the same state of traumatization, effectively retraumatizing the person each time, often seemingly without warning or reason.

Sometimes the pain of trauma kept in the body results in the coping reaction of dissociation. This is the "freeze" function that accompanies the more well-known "fight or flight" responses. The brain, in a sense, detaches from the body, leaving the person disconnected from their body, unable to feel sensations or identify needs or desires within themselves. Just as the body might react to trauma with violent intensity in a cry for help, it may also completely disengage to shield itself from the pain. In an attempt to shut down the pain, it may shut down all feeling and connection altogether. When the brain is unable to narrativize and process the stimuli of trauma, it may cease to narrativize and process any stimuli at all. But identifying and experiencing feeling is a necessary part of its processing. Bessel van der Kolk says that "trauma victims cannot recover until they become familiar with and befriend the sensations in their bodies" (102). Recognizing the locus of trauma in the body means one must have access to one's own body to work out the trauma therein.

The inability to process stimuli that characterizes trauma is both what causes the survivor's ongoing distress and what makes it so challenging to overcome. Van der Kolk explains that "it is enormously difficult to organize one's traumatic experiences into a coherent account," and so survivors will create a consumable "cover story" that allows them to talk about the event but nonetheless does not actually address the underlying, embodied trauma (43). Thus, it becomes easier for the survivor to organize the event into a narrative that can be shared and explained but harder to "notice, feel, and put into words the reality of their internal experience" (van der Kolk 47). The ability to narrativize the trauma does not necessarily translate into the ability to heal the ongoing somatic effects of the trauma. An embodied problem requires an embodied solution. In fact, van der Kolk suggests that it is possible for people to heal from trauma without narrativizing or talking about it at all and that certain embodied therapies can be effective even without an established, trusting relationship between the therapist and the patient (255).

As a rupture of proper somatic and cognitive memory, traumatic incidents can be difficult to process. Healing after a traumatic incident therefore does not occur in a simple, straightforward, or linear manner. Scaer explains that "trauma cannot be cured by words and cognitive processing alone. The sensory experiences of the body must be introduced in the ritualistic extinction of the brain/body traumatic connection" ("Neurophysiology" 58). What he means by "ritualistic extinction" is the repetitive, iterative mode of working out and neutralizing the unprocessed trauma. It requires a multifaceted approach that integrates all aspects of the person, for all aspects of the person are affected by trauma. Trauma, experienced in the body, must be worked out in, through, and by the body. Briana Whiteside's chapter in this volume discusses further the role of the body as the locus of trauma and also the locus of healing, and how this is expressed in Octavia Butler's work.

Therapists have found multiple embodied avenues for processing trauma. Researchers and therapists discuss bodywork, massage, dance, yoga, and gardening as examples. These practices ground people into their bodies in the present moment, which allows for the freer flow of feelings so that trauma can be processed. Scaer, van der Kolk, and others even consider the increasing popularity and success of eye movement desensitization and reprocessing (EMDR), a therapy developed by Francine Shapiro, wherein the patient follows the therapist's fingers with their eyes in a repetitive motion that seems to jolt or budge the "stuck" trauma out of its rut. The movement of the eyes somehow allows patients to access and encounter painful trauma feelings in their bodies and, as a kind of exposure therapy, subsequently desensitizes them so that they can be worked out.

In their thorough anthropological study of disaster rituals, Paul Post and his coauthors define disaster as a collective trauma. "A disaster is a collective occurrence," they explain, "it overcomes a group, and not an individual. This means that people cannot approach the consequences of a disaster on the individual level alone" (Post et al. 23). In the same way the embodied nature of trauma must be worked out in an embodied manner, the collective nature of shared traumas must be worked out in and as a group. Ritual, therefore, can serve as a method of collective embodied processing and healing of collective embodied trauma.

Trauma and Ritual

Since trauma fragments the victim's physical experience, keeping them from processing stimuli and resultant emotions in the moment, healing that trauma involves accessing the stuck feelings, both emotionally and physically. There are multiple ways of doing this. Gordon-Lennox explains that ritual is one way to "regularize the perception of time and allow people to stay in the present to experience harmonious relations (emotional attachment) with other people" (Gordon-Lennox, *Crafting Secular Ritual* 35–36). By participating in rituals—established, traditional ones or ones created brand new out of necessity—people are invited to engage in embodied practice that can help them unlock and experience the trauma left in their bodies in a safe environment in order to begin the process of healing. One example of an embodied ritual that I will not discuss here is pilgrimage, but Sarah Wood's chapter in this volume talks about pilgrimage as a metaphor for the process of healing.

At the outset, we should be clear (as Gordon-Lennox is) that "therapy is not the end purpose of ritual" and that "ritualizing is often therapeutic, but it should not be confused with therapy" (Gordon-Lennox and Russo 45). While ritual can be a powerful tool in the ongoing process of dealing with trauma, it will most likely not be sufficient to do all the complex work of healing. Further, while ritual may indeed have a therapeutic effect, that is not its primary purpose, and ritual serves other functions that are not necessarily related to handling trauma. Indeed, many ritual theorists resist a narrative that imposes purpose or function on ritual at all, insisting, like Grimes and others, for example, that "rites are purposeless and beautiful. They do not belong to the category of utility, function, purpose, and profit"; they are essentially "without point" and yet "not without meaning"

(Post et al. 50). Theorists critique the fact that "present-day rituality is readily judged on, and legitimated by, purpose and function" and that, for example, "funerary ritual is praised therapeutically as grief processing" (Post et al. 243). But still, it remains true that ritual does indeed entail the body engagement, time regulation, and communal cohesion that are vital elements of effective trauma treatment and so can serve as a therapeutic supplement. These three aspects of ritual—the body, time, and community—each contributes in unique ways to processing and healing trauma.

Body

We've discussed above how trauma affects the physical body of the victim. There are integral ways that ritual works with and on the body as well. Gordon-Lennox says that "authentic ritual is an encounter with the senses and sensemaking" (Gordon-Lennox and Russo 30). All ritual is embodied. It combines components that require and interact with all of our bodily senses—visual images, music or spoken words, incense, food and drink, grasping hands, kneeling, sitting, or moving. The embodied activity is central to ritual just as it is central to trauma therapy, and so these two can function concomitantly. Mount Shoop advocates for "healing liturgies that focus not on words but on embodied practices like anointing with oil, laying on of hands, or sacred movement," asserting that "these embodied practices are of utter necessity since body language does not yield complete comprehension. Embodied healing needs space for its expression even in its mystery" (38). Ritual can provide at least some of the embodied practice that trauma requires to heal. Just as EMDR therapy can engage and dislodge the trauma in the body without using words, ritual can work out the emotions in the body through movement and the senses.

Time

One of the key characteristics of ritual is the way it plays with time. Occurring both inside and outside of time, set apart and yet within the linear stream, ritual is, necessarily, what the anthropologist Victor Turner calls a "liminal space." It both is and is not real; it is both part of and yet distinct from the whole of life. It is in between. Part of trauma is the muddling of and disconnection with time as it tends to be experienced typically. It arises in part from not being able to process events in real time and manifests in disconnection from experience-in-time as well as flashbacks and feeling as if the past is in the present. The particular, structured timekeeping of ritual can serve as a way to reorder the disordered time of trauma. Gordon-Lennox explains that funeral rituals, for example, allow safe space and time for mourners to "oscillate" between sadness and happiness, to feel the feelings and discharge them safely, and then return to the real world "anchored in a new reality" (*Crafting Secular Ritual* 76–77). Rituals provide a time out, a pause button for the continuous onslaught of reality, and a space to process that may not be afforded in the moment.

Community

Ritual both creates and preserves a social reality. Victor Turner identified the particular social nature apparent in ritual as "communitas"—a group united in their common experience of the ritual practice. In times of tragedy, the creation or preservation of a community of support offered by ritual is vital for moving from trauma to healing, both for the traumatized individual and for a traumatized community. Post et al. say that "ritual has a robustly collective dimension; the acts are performed by a group, a community, and that community is in turn bound together by the ritual act" (40). The binding together of a community in crisis, or the binding of an individual in crisis to a larger community, anchors persons in a stabilizing reality that creates a safe and compassionate environment for processing the trauma. The ritual can bolster the identity of the community, which allows for a robust sense of belonging and consistency in the face of the alienating and dismembering action of trauma. Further, ritual links the community to the communities of the past, to the context and culture in which the community is and has been grounded. The continuity of community that ritual evokes facilitates the collective process of mourning as well as provides the collective comfort and stability needed to heal the trauma.

Given what we know about trauma, as well as the way ritual works with the body, time, and community, the value of ritual for processing trauma should be apparent. Ritual practices can be an effective method for dealing with trauma, and indeed, though it is not the primary function, ritual can be used in a therapeutic manner. The benefits of ritual for dealing with trauma are such that so many traumatized people seem to reach impulsively for ceremony and symbolic gesture to help them cope, even creating new rituals from scratch if no properly relevant practices exist.

Ritual and Trauma in the Parables

The narrative told in Octavia Butler's *Parable of the Sower* and *Parable of the Talents* begins in 2024, in a United States not terribly unlike our own that is becoming increasingly dystopic. A changed climate has resulted in a severely drought-afflicted Southern California, where food is scarce, water is expensive, and the drug-addled poor roam the streets outside the walled communities of the middle class, who are only marginally better off. The struggle that arises from this landscape is the soil from which sprouts a new religion. The protagonist, Lauren Oya Olamina, is the daughter of a Baptist minister, and where she finds her father's Christianity insufficient for addressing the terror in which they live, she develops—or rather, she would say, discovers—a new set of beliefs and practices she calls Earthseed.

Given the embodied nature of trauma and the value of ritual for dealing with it, the remainder of this chapter will analyze the text of the Parable books to bring to the fore the trauma suffered by the characters and the ways they employ rituals to process it. I will discuss the traditional Christian rituals that appear in the text but will focus more closely on the new rituals that emerge from the experiences of the Earthseed community, because the Earthseed rituals (and indeed Earthseed itself) arise directly from the characters' attempts to deal with their trauma, heal from it, and find a better way forward.

Olamina's close ties to her minister father all but destine her to a religious life. Born on the same day, Olamina and her father are both characterized by an inherent religiosity that does not necessarily manifest as zealousness but is more simply a matter-of-fact integral piece of their being. It is perhaps this connectedness that leads Olamina, against her better judgment and her true beliefs, to be baptized into the Christian church. She blames cowardice, admitting, "I let my father baptize me in all three names of that God who isn't mine anymore" (*Sower* 7). She does not believe in her father's God, and yet her love for her father and his community are sufficient motivation for her to subject herself to the initiation ritual of baptism. She wishes she could have resisted, been honest about her conflicting beliefs about her God and her father's, but the importance of the ritual to him and to the community of his church, both of which she is bound to, and the cohesive function of the ritual override any sense of self-righteous self-preservation that might have kept her from participating. Olamina's need for the community in this dangerous time, particularly as a fifteen-year-old girl, makes her vulnerable, and participation in the ritual of belonging solidifies her position in a group that can protect her.

Besides the explicit Christian rituals of the Robledo community, there are other practices that take on a kind of religious ritual function in the apocalyptic setting of the Parables. One such ritual is gun-handling instruction and target practice. Olamina explains that learning how to handle a gun is part of the curriculum at her home school, which is attended by many of the community's children, and that once the children turn fifteen and have passed that instruction, they are taken regularly for target practice. "It's a kind of rite of passage for us," she says (*Sower* 39). The "rite" of one's first target practice is consistent with the dangerous context of the community. As adolescents age into adulthood, they take on a portion of the responsibility for the defense of the group. That this rite corresponds with Olamina's baptism is not insignificant. Both are reflective of the need for a cohesive community in times of suffering, and the solemnity or distinction of ritualizing these moments of initiation serves to make clear the importance of the individual to the community as well as the community to the individual. The rituals engender a sense of obligation as well as a promise that solidifies the individual's place in the community and strengthens its cohesion.

Perhaps one of the most important scenes of ritual in the books, the scene when Olamina steps into her identity as a religious leader, is the Sunday morning service that becomes an "impromptu funeral" for her father after his disappearance. Her own power and presence take the reins, though she is still in her father's Christian church and preaches a Christian message from the Christian Bible. But she identifies in that moment, when "people came for church, all uncertain and upset, not knowing what they should do," that she could lead people who needed leadership and that religious ritual could help in these times of desperation. Though her father is still missing, the community gathers at their home, as is their habit. "They were uncertain and hesitant," Olamina says, "but they came" (*Sower* 134). The consistency of ritualized, routine gathering carries the people to their place of worship, even, or especially, when they are frightened and unsure. And so Olamina leads them through a more or less typical service. She preaches a sermon, "if an unordained kid can be said to preach a sermon," and they sing a song (*Sower* 134). Afterward, she recognizes, "That was Dad's funeral that I was preaching." At the beginning of the following chapter, they hold a "proper" funeral for him, but Butler goes into far less detail about it—only a few lines. It is clear that the real funeral, the one with the most meaning and weight, was the service that emerged in the course of the community's typical ritual practice, with Olamina's leadership and preaching. What is more, the other funerals that take place in Robledo—for three-year-old Amy Dunn and for Olamina's brother Keith—garner the scantest mention. It is clear that, for Butler, the focus is not on the traditional Christian rituals, though they are present. The minimal mention reflects the inadequacy of these rituals to truly do the work of addressing the needs of the traumatized community. They observe them, because they are available and they are what the community knows, but it is apparent from the dearth of description that more is desired and required.

Once she leaves Robledo, forced out in a violent and fiery attack that leaves her family and much of the community dead, their homes burned and looted, Olamina begins formalizing her new religion. She develops Earthseed, conscious of the spiritual and psychological needs it must address for herself and the new community that gathers around her on the road. "Earthseed deals with ongoing reality, not with supernatural authority figures," she insists, distinguishing between the beliefs about God as change and the physical practices of the religion. "Worship is no good without action. With action, it's only useful if it steadies you, focuses your efforts, eases your mind" (*Sower* 219). When Travis Douglas, still skeptical about Olamina's ideas, objects that all God is good for is for propping struggling people up, Olamina answers, "That isn't what God is for, but there are times when that's what prayer is for" (*Sower* 220). She is convinced that God as an idea, "God is Change," is neutral, chaotic, no respecter of persons. But religious practice—ritual—is useful and necessary for human wholeness. Later, when asked what they pray to, she answers, "Ourselves. What else is there?" (*Sower* 238). It is not a supernatural authoritative being that offers palliative care to the suffering, but it is the ritual practices grounded in reality and physical activity that can result in true healing. In *Parable of the Talents*, Asha Vere wonders how "a belief system like Earthseed—very demanding but offering so little comfort from such an utterly indifferent God—should inspire loyalty at all" (47). She—like so many others Olamina encounters and tries to explain Earthseed to—does not understand how one can find comfort if there is no supernatural "big-daddy-God" (*Sower* 15). But Olamina is clear: it is not the belief that comforts and strengthens; it is the action. She says in one of her Earthseed verses:

Only actions
Guided and shaped
By belief and knowledge
Will save you.
Belief
Initiates and guides action—
Or it does nothing. (*Talents* 348)

It is interesting that Asha Vere cannot reconcile this perceived disconnect, particularly given her own involvement in the church choir despite her lack of belief in her adoptive parents' religion. She still finds that "the choir provided relief" from her own trauma by the habitual involvement in church—the time set apart in rehearsal and performance (out of the house and away from her abuser), the physical act of singing (in which she finds the strength of her own voice), and the community provided by the choir (who value her being there) (*Talents* 349–350). She feels connected to this community and "didn't want to be free of it. . . . Everyone needs to be part of something," she says (*Talents* 378). Though she resists the God of her adopted parents, she feels a part of the community and finds comfort in participating in its ritual activities.

After the attack on the nascent Earthseed group's camp that leaves Jill Gilchrist dead and several others wounded, Olamina says they spent the morning gathered and reading Earthseed verses. "It was a calming thing to do—almost like church," she says. "We needed something calming and reassuring" (*Sower* 294). The set-apart time to gather and read and talk about Earthseed makes space for the community to process the trauma of the previous day, to come together to rest and support one another.

At the end of *Parable of the Sower*, having arrived on Bankole's property to establish their community, the people of Earthseed develop their funeral rite. They have all lost so many loved ones and been through so much; a proper ritual was natural and necessary. "Most of us have had to walk away— or run—away from our unburned, unburied dead," Olamina says. "Tomorrow, we should remember them all, and lay them to rest if we can" (*Sower* 326). The constant struggle, the running, the fighting, the moving, keeps the members of Earthseed from being able to properly process the trauma and loss they had endured. They had to carry it with them as they fought for their own lives, unable to truly face the horrors they had endured. But once they were able to settle in a safer place, they could take the time to pause, to come together intentionally as a community and observe their collective and individual grief. And as an emerging religious community in its own right, Earthseed develops their own distinct funeral rite for their dead.

In creating the funeral ritual for Earthseed, Olamina starts, as Grimes recommends, literally with stuff from her backyard—acorns. "I have acorns enough for each of us to plant live oak trees to our dead," she plans. "I would like to give them a grove of oak trees. Trees are better than stone—life commemorating life" (*Sower* 326). They cobble together words from what they have—"Bible passages, Earthseed verses, and bits of songs and poems"—to lay their loved ones to rest, and they join together in the physical act of planting the acorns in the ground (*Sower* 328). This ritual affords the community the opportunity for processing their grief and getting some measure of closure after their protracted, incessant suffering. The pause to look back, to remember their friends and families, is vital for healing, for being able to continue even in the midst of continued struggle.

As Earthseed becomes more established, growing their roots into the Acorn community, developing their school and their work, birthing and raising children, their rituals become more established as well. The ritual of initiation, or "welcoming," is one of the most important. The joining of the individual with the community is crucial for healing in the apocalyptic setting of the books. Olamina explains that "everyone in Acorn has a horrible, ordinary story to tell" (*Talents* 56). They continue to take in traumatized people who have lost so much, and the welcoming ritual formalizes the realization of a new kind of attachment, a new family. They choose new people to be tied to, who stand beside them during the ritual, while words are spoken and promises made. They become "Change-uncles" and "Change-aunts" of children, "Change-brothers" and "Change-sisters" to each other. Gifts are given and songs are sung. "No words are good enough," Olamina says, to sufficiently welcome a child into the world, into the community, "and yet, somehow, words are needed. Ceremony is needed" (*Talents* 65). A simple practical decision to stick together is not adequate in this violent, transient world. Ritual is required to process the reality of the community, to come to terms with the way things are in order to create a better way for things to be.

The rituals in the community of Earthseed give its members a special ability to survive. "We're survivors," Olamina explains to Len, one of her companions after the dissolution and dispersal of the Acorn camp. "All of Acorn was. We've been slammed around in all kinds of ways. We're all wounded. We're healing as best we can. And no, we're not normal. Normal people wouldn't have survived what we've survived" (*Talents* 346). The involvement in the cult, this ritualized community, is what marks the members of Earthseed as "not normal," and yet it is exactly this nonnormativity that allows them to heal and survive. The time, movement, and community provided by the rituals of Earthseed give its members tools for processing the traumas of their apocalyptic world. This is perhaps also why Earthseed becomes so successful after the acute "Pox" is over. It becomes clear that "people are ready for something new and hopeful" and that "some of these dissatisfied people are finding what they want and need in Earthseed" (*Talents* 392–393). In the course of the Pox, virtually the entire country had been traumatized, and the new rituals of Earthseed, which had been developed precisely to address the specific traumas people had endured in this time, proved to be quite appealing and effective, even on a larger scale.

Conclusion

Given what we know about the embodied nature of trauma and the benefit of ritual for processing it, it makes sense that the establishment of a new religion from the individual and communal suffering of an apocalypse would include integral rituals for addressing its members' trauma. Engaging in rituals that set aside sacred time for gathering, welcoming, and remembering their dead allows them to participate in the physical movement of their bodies and knits them together as a strong and supportive community. Therefore, the members of Earthseed are able to better process their traumas, work toward healing, and ultimately survive the Pox and thrive into the future toward their Destiny. The brand newness of Earthseed allows for the creative shaping of rituals that could meet the specific needs of the traumatized community, using their own symbols, language, and context and resulting in an even more effective therapeutic ritual. In the end, it is not a personal, supernatural God that saves the Earthseed community but the communal activity of mutual comfort and support through ritual that helps them heal and survive. They are able to withstand their pain, shape God, and mend their hearts and bodies so that they could continue to shape the world for the future.

WORKS CITED

Butler, Octavia E. *Parable of the Sower*. Grand Central Publishing, 2000.
———. *Parable of the Talents*. Seven Stories, 1998.
Gordon-Lennox, Jeltje. *Crafting Secular Ritual*. Jessica Kingsley Publishers, 2016.
———. "Rhyme and Reason of Ritualmaking." *Emerging Ritual in Secular Societies*, edited by Jeltje Gordon-Lennox, Jessica Kingsley Publishers, 2017, pp. 70–86.
Mount Shoop, Marcia W. *Let the Bones Dance: Embodiment and the Body of Christ*. Westminster John Knox Press, 2010.
Post, Paul, et al. *Disaster Ritual Explorations of an Emerging Ritual Repertoire*. Peeters Publishers, 2003.
Scaer, Robert. *The Body Bears the Burden*. Routledge, 2014.
———. "The Neurophysiology of Ritual and Trauma: Cultural Implications." *Emerging Ritual in Secular Societies*, edited by Jeltje Gordon-Lennox. Jessica Kingsley Publishers, 2017, pp. 55–69.
Turner, Victor W. *The Ritual Process: Structure and Anti-Structure*. Aldine Publishing, 1969.
van der Kolk, Bessel. *The Body Keeps the Score*. Penguin Books, 2015.

8

Migration, Spirituality, and Restorative Spaces

Shape-Shifting to Heal in Octavia Butler's Wild Seed

BRIANA WHITESIDE

Your silence will not protect you.

—LORDE, *Cancer Journals*

Caring for myself is not self-indulgence, it is self-preservation, and that is an act of political warfare.

—LORDE, *Burst of Light*

Octavia Butler's *Wild Seed* (1980) models engaging discourse on how Black women can use their bodies as sites of trauma and therefore sites of healing that can shape-shift to resist subsequent oppression or even prevent it. Butler acknowledges that power in unhealed hands is dangerous, and she challenges Black women to do the work of identifying and healing emotional and spiritual wounds. Where such authors as Gloria Naylor, Alice Walker, and Toni Morrison, to name a few, provide community for their Black women protagonists to heal, Butler tasks her protagonist Anyanwu to create a healing space within herself to respond immediately to her trauma. Consequently, she writes Black women's bodies as recovery spaces that double as "borderguard[s]"[1] (borrowing from Toni Cade Bambara) for spiritual safety and healing privacy. In this way, Butler enters into larger discussions pertaining to Black women's agency and political power, for healing is an act of political warfare. In this chapter, my reading of the healing agency and its political nature builds on Tarshia L. Stanley's and Keegan Osinski's attention to how religion and politics can be used to unpack personal and social trauma, respectively.

Black women's healing scholarship has covered considerable ground. Such scholars as Farah Jasmine Griffin, bell hooks, Courtney Thorsson, and Patricia

Hill Collins highlight how the texts that Black women create historicize social constructions of what's "wrong" with Black womanhood, the impact of storytelling for healing, the constant need to attend to women's "inner nation,"[2] and the importance of communal "safe spaces." Their works are positioned within studies of how slavery continues to affect Black women. In the vein of Black women's narratives, Butler's gateway novel *Kindred* (1979) has received significant attention for her examination of slavery's aftermath on the enslaved's descendants and their ongoing healing struggle (Dutta; Hua; Obertson; Popescu; Flagel; Guha-Majumdar). Comparatively speaking, though, *Wild Seed*—a novel that explores how enslavement influences relationships between men and women, and Black women's attempt to heal from relational trauma—has been underexplored. Subsequently, we have missed how Butler intervenes on discussions concerning Black women's relational traumas and how she extends Black women's healing narratives.[3]

Wild Seed follows Anyanwu—a 350-year-old oracle—as she migrates from a small Neolithic community outside of an Ibo village to the shores of Africa where Africans are sold, through the Middle Passage, to eighteenth-century New England—more specifically, Wheatley, New York, where she will live on the Wheatley plantation. By the end of the novel, Anyanwu eventually arrives at Avoyelles Parish plantation in nineteenth-century southern Louisiana and then relocates to California. The narrative begins in 1680 and ends around 1858, before the Civil War, and tracks an unlikely emotional/ tense/strained affair between two immortals—Anyanwu, a shape-shifter, and Doro, a vampire-like body-snatching spirit entity who intentionally establishes a superhuman race by selectively breeding those with special abilities. As "wild seed"—people too valuable to be killed casually—Anyanwu has dreadfully unexpected experiences en route to, and once she reaches, the Wheatley plantation. Among other things, Doro breeds her as an animal and trades her to his son Isaac.

Yet, despite Anyanwu's experiences, Butler explains in her Huntington Library notes that Anyanwu is the personification of power and "is very much in control—not necessarily of the situation but of [herself]."[4] Granted, her power is no match for Doro's, but she is not powerless. In fact, her shape-shifting capability allows her to showcase just how powerful she is when she creates a safe place of healing by metaphysically migrating from one form to another. Through metaphysical migrations, Butler models how she reconstructs the protagonist's body as a recovery space and explores how the spatial symbolism of escape provides insight into how Black women can begin the healing process.[5] Here, metaphysical migrations build on the in-betweenness theory, which refers to being neither in one state nor the other but a territory of blurring amid two places. According to Carole Boyce Davies, the in-between is the place "that defies the sense of a specific location" (1), permitting the agent a sense of mobility that was not possible previously. Anyanwu embodies the essence of in-betweenness when she moves physically and spiritually within and outside of historically traumatic physical locations, further revealing the complex relationships between Black women, healing, and geographical places. Moreover, by remaining a Black woman in essence, Butler uses her to gesture toward the power and agency of Black female bodies in wholeness.

When Anyanwu shifts into other shapes, she uses those outward shells as mechanisms of defense to create healing spaces as she moves externally. In the text, she has experiences in Africa that encourage her to cease to be woman; aboard the Middle Passage, she must cease to be human; on southern Louisiana soil, she must cease to be Black and woman. Particularly in her seventeenth-century village, Anyanwu transforms into a "small, well-muscled man" (16) to defend herself against seven men who come to kill her. Butler explains that Anyanwu is "cut almost in half" (22) by a machete but uses her hands to fend off the male attackers: Anyanwu sadly explains, "They were my people" (22). In male form, she symbolically divorces herself from women's social vulnerability and the tragic circumstances of communities that dismiss the degradation that Black women experience. Though outnumbered seven against one, Anyanwu gains through transformation the supernatural strength that compensates for the disadvantage. Ultimately, she leaves the abusive hegemonic community that threatens her livelihood as woman and fights within the community as male. Here, Butler writes upon the Black female body to acknowledge and corroborate the complexity of physical intrarelational violence, and by naming bodily mutilation, she explores resistance and freedom strategies.

Certainly, Anyanwu's physical manifestation doubles as a space for her to "do the work," borrowing from Iyanla Vanzant, of resisting by physically fighting and triumphing over the oppressive forces that attack her.[6] In addition, her outward cast allows her to attend to her inner female wounds for Anyanwu is still spiritually a Black woman. Long is the struggle of Black women's battle with intraracial male violence, and Butler uses the village scene to comment on the reality. By acknowledging this, she uses Anyanwu to provide social commentary on the Black female body, uses naming to confirm that physical injustices happen, and then removes the associated shame. At the same time, Butler moves one step further in demonstrating Anyanwu's ability to create community within herself by unveiling how metaphysical migrations serve as safe spaces that assist Black women's healing.

Still, slavery is the historical wound that continues to threaten and manipulate contemporary gender and racial politics even in the lives of the free. The historical reimagining of chattel slavery and the transatlantic slave trade's wounding of Black women's bodies has encouraged substantial critical introspection of the double subordination that conflates Black women's needs with African American needs as a whole. Concerning this, Butler offers careful examination of the Middle Passage and emphasizes the feelings of Black women who were torn away from their homelands. For instance, Anyanwu's despair while en route to the New World coincides with African women's struggles aboard slave ships: "[Anyanwu] felt completely alone on this huge vessel at the edge of endless water. Loneliness . . . She gripped the rail, eyes on shore. . . . She would leap into the sea. Its waters would take her home, or they would swallow her" (57–58). Though physically a clean break, the Middle Passage psychologically serves as a spatial continuum, and the mental and emotional trauma of the experience prompt Anyanwu's leopard transformation when she encounters Lale Sachs, Doro's white son who has telepathic abilities.

Butler uses Lale to continue providing insight into Black women's spiritual and psychological trauma. In the text, Lale has the ability to exercise mental control over others by telepathically changing and controlling their thoughts, which distorts their perceptions of truth and reality. On the one hand, his imaginative conjuring ability reflects the enemy's strongholds that cause people, more specifically Black women, to digress mentally from spiritual leadership.[7] On the other hand, his power mirrors the tactics of slavers, who mentally and physically beat enslaved Black women into submission. On the ship, Lale injects sexual images into Anyanwu's mind that correspond to historical raping incidents: "[Anyanwu] saw herself engaged in wild frantic sexual intercourse, first with Isaac [his white brother], then with this ugly green-eyed man whose name was Lale" (69). Victims of brutal rapes and general sexual abuse during the Middle Passage journeys, enslaved women resisted sexual and reproductive oppression by abortion and infanticide; likewise, Anyanwu uses her body as a weapon of resistance. In response, she creates a place of physical and emotional refuge to protect her womanhood, and she defensively kills Lale. Butler writes of Anyanwu's reasoning, "Best to kill [Lale] now before he could . . . control her thoughts again. . . . He might kill her. . . . With a snarl, she tore out the throat of the being under her feet" (70). Indeed, her decision to kill him is political, for she uses the leopard form to dismantle spiritual and patriarchal oppressive powers that traumatize Black women. Anyanwu also shifts authoritative power by decapitating Lale, and she frees herself of psychological bondage by dismounting the imperialist, capitalist government that subordinates and terrorizes Black women.

Regarding healing, the leopard form is an embodiment of a restorative space. Metaphysical migrations give Anyanwu the opportunity to focus on Thorsson's "inner nation," and she is able to heal the intimate traumas that Black women aboard the Middle Passage experienced. Butler writes that "in [Anyanwu's] leopard form, Doro had discovered that his mind could not find her. Even when he could see her, his mind, his tracking sense, told him she was not there. It was as though she had died, as though he confronted a true animal—a creature beyond his reach" (84). In the introspective space within the leopard shell, Anyanwu makes the internal changes "that those watching could not be aware of" (82), further demonstrating how the ritualistic practice of healing is important for the individualized self. Again, Doro's inability to access Anyanwu while she heals cements the power of the borderguard that serves as a buffer for Black women's contemplative space to tend to their inner needs.

While Anyanwu's ability to heal speedily from hurts that challenge her identity is noteworthy, Butler does not assume that all healing happens quickly. Black women characters, especially on American soil, overwhelmingly suffer from strength and many times silently suffer. Trudier Harris refers to it as "this disease called strength" (iv). The dis-ease is highlighted in Black literary women's denial of vulnerability and weakness. Such denial exalts them to superhuman status, further negating their need for assistance. I add to Harris's assertion that, though Black women characters may experience dis-ease, the decision to adopt the position of strength is still within their control. In *Wild Seed*, Butler examines the ramifications of strength, and she yields Anyanwu the opportunity to heal alongside her oppressor to truly grant her an opportunity to rise above systemic forms of oppression.

To illustrate the point on strength: it is not surprising that, when Anyanwu withstands numerous attacks on her personhood in America, she endures silently. After Doro gave her to his son Isaac and commanded children from them and when "he took her from Isaac's bed to his own and kept her there until he was certain she was pregnant" (145), she obliges. After he commands her to be with Thomas as punishment, "a man with a long sparse beard . . . and long black hair clotted together with the grease and dirt of years from neglect," (146) who later "cursed her and reviled her blackness" (147), Anyanwu's spirit does not outwardly break. When Doro forces Thomas's soul from his body and orders Anyanwu to bury Doro's old body with her bare hands while pregnant, she remains in the community. Even when he rapes her—"when she was finished, he made her undress and lie with him" (161)—Anyanwu abides. Butler writes that when Doro violates her body, she "did not weep because she thought that would please him. But afterwards, for the first time in centuries, she was uncontrollably sick" (161). Across these scenes,

Butler floats how Black women indirectly participate in their own oppression by upholding false perceptions of strength that silence them.

Subsequently, Butler uses Isaac and Anyanwu's daughter Nweke's sudden death to expose the grave consequences of Anyanwu's decision to delay shape-shifting in the face constant abuse. On the day of their funerals, Anyanwu has a nervous breakdown and disappears, and "to Doro's tracking sense, it was as though she had ceased to exist" again (179). She takes the shape of several animals, including a dolphin, a large bird, a werewolf, and large dog, when she physically leaves the community as a Black woman for a century and a half. I submit that Anyanwu's extended nonhuman existence reflects the long-term detrimental impact of strength for Black womanhood and reveals how slow and strenuous recovery is a result of unaddressed trauma. Indeed, her recovery time is similar to Black women characters that die before healing, specifically Great-Gram and Gram in Gayl Jones's *Corregidora* (1975)—but, because of longevity of life, she has the opportunity to heal and reenter the community after 150 years. Consequently, the longevity of the healing experience also uncovers how deeply Black women's bodies and psyches are wounded, and Butler not only comments on Black women's oppression, but through Anyanwu's absence, she critiques Black women's history of healing negligence that binds them to victimhood.

Moreover, Butler challenges Black women's subjectivity in the American imagination when she uses Anyanwu's healing power to move her from the margin to the center. Perhaps the most dramatic revision of history occurs when Anyanwu transforms into a successful, eligible white planter in 1840 Louisiana. On the Warrick plantation, Anyanwu embodies the planter class lifestyle by living in a "large white frame house with tall, unnecessary columns and a porch with upper and lower galleries" (184), and she breeds supernatural beings who people the land.[8] Though "Anyanwu owned no slaves" (199), her actions do mirror those of former slaveholders who utilized sharecropping systems after the Civil War.[9] For example, if her "field hands" (201) disobeyed, Anyanwu exiled them though she knew it meant certain death for individuals whom society deemed "misfits, malcontents, [and] troublemakers" (200). Ultimately, when she casts them off the plantation, she uses those who disobey to indirectly threaten others by deeming insubordinate people unworthy of living. While she does not slaughter those who people her plantation, she figuratively sends them to their death.

At any rate, by allowing the protagonist to wear a southern gentleman's skin, Anyanwu becomes a trickster to undermine slavery, and she reclaims Black women's reproductive control. In this case, Anyanwu explains to Doro that as a white man, she married a white woman and has the ability to father white children: "I could give [my wife] girl children of my own body. Girl children who would have [white] coloring" (199). Her ability to manipulate the gender and ethnicity of a child is noteworthy because it unpins white society's control over Black women's bodies, and it gives Anyanwu power to limit the birth of white southern males who may grow to rape enslaved Black women. When Anyanwu reveals that if she carelessly genetically coded a child's body she "could have given her a monstrosity" (199), her concern dually reflects historical southern anxieties of the planter class and the enslaved. On the one hand, the "monstrosity" reflects white southern fears of biracial children intermixing with the "pure" white race, and Butler complicates and erases boundaries between the nationally acceptable and the nationally threatening in American culture. On the other hand, for African Americans, the presence of a white male on the plantation and his eventual harmful actions toward Black people echo historical fears of what is considered monstrous. In this scene, Butler rewrites history in a way that extends healing not only to Black women but to an entire community.

Nevertheless, healing is not erasure and demands an individual's constant attention and effort.[10] Though Butler's modeling of Anyanwu's healing capability is noteworthy, it does not provide true freedom, which is why Anyanwu contemplates suicide at the end of the narrative. When Doro questions her decision, she tells him, "It's the only way I can leave you. . . . You are all I have, perhaps all I would ever have. . . . And you are an obscenity" (245). She is not merely speaking about their immortality but the fact that wholeness requires reconciliation and that freedom rests in conciliation with Doro.[11] Anyanwu's struggle is also reminiscent of the underlying message in Minnie Ransom's statement to Velma Henry in Bambara's *The Salt Eaters*—published the same year as *Wild Seed*—that "wholeness is no triflin matter. A lot of weight when you're well" (5). In essence, both Bambara and Butler suggest that healing and wholeness are multilayered and involve harmony restoration, which would allow Black women to unburden themselves completely. In this scene, Anyanwu strategically uses vulnerability with Doro, who is wearing a Black male body at this point, to begin the reconciliation phase.[12]

On the one hand, Anyanwu uses vulnerability to continue rejecting the monument of strength image associated with Black women in relationships. On the other hand, she utilizes it as a tool to shift the power dynamics between her and Doro. Her healing prompts a new awareness within him, one that challenges him to grow and realize her importance to his very existence. For instance, as she prepares to kill herself, he pleads with her,

"Anyanwu you must not leave me!" . . . "Please, Anyanwu" . . . "Listen to me. There isn't anything I wouldn't give to be able to lie down beside

you and die when you die. You can't know how I've longed . . ." He swal-
lowed. . . . He wept. He choked out great sobs that shook his already
shaking body almost beyond bearing. . . . He would not stop. (251)

Though Doro remains an absolute power, he realizes that his power is worth-
less if Anyanwu dies. Whereas the ramifications of enslavement pit Black
men and women against one another, Butler affirms that their highest potential is only obtainable through partnership. Yet this is not affirmed without
first providing Doro space to air his weaknesses, exposing the pain that Black
men carry behind masks of strength and dominance. And like many African American literary women, Anyanwu decides to live because living—not
surviving—is her responsibility. Since part of her story is about continuing
to live despite torture and abuse, it follows that she has to continue living,
even though her former abuser also continues living. Anyanwu lives with
Doro after she has healed / gained agency, just as Black women will live *in
the world with* the legacies of their own horrific past and perpetrators of their
recent abusive experiences. Interestingly, scholars have overlooked how her
decision mitigates Doro's power and mobilizes her to regain control of her
identity, which ultimately frees Anyanwu from the external forces that once
commanded her subjectivity.

In the epilogue, Butler marries the power of Anyanwu's ability to heal
the wound between the *real self* and the projected self with the importance
of reconciliation. She writes,

There had to be changes. . . . [Doro] did not command her any longer. She was no longer one of his breeders, nor even one of his people
in the old proprietary way. He could ask her cooperation, her help,
but he could no longer coerce her into giving it. There would be no
more threats to her children. He would not interfere with her children
at all. (252)

Anyanwu's choice to reconcile with Doro contributes to the tonal shift in the
novel; her compromise transforms her self-awareness and self-perception. In
the end, she realizes that she, too, is powerful, and her migration from the
margins to partnership with Doro has long-term benefits. Though initially an
individual choice because, as Bambara reminds us in *The Black Woman* (1970),
"revolution begins in the self and with the self" (109), we see that Anyanwu's
decision is advantageous for the entire community.[13] Significantly, when metaphysical migrations are considered, it is possible to understand how Anyanwu
emerges not as a survivor but a Black woman in control of her destiny. Her

spiritual movements also attest to the rich opportunity to move beyond historic possibility to engage larger concerns for Black women's need to combat oppression and function in wholeness. By first writing against the traditional pattern of the migration narrative—traveling from south to north—to include a Black woman who can move metaphysically in order to come to terms with physical and mental traumas, Butler challenges and expands the master narrative of migration.[14] Secondly, by reimagining black women's healing strategies, she provides scholars space to contemplate how spiritual mobility lends Black women room to heal inner wounds and reenter society in wholeness.

By and large, Butler's participation in exploring migration narratives that discuss Black women's bodies as resistant healing sites is in line with modern-day healing justice initiatives. Healing justice, according to Loretta Pyles, "is the framework that allows activists to find ways to liberate and empower individuals by attending to the impact of violence and intergenerational trauma, the body, emotions, and spirit that in turn facilitates deeper understandings, connection, and sustainability" (xviii).[15] It is both the paradigm and set of practices that invite practitioners to heal themselves at the same time that they heal the world by drawing on communal ways of healing to provide justice to marginal communities. As Pyles notes, "since oppression creates deep trauma, it only makes sense that disrupting oppression and healing from it will require more than political and intellectual processes; it will also require embodied ones" (9), and Butler's text can be used as a reputable model. While the Westernized view of justice privileges criminalizing individuals to right their wrongs, healing justice focuses on individual identity, restoration, and peace that allow activists to fight for social justice more effectively. Ultimately, Butler's encouragement to consider the long-lasting impact of ignoring Black women's marginalized emotions and spirits, and how the negligence impedes on liberation, is an attempt to grant justice through healing.

Altogether, Anyanwu, as a healer, offers some answers to the imaginative ways that healing operates, and her decision to take advantage of the restorative space within herself provides an opportunity for her to forgive, reconcile, and ultimately restore the harmony in her life. Not to mention, since healing metaphorically represents the act of reclaiming one's body and reconfiguring it to serve a greater purpose, Butler's text serves as a representative model of a revisionist text. By migrating to a place free of oppressive powers, the protagonist overcomes injustices that distort her sense of self-worth and identity, which explicitly reveals that emotional healing is as important as physical healing. Overall, there is rich opportunity here to explore the imaginative areas of healing and the impact on a protagonist who has the power to cease to be Black, woman, and American.

NOTES

1. In *The Salt Eaters*, Toni Cade Bambara comments on the protagonist Velma Henry's desire to call in the borderguard, which is a deep-seated desire to "withdraw the self to a safe place where husband, lover, teacher, workers, no one could follow, probe. Withdraw herself and prop up a borderguard to negotiate with would-be intruders" (5). The borderguard is a barrier of protection that would allow Velma to create an in-between space within herself.

2. Courtney Thorsson borrows the concept of "inner nation" from Bambara's *The Salt Eaters*. Bambara redefines nation as a varied, practiced, and multifocal entity. If outer nation represents Black communities and collectivity, inner nation constitutes internal collectivity and wholeness. Both inner and outer nations affect one another and must be in concert in order to prompt personal synchronization. For Thorsson's complete explication, see Thorsson 2013.

3. There are a few articles written on Butler's *Wild Seed*: Wood; Dubey; Afful; Matthews; Jones.

4. See Octavia Butler Journal, 1979, box 178, OEB 3219, Huntington Library, San Marino, California.

5. The metaphysical can also encompass internal movements and states of being that would allow one to have a spiritual experience while one's physical self is stationed elsewhere. Perhaps a better way to understand this would be to consider an out-of-body experience.

6. The American inspirational speaker Iyanla Vanzant is known for encouraging her viewers to "do their work." The phrase means to be willing to listen and to be wrong, to be honest, and to heal from issues that may stymie an individual from having strong relationships with others and themselves. Vanzant asserts that individuals must do the work necessary to become whole.

7. For an understanding of spiritual warfare see *English Standard Version Bible*, 2 Cor. 10:3–5.

8. In the text, both Doro and Anyanwu's husband, Mgbada, accuse her of intentionally breeding people with supernatural capabilities to people her plantation.

9. Anyanwu's plantation is peopled with supernatural "field hands" (201). Though she frees them in theory, they are hired help and are used at her disposal. While she does not whip those who disobey her, she does exile them though she knows that it would mean that they would die a quick death.

10. For a complete examination of healing, see Griffin 524.

11. In her notes at the Huntington Library, Octavia Butler is adamant that Anyanwu is not a victim and that book 3 of *Wild Seed* explores Anyanwu's quest for reconciliation in freedom. See Octavia Butler Journal, 1979, box 178, OEB 3219, Huntington Library, San Marino, California.

12. I mention Doro's flesh here because he usually wears white skin in the narrative. At one point, he even remarks that it is easier to wear a white body when he travels.

13. Though the importance of Anyanwu's partnership with Doro is more pronounced in the sequel *Mind of My Mind* (1979), Butler hints at it in the epilogue. Simultaneously, she corroborates bell hooks's assertion that "when black women recover fully and exercise our will to be compassionate, to forgive, this will have a healing impact on black life" (128). For an extended commentary on women's introspective spaces, see hooks.

14. In addition, the realm of science fiction broadens imaginations to the expansive possibilities of life by exploring alternatives to social and historical events. Significantly, Butler challenges values placed on Black womanhood and deconstructs notions that subordinate Black women by centering and lending female protagonists extraordinary superpowers in her narratives, which is in correlation with the neo-slave-narrative tradition.

15. See Pyles's explanation of healing justice and its importance.

WORKS CITED

Afful, Adwoa. "*Wild Seed*: Africa and Its Many Diasporas." *Critical Arts*, vol. 30, no. 4, 2016, pp. 557–573.

Bambara, Toni Cade. *The Black Woman*. New American Library, 1970.

———. *The Salt Eaters*. Vintage, 1980.

The Bible. English Standard Version, Oxford University Press, 1998.

Butler, Octavia. *Seed to Harvest: Wild Seed, Mind of My Mind, Clay's Ark, and Patternmaster*. Grand Central Publishing, 2007.

Collins, Patricia Hill. *Black Sexual Politics: African Americans, Gender, and the New Racism*. Routledge, 2005.

Davies, Carole Boyce. *Black Women, Writing and Identity: Migrations of the Subject*. Routledge, 1994.

Dubey, Madhu. "Octavia Butler's Novels of Enslavement." *Novel*, vol. 46, no. 3, 2013, pp. 345–363.

Dutta, Suchismita. "Indelible Race Memories and Subliminal Epigenetics in Octavia Butler's *Kindred*." *Intersections*, vol. 21, 2018, pp. 86–103.

Flagel, Nadine. "'It's Almost Like Being There': Speculative Fiction, Slave Narrative, and the Crisis of Representation in Octavia Butler's *Kindred*." *Canadian Review of American Studies*, vol. 42, no. 2, 2012, pp. 216–245.

Griffin, Farah Jasmine. "Textual Healing: Claiming Black Women's Bodies, the Erotic and Resistance in Contemporary Novels of Slavery." *Callaloo*, vol. 19, no. 2, 1996, pp. 519–536.

Guha-Majumdar, Jishnu. "The Dilemmas of Hope and History: Concrete Utopianism in Octavia E. Butler's *Kindred*." *Palimpsest: A Journal on Women, Gender, and the Black International*, vol. 6, no. 1, 2017, pp. 129–152.

Harris, Trudier. *Saints, Sinners, Saviors: Strong Black Women in African American Literature*. Palgrave, 2002.

hooks, bell. *Sisters of the Yam: Black Women and Self-Recovery*. South End Press, 1993.

Hua, Linh U. "Reproducing Time, Reproducing History: Love and Black Feminist Sentimentality in Octavia Butler's *Kindred*." *African American Review*, vol. 44, no. 3, 2011, pp. 391–407.

Jones, Cassandra L. "Memory and Resistance: Doro's Empire, Mary's Rebellion, and Anyanwu as *Lieu De Mémoire* in Octavia E. Butler's *Mind of My Mind* and *Wild Seed*." *Women's Studies*, vol. 47, no. 7, 2018, pp. 698–718.

Lorde, Audre. *Burst of Light and Other Essays*. Ixia Press, 1998.

———. *The Cancer Journals*. Aunt Lute Books, 1980.

Matthews, Aisha. "Gender, Ontology, and the Power of the Patriarchy: A Postmodern Feminist Analysis of Octavia Butler's *Wild Seed* and Margaret Atwood's *The Handmaid's Tale*." *Women's Studies*, vol. 47, no. 6, 2018, pp. 637–656.

Morrison, Toni. *Beloved*. Vintage, 1987.

Naylor, Gloria. *Mama Day*. Vintage Books, 1988.

Obertson, Benjamin. "'Some Matching Strangeness': Biology, Politics, and the Embrace of History in Octavia Butler's *Kindred*." *Science Fiction Studies*, vol. 37, no. 3, 2010, pp. 362–381.

Popescu, Irina. "Empathetic Trappings: Revisiting the Nineteenth Century in Octavia Butler's *Kindred*." *Journal of Human Rights*, vol. 17, no. 2, 2018, pp. 184–198.

Pyles, Loretta. *Healing Justice: Holistic Self-Care for Change Makers*. Oxford University Press, 2018.

Sawatsky, Jarem. *The Ethic of Traditional Communities and the Spirit of Healing Justice Studies from Hollow Water, the Iona Community, and Plum Village*. Jessica Kingsley Publishers, 2008.

Smith, Catherine. "Between-ness: Theory and Practice within the Margins of Excess." *IDEA Journal*, vol. 1, no. 4, 2003, pp. 131–144.

Thorsson, Courtney. *Women's Work: Nationalism and Contemporary African American Women's Novels*. University of Virginia Press, 2013.

Walker, Alice. *The Color Purple*. Harcourt, 1982.

Wood, Sarah. "Subversion through Inclusion: Octavia Butler's Interrogation of Religion in Xenogenesis and *Wild Seed*." *Femspec*, vol. 6, no. 1, 2005, pp. 87–99.

9

"We Trade the Essence of Ourselves"

West African Spirituality in Xenogenesis's Oankali

Ebony Gibson

Early in Octavia Butler's novel *Dawn*,[1] the alien Jdahya attempts to describe to the protagonist Lilith Iyapo the process of gene trading that guides the Oankali way of life. He explains, "We trade the essence of ourselves. Our genetic material for yours" (40). Even in these two short sentences, science is suffused with spiritual connotations attached to the meanings of "essence." It reflects these extraterrestrials' genetic drive to merge their body and spirit with others as a way of life—and to shape new life.

The debate over the intentions and actions of the Oankali has been dynamic among scholars and writers. This alien race has been called "slavers," "colonizers," "seducers," and "wastrels."[2] At best, the Oankali's actions are often viewed in ambiguous terms: Naomi Jacobs describes them as "benevolent tyrants." She argues that "the humans are outclassed by the aliens' greater capacities. . . . [Furthermore,] . . . the Oankali believe greater powers and knowledge give them the right to choose what is best for the humans and to act accordingly" (97). Early in his article when describing how the Oankali way of life is presented to humans, Jeffrey Tucker frames it with the competing verbs "offer/impose" (164). Christina Braid asserts the Oankali "sympathiz[e] only half-heartedly" for their costly errors against humans (56). In his biocritical text *Octavia E. Butler*, Gerry Canavan provides a thorough review of the Oankali debate. He admits that he "genuinely love[s]" the Xenogenesis series. And near the conclusion of his argument, which is one of the most adamant critiques against the Oankali, he asserts, "For all of their supposed difference and for all their self-inflating rhetoric, [the Oankali] are as much the final perfection of human destructivity as an alternative to it" (119). Canavan argues that, when stripped of science fiction elements, the trilogy is "a plain retelling of the brutal history of imperialism" (106).

While Canavan's position is clear, earlier in the chapter when reviewing the position of Oankali supporters, he also points out that a common thread among those who are "pro-Oankali" is a belief in the Human Contradiction (113). The Oankali believe that human bodies are "fatally flawed." Humans are intelligent yet hierarchal. Jdahya argues that these are "a mismatched pair of genetic characteristics. Either alone would have been useful, would have aided the survival of your species. But the two together are lethal" (*Dawn* 38). Thus, while humans are intelligent, we are still genetically wired to impose hierarchy even at the cost of our own demise.

I have never doubted I am *pro*-Oankali. Yet reading Canavan's work led me to carefully consider what in my lived experience contributes to my easily embracing the Oankali way of life. First, I agree with the Oankali's assertions that humans are "fatally flawed." Moreover, I may more easily embrace that position because I have the lived experience of a dark-skinned African American woman in academia, teaching and researching on work that intersects African American literature, African American studies, and Black feminist thought—and I practice a lesser known (non-Western) spiritual system. In other words, I have overlapping sites of privilege and lack of privilege (as most human beings do); however, my same training and education that provide me spaces of privilege also make me hyperaware of when the things that I value or that reflect my experience are diminished or dismissed. Secondly, I am influenced by my lived experience as a practitioner of Ifa—an ancient spiritual system that originated in southwest Nigeria. Moreover, many of its practitioners—including myself—describe it not just as a spiritual system but a way of life. It is an entire world view. Most rituals are built around community and consensus, drawing on the energy of many to gain agency and diverse perspectives.

In this chapter, I will examine Butler's use of Yoruba culture in Xenogenesis. Furthermore, I will use my own experience with ritual and culture as a practitioner of Ifa in examining several Oankali cultural practices: use of consensus, ancestral reverence, and the value of memory and knowledge. These practices reflect a sense of spirituality—a knowing, a way of life—created through a deep biological drive. It is a vision of healing, guided by a sense of sacrifice and constant revision and most reflected in the Oankali's desire to resolve the human fatal flaw—something so *fatal* that Lilith's child Jodahs equates it to a man "walk[ing] off a cliff simply because he could not see it—or because he, or rather his descendants, would not hit the rocks below for a long time" (*Imago* 531).

Much of what I have learned of Ifa as a general practitioner and during my ongoing training as an initiated priest is through conversations and verbal lessons, reflecting the oral culture of the spiritual system;[3] therefore, I will cite personal anecdotes and observations as much as "traditional" academic texts. Furthermore, this chapter will incorporate stylistic choices that merge an academic essay with a personal essay; it is an intersection of literary criticism, cultural commentary, and personal narrative.

"The Oankali Are Not Evil. They're Just Driven": Xenogenesis Series

In 1987, the science fiction writer Ian Watson wrote a letter to Butler raising his suspicions about the motives of the Oankali and wondered if they had caused the war that destroyed the world. In her response, Butler explains they had not and that "[t]he Oankali are not evil. They're just driven by their own biology to do certain things—just as we humans are driven by our biology to do certain things. Very different things."[4] They are biologically driven to gene trade. They give their whole self, combining with other species—in this case, with humans.

Dawn begins 250 years after a nuclear war that has destroyed most of Earth. The Oankali have saved as many humans as they can. Lilith Iyapo is forced into the role of being the first person to prepare humans to return to Earth. Humans have been healed and nourished but also isolated and studied. Oankali are both attracted and repelled by the contradiction within humans of intelligence and hierarchy. Oankali believe "trading" will help to control that. Humans are mistrustful of their captors and soon learn that they must make a choice concerning the new Earth that awaits them: create a new race by genetically combining with the Oankali or return home to have a healthy and very long life but never be able to give birth to children.

Adulthood Rites follows the birth of Lilith's son Akin. Akin is the first male born to a human woman. The families in trade villages are different: a male and female Oankali parent, a male and female human parent, and a third gender of the Oankali—an ooloi. It combines the genetic material, "mixing" a child. Akin is kidnapped by human resisters when he is very young. He lives among them for over a year, and Akin gains a new respect for humans and an understanding of why they resist. He later learns that he was left with humans for so long due to an Oankali consensus—that his family vehemently objected—to better understand human culture. When he is older, Akin is able to use the Oankali process of consensus to petition for humans to receive a colony on Mars—a human world where they can have children. And *Imago* takes place fifty years after the Mars colony begins. Lilith's child Jodahs becomes the first ooloi born to a human. Oankali and humans watch carefully to see if Jodahs can learn to control the overwhelming power of being able to manipulate with a simple touch any living entity at the genetic level.

Yoruba Aesthetics and Ifa

In *Dawn*, Butler uses Yoruba culture to create layered meanings of tradition, loss, and survival. Lilith recalls the memory of her husband's and son's deaths in a car accident before the war. She was married to Sam, a first-generation Nigerian American.[5] His parents "had sent him to visit their families in Lagos when they could. [And they] had hoped he would marry a Yoruban girl" (77). They disapproved so much of Lilith that they never met their grandson Ayre before he died in the crash. Her in-laws clung to a traditional way of life and were not willing to adapt or find common ground. In their rejection of their son, they lost the opportunity to ever know their grandchild. And in traditional West African culture, children are *everything*. Sam suffers a brain injury in the same accident; he comes in out of consciousness, taking three months to die. She remembers the vacant look in Sam's eyes as he lay in a hospital bed, staring through parents he did not seem to recognize. Lilith recalls this moment as she considers whether to let Nikanj chemically change her brain so that she has an eidetic memory. Lilith fears the worst. What if Sam was trapped inside, unable to communicate? She is terrified of losing the essence of herself and who she is. Lilith replays this memory as she decides how much she is willing to risk for survival.

Lilith sees her brain being changed as destruction of self. The Oankali see this genetic change as no different than healing her cancer. While she worries that she will lose the essence of who she is, they envision this genetic change as something that allows her to access more knowledge and by extension grow to her full potential. Memory and knowledge are spiritual to the Oankali. They know what they know and move through life with no difference between their thoughts and actions.

In *Adulthood Rites*, Lilith gives her son Akin a Yoruba name. He is the first Oankali construct (a genetic combination of Oankali and human) male born to a human woman. Akin explains two meanings provided for his name: "It means *hero*. If you put an *s* on it, it means *brave boy*" (*Rites* 351). Aparajita Nanda explores several significant meanings of his name: "A 'kin' to Oankalis [sic] and humans, Akin is 'akin' (not 'a-kin' to any one species)." Secondly, she offers that his "name foreshadows and presages his purpose."

He will "become someone brave and heroic on behalf of his kinsmen, his kinfolk" ("Re-writing" 123). Another perspective is offered by Theodora Goss and John Paul Riquelme. They consider a possible impact of first believing Akin is pronounced "a kin" but learning that it is pronounced "Ah-keen" (*Rites* 351): "The new pronunciation in relation to the old one, which we are unlikely to be able to suppress entirely, creates a heteronymous situation in which the same group of letters carry different meanings. In this case, the meanings merge. This posthuman male with an African name is also a kin, however alien he may seem. . . . By registering the blurred character of apparent opposites, such as *akin* and *alien*, this kind of double vision undercuts hierarchical thinking, which depends on binaries" (451). Thus, Akin's name (like his very existence) may read to signify the posthuman blending that offers hope of human and alien Oankali coexisting. Moreover, Akin's internal struggle is reflected and affected by the external struggle he observes between resisters and Oankali. The Oankali reached a consensus to leave Akin with the resisters so that the Oankali would gain more knowledge of humans; eventually, Akin is able to offer a path that offers some healing—but by no means all—of the cultural divide and pain humans have toward Oankali.

Another interpretation would be to consider similar pronunciations in Yoruba. Akin ("ah-keen") is very close to *ikin* ("ee-keen"). Ikin is a palm nut used as a divination tool by high priests of Ifa.[6] Ikin are considered sacred because of the connection to the prophet Orunmila of Ifa. They are symbolic objects that represent his presence on earth (Karade 91). In *Adulthood Rites*, Akin becomes a prophet that delivers to humans the possibility of having children again. He gives them life. Ikin is a symbolic representation of Orunmila the prophet, "who developed and expounded upon the system of esoteric worship known to this day as Ifa" (7). He provided a spiritual life and new path. This reading adds a deeper West African richness and connection beyond the classical Western archetype of a prophet.

Butler studied Yoruban mythology "to make use of it." She explains in an interview: "Everyone makes use of Greek mythology, so I've been fooling around with Yoruban" (Piziks 50). In other words, she was specifically seeking to weave a non-Western mythos into her work.[7] Yet critics' readings of the Oankali more often focus on race, enslavement, colonialism, and/or postcolonialism as opposed to a Yoruba aesthetic.

However, in his analysis of *Dawn*, Gregory Jerome Hampton uses a Yoruba aesthetic. He uses Wole Soyinka's "The Fourth Stage," which juxtaposes the Yoruba tragedy against the Greek tragedy in a framework to examine *Dawn*. Hampton analyzes *Dawn* as a tragedy using the Yoruba *orisha*[8] Ogun and Obatala instead of Nietzsche's Greek Apollo and Dionysus. Hampton seems to accept the Human Contradiction and views the humans' resistance as disastrous: "Tragically, the humanity of the past was not able to accept ambiguity even when it resided at the core of human existence on a genetic level. It is the non-Western thinking/non-human/alien Oankali characters who teach the sole survivors of humanity to embrace something very similar to Yoruba aesthetics" (72). In this case, I use his assertion to open the door to a deeper exploration between Yoruba religion—Ifa—and the Oankali.

In her theoretical and critical text *The Spirit and the Word*, Georgene Bess Montgomery offers a clear and accessible description of Ifa: "an ancient spiritual system of cosmology, worldview, and philosophy. Although dramatically simple, Ifá is a 'complex combination of theology and ritual' ("Moral" 1). As such, it is a microcosm of African life, thought, and cosmology, based on a profound spirituality that emphasizes the intimate and inherent connection between all living and nonliving things" (8). Thus, she encapsulates that Ifa is way of life that considers the divinity in all things—not just humans. This reflects some of the Oankali's core beliefs of reverence for all life.

In this chapter, I am pulling from one spiritual system as a way to provide clear form and concrete examples of common philosophies, rituals, and practices in West African spirituality (as well as other traditional spiritual systems). I am pulling from a culture Butler deliberately integrated into her work. Finally, I am extending ideas in Hampton's analysis. He acknowledges the presence of a Yoruba aesthetic in his reading of the Oankali, but his use of Soyinka's work creates a framework based primarily on an artistic use of Yoruba religion. I will move beyond artistic aesthetic to the lived experiences of a practitioner.

Consensus

The initiation of an *olorisha* (a priest initiated to an orisha) generally takes seven days. On the sixth night, the *ita* takes place. This new priest (called an *iyawo*) is given messages to guide her journey through life. Messages may be related to health, family, and career—but it is most specifically related to her lifelong journey of *iwa pele* (good character).[9] The ceremony is a long process. My ita took so long it had to be completed on a second day.

The process is organized according to the orisha vessels (or pots)[10] the priest has received, starting with Esu,[11] then the orisha the priest was initiated to, and then any other vessel the priest has received. For each orisha, four *odus*[12] are divined using a system of sixteen cowrie shells.[13] For each odu, every priest present is given the opportunity to add their knowledge. This itself may become an extensive conversation. My ita had four priests present. I have participated in itas with ten priests present. It is a long process that requires patience, thoughtfulness, and focus from all involved; it is deeply personal, and while rewarding, it is emotionally draining and at many moments overwhelming. An iyawo is given an incredible amount of guidance from a wide variety of lived experiences. At my ita, even with just four priests—in addition to my own instincts—I was practicing a form of consensus. I had to interpret a large amount of information being given to me and reach an understanding of how to guide my life. I understood this interpretation would evolve over time with new experiences, and I must be prepared to adapt and change.

The Oankali do not have a central government; major decisions are reached through consensus. It is a neural joining that leaves no room for deception. Not everyone agrees, but a decision is reached. It is an evolving process always open to the possibility of future change. It was consensus that humans who did not mate with Oankali would not be able to give birth due to the fatal flaw (or human contradiction). All Oankali do not agree, and the decisions sometimes have horrible outcomes. Christina Braid asserts, "[The Oankali] are always willing to learn from their mistakes but deem insignificant the consequences of their actions. No one Oankali seems to be held accountable for any *faux pas*, an interesting side-effect of their government without responsibility. The democratic nature of the Oankali seems wrought with difficulty throughout the text, even while the violence caused by certain alien actions is safely hidden by the placid and nonchalant Oankali disposition" (55). However, I would argue that the Oankali are not hiding or indifferent but simply live in a space that accepts mistakes or change as a natural part of learning. They accept the wounding of egos, ideas, and even bodies as a natural part of the process. They accept sacrifice as a natural part of growth. A bad decision in a consensus is the reason Lilith is brutally attacked and nearly raped. But because Nikanj's warning came true, the Oankali began to respect his input despite his age, and others acknowledged his understanding of humans. However, Oankali are also willing to sacrifice other Oankali to reevaluate a stance. For instance, because Akin is left with resisters, he is unable to bond with his sibling, and the impact on him is devastating for years. On the other hand, because Akin spent over a year with resisters, he was able to understand humans better and eventually convinces the Oankali—through consensus—that humans should be given a chance to change and adapt.

Ancestral Reverence

Most ancestor shrines have several main elements: they have a piece of white cloth, a white candle, a glass of water, and pictures of family members that have died.[14] I also added things such as a cigar for my grandfather, saltwater taffy for my father and the clarinet he played in the army, one of my grand-mother's hats, and a bottle of perfume she loved. And I add from time to time additional things that my family members would treasure.

Most of this does not seem unusual. It is common in many cultures in the African diaspora and Eastern spiritual systems. And it is not even uncommon for those who practice a wide variety of faiths (or none at all) to save a funeral program and sentimental item or to cook a favorite meal to remember those they have lost. My practice is simply a more intentional and openly acknowledged ritual.

Another essential element of this shrine is a list of names of those who have died. My list begins with the most recent death in my bloodline and moves to the longest ago that I know by name. One near the end of the list is my great-grandmother who over a century ago bought hundreds of acres of land in Mississippi that still remain in the family. And it begins with her son, my maternal grandfather who died at ninety-one surrounded by his loving children. At least once a week, I say each name aloud. If available, I provide a few concrete details or a memory that encapsulates him or her.[15] I recite prayers in Yoruba and others in English.

Ifa—like many traditional religions—practices ancestral reverence. To be clear, it is not worship. Ancestors are my first line of defense. I go to them with questions before I go to the orisha. I talk to them every day. I cook them meals they enjoyed when they were alive. I fix their favorite drink and place it on the ancestor shrine. I speak their names aloud to let them know they are remembered. In *Egun: The Ifa Concept of Ancestor Reverence*, Fa'lokun Fatunmbi explains, "*Ifa* teaches the idea that you cannot know who you are if you cannot call the name of your ancestors going back seven generations. The ability to call the names is believed to make it possible to seat your *ori* (consciousness) in the world" (1). However, after hours of research, I can only trace back three generations on my paternal side and five on my maternal. The transatlantic slave trade makes it difficult. However, all Oankali know their entire genetic line. The information is "passed on biologically." They remember every "division" that has taken place in their family since they left their home world so long ago that it probably no longer exists (*Dawn* 36, 37). The Oankali are biologically connected to the past. In this case, the importance and power of family are moved from mysticism and myth to genetic and biological. They live in a space where the past is always with them, yet they are driven to constantly evolve. Hampton makes a similar allusion about the Yoruba aesthetic: "The past, present, and future or the ancestors, the living, and the unborn, are all woven together in a oneness that permeates

Yoruba aesthetics. Each mode of time helps to explain the next in contexts of art, religion, life, and the metaphysical order of the Yoruba world" (74).

Value of Memory and Knowledge

When a child is born into the culture of Ifa—even in the United States—she learns rituals by watching her family and community. She hears the songs, drums, and prayers. Therefore, she learns Yoruba as she learns English. She watches the rituals. She performs simple but significant tasks from an early age, such as changing the water on shrines, gathering supplies for rituals, and cleaning after ceremonies. Most importantly, she quietly observes.

I was not born into this way of life. Like Lilith I continue to play catch up with rituals, cultural expectations, and language. Some prayers are written down, but many are not. It depends on the teaching philosophy of the priest from whom you are learning. Moreover, Yoruba is a tonal language full of inflections; prayers and chants are almost sung more than spoken. And of course songs are also a key part of rituals. The nuances at times seem endless. It is my beautiful ambition. It is a lifelong journey to learn as much as you choose to learn.

I envy the Oankali as I face the challenge to learn a culture I was not born into. The Oankali have eidetic memory. What they learn once is always remembered. I agree with Sarah Outterson that "learning is natural to their bodies. It is as inevitable as the Clayark drive to infect or the human hierarchal impulse that Butler depicts. [Additionally,] this Oankali pedagogical philosophy explains their odd aversion to human writing" (446). For example, Lilith perceives the choice to not provide her with writing tools as a punishment; and as Outterson points out, the Oankali "refusal to allow Lilith the tools of that external culture whets her hunger for the greater connections that only they can provide" (446). They want her to learn the world their way. At a moment of frustration, Lilith screams, "I don't have a disease! Forgetting things is normal for most humans! I don't need anything done to my brain!" (*Dawn* 76). But forgetting is not normal for Oankali. And Lilith becomes the bridge to the posthuman children that follow.

Lilith eventually makes the choice to have the procedure while she still has some agency in the decision. Sometime later, after Lilith is chemically changed, she is given books and other writing materials as a peace offering from the ooloi Kahguyaht. Moreover, in the third part of *Dawn* entitled Nursery, the dossiers are an essential tool for Lilith as she chooses whom to awaken. She spends days looking through the papers, knowing the wrong decision may kill her. The dossiers also transform to keys. Lilith must rub the picture from the dossier across the wall to locate each body within and release the long green plants from the wall containing humans. She regains the material connection but with the enhanced technology of the Oankali. Even this is trading.

For Oankali, memory and knowledge are the platform to pursue inner enlightenment. They constantly adapt their way of thinking and their physical bodies to serve the needs of the community and their biological imperative. Katherine Broad asserts that the Oankali value the "biological over linguistic epistemologies" (147). Moreover, she explores Foucault's formulation of ranked knowledges. What is considered "erudite" or "disqualified knowledges" is determined by those in power (147). She observes that the Oankali knowledge of "how to live in sync with the environment" would "generally [be] considered negative, low-hierarchy knowledge" in current Western society. However, within the novels, "Oankali knowledge of the body . . . is also categorized as erudite, more accurate and discerning than what could be determined by human knowledges that retain a self/other divide through language and physical touch. [Yet,] humans' insights into their own selves and bodies is shown to be disqualified knowledge, subjugated or naïve knowledge" (147). Consequently, Broad later warns that "the peaceful Oankali society predicated on a valuation of difference is preferable to humans' xenophobia and war, but the seductiveness of the Oankali world order should not blind us to the fact that their incorporation of difference is also in eradication" (151). Thus, Broad gives voice to the devaluing of human culture and choice—irreparable loss.

Oankali see change; they *must* change to meet the needs of the trade, the ship, and biological drive. And every change is remembered in their genetic code—millions of years of change.[16] Humans cannot understand that. They do not have a language for it. And the Oankali believe they will not understand it. True understanding will only come from children who are both Oankali and human. The posthumans to come will have access to the memories.

In *Race in American Science Fiction*, Isiah Lavender III points to the othering of the human beings and the Oankali. He explains, "It is fascinating to contemplate humans positioned as the colonized 'other' by the Oankali. Just as humans are configured as other, the Oankali are others too, as they make use of living technologies to travel the stars and forcibly trade with various life forms" (72). In this case, Lavender seems to allude to several points of fascination. Human beings who generally see themselves in a position of power are marginalized; their needs and ideology are seen as secondary to others. However, the Oankali—despite their immense power—are othered too. While the othering is most apparent in their appearance, the Oankali's cultural beliefs and biological drive to embrace change and genetically combine with others are ideologies that create the most distance, especially from common Western ideologies of individuality, power, and privilege.

I agree that the Oankali's actions are flawed. Having power does not eliminate mistakes. It increases the impact of them. Their assuredness of what is right and their intent to heal are still oppressive to humans who have lost so much of their power. However, I see the struggle of healers who eventually must accept the free will of humans. And it does not negate that I am still more drawn to their way of life because I see elements of my life within the Oankali. I see much of the humanity that I aspire to—in the aliens.

NOTES

1. The Xenogenesis trilogy comprises *Dawn, Adulthood Rites,* and *Imago.* It was repackaged as *Lilith's Brood* in 2000. For specificity in citations, the novel titles will be used.

2. See Canavan for "wastrels" and "seducers." See Lavender for "slavers." See Canavan and both articles by Nanda for "colonizers."

3. I was initiated as a priestess of Yemonja in 2016 in the Osabi Ferososi lineage by Ile Tiwalade.

4. Letter to Ian Watson, January 6, 1988, OEB 4429, Huntington Library, San Marino, California. Image reprinted at Canavan 114.

5. Lilith's married name is Iyapo, which means "many trials," foreshadowing the endless challenges she must face. "Trials" also hints at judgment, not just physical trials. It is also phonetically close to the female name Iyabo, which means "mother has returned." Lilith is forced into the role as surrogate mother and leader to humans; she has no desire for this role.

6. There are several levels to which a priest may aspire. A high priest is generally the highest level and performs specific ceremonies and rituals. The order, initiation process, and training vary from lineage to lineage. But there is more overlap than difference. For information on the stages, see Karade 101–105.

7. Canavan mentions that Butler took courses on African literature and African history (36). However, no additional details are provided.

8. Energies that in Yoruba religion represent various aspects of Oldumare—Ifa's name for the Supreme Being. They are sometimes compared to angels or saints.

9. "Above all, Ifá stresses ìwà-pẹ̀lẹ̀, 'good character.' Ìwà-pẹ̀lẹ̀ is motivation behind all actions—ritual, sacrifice, initiation, ancestor reverence, Òrìṣà worship—and is the guiding principle by which Ifá practitioners live" (Montgomery 9).

10. Pots for an orisha are created through a complex ritual using herbs, specific items for the respective orisha, and songs and prayers performed by priests. They are not considered the actual orisha (which is a common misconception); they are an instrument to more directly connect. For example, many who practice Christianity believe you can talk to God anywhere but have a stronger connection at a church or altar.

11. An orisha in the Ifa spiritual system. While he is often referred to as a trickster god, this is an oversimplification. He is also the messenger; he carries messages to heaven and must be appeased before all other orisha in rituals.

12. Lessons from the sacred Ifa corpus, which contains "256 *Odù*, each representing a particular energy. These Odù are scared stories, verses, and scriptures that provide wisdom and moral guidance" (Montgomery 9).

13. See Bascom; Olupona and Abiodun.

14. This may vary due to lineage practices and is also adapted to suit practical needs of space, material resources, and stylistic preferences.

15. For more details about the process, see Fatunmbi.

16. Jdahya explains to Lilith, "Your people have something we value. You may begin to know how much we value it when I tell you that by your way of measuring time, it has been several million years since we dared to interfere in another people's act of self-destruction. Many of us disputed the wisdom of doing it this time. We thought . . . that there had been a consensus among you, that you had agreed to die" (*Dawn* 16).

WORKS CITED

Bascom, William Russell. *Ifa Divination: Communication between Gods and Men in West Africa*. Indiana University Press, 1991.

Braid, Christina. "Contemplating and Contesting Violence in Dystopia: Violence in Octavia Butler's *XENOGENESIS* Trilogy." *Contemporary Justice Review*, vol. 9, no. 1, Mar. 2006, pp. 47–65.

Broad, Katherine R. "Body Speaks: Communication and the Limits of Nationalism in Octavia Butler's Xenogenesis Trilogy." *The Postcolonial Fantasy: Essays on Postcolonialism, Cosmopolitics, and Science Fiction*, edited by Masood Ashraf Raja, Jason W. Ellis, and Swaralipi Nandi, McFarland, 2011, pp. 141–155.

Butler, Octavia E. *Bloodchild and Other Stories*. Seven Stories Press, 2005.

———. *Lilith's Brood (Dawn, Adulthood Rites, and Imago)*. Grand Central Publishing, 2007.

Canavan, Gerry. *Octavia E. Butler*. University of Illinois Press, 2016.

Fatunmbi, Fa'lokun. *Egun: The Ifa Concept of Ancestor Reverence*. CreateSpace Independent Publishing Platform, 2013.

Goss, Theodora, and John Paul Riquelme. "From Superhuman to Posthuman: The Gothic Technological Imaginary in Mary Shelley's *Frankenstein* and Octavia Butler's Xenogenesis." *MFS Modern Fiction Studies*, vol. 53 no. 3, 2007, pp. 434–459. *Project MUSE*, doi:10.1353/mfs.2007.0068.

Hampton, Gregory Jerome. *Changing Bodies in the Fiction of Octavia Butler: Slaves, Aliens, and Vampires*. Lexington Books, 2010.

Jacobs, Naomi. "Posthuman Bodies and Agency in Octavia Butler's Xenogenesis." *Dark Horizons: Science Fiction and the Dystopian Imagination*, edited by Raffaella Baccolini and Tom Moylan, Routledge, 2003, pp. 91–111. *EBSCOhost*, search .ebscohost.com/login.aspx?direct=true&db=mzh&AN=2005532592&site=eds-live &scope=site.

Karade, Ifa. *The Handbook of Yoruba Religious Concepts*. Weiser Books, 1994.

Lavender, Isiah, III. *Race in American Science Fiction*. Indiana University Press, 2011.

Montgomery, Georgene Bess. *The Spirit and the Word: A Theory of Spirituality in Africana Literary Criticism*. Africa World Press, 2008.

Nanda, Aparajita. "Power, Politics, and Domestic Desire in Octavia Butler's *Lilith's Brood*," *Callaloo*, vol. 36, no. 3, 2013, pp. 773–788. *JSTOR*, www.jstor.org/stable/24264846.

———. "Re-Writing the Bhabhian 'Mimic Man': Akin, the Posthuman Other in Octavia Butler's *Adulthood Rites*." *ARIEL*, no. 3–4, 2010, pp. 115–135. https://scholarcommons.scu.edu/cgi/viewcontent.cgi?article=1128&context=engl.

Olupona, Jacob K., and Rowland Abiodun, eds. *Ifá Divination, Knowledge, Power, and Performance*. Indiana University Press, 2016.

Outterson, Sarah. "Diversity, Change, Violence: Octavia Butler's Pedagogical Philosophy." *Utopian Studies*, vol. 19, no. 3, 2008, pp. 433–456.

Piziks, Steven. "An Interview with Octavia E. Butler." *Marion Zimmer Bradley's FANTASY Magazine*, no. 37, 1997, pp. 46–51.

Tucker, Jeffrey A. "'The Human Contradiction': Identity and/as Essence in Octavia E. Butler's 'Xenogenesis' Trilogy." *Yearbook of English Studies*, vol. 37, no. 2, 2007, p. 164. *EBSCOhost*, search.ebscohost.com/login.aspx?direct=true&db=edsjsr&AN=edsjsr.20479308&site=eds-live&scope=site.

10

The Healing and Harmful Effects of Work in Octavia Butler's Short Stories "Crossover," "The Book of Martha," and "Speech Sounds"

Jennifer L. Hayes

In the Gospel of Luke, a familiar story about women and work is presented:

> Now it came to pass, as they went, that he entered into a certain village: and a certain woman named Martha received him into her house. And she had a sister called Mary, which also sat at Jesus' feet, and heard his word. But Martha was cumbered about much serving, and came to him, and said, Lord, dost thou not care that my sister hath left me to serve alone? Bid her therefore that she help me. And Jesus answered and said unto her, Martha, Martha, thou art careful and troubled about many things: But one thing is needful: and Mary hath chosen that good part, which shall not be taken away from her. (KJV Luke 10:38–42)

Martha chastises her sister Mary for not contributing to the work required of women in the home. Service can be viewed in two ways through the characters of Mary and Martha. Mary's work is seen through her attentiveness to Jesus while Martha's service is seen through the work she accomplishes within the home. Jesus's response sets forth an idea about the role of women within the church and society more broadly. While both women represent servants of the Lord, one woman seems to be more burdened by her duties, and Jesus does not allow a space for her feelings of being overwhelmed. In this chapter, I examine work as a trope that Butler uses to address the trauma of expectations for women within religion. The juxtaposition of Mary and

Martha highlights the different reactions to women workers in biblical lore as well as Butler's short fiction. While Black women have been socialized to value Christian beliefs, some struggle with a tradition that does not value their contributions.

In this chapter, I apply a Black feminist reading to three Octavia Butler short stories: "Crossover," "The Book of Martha," and "Speech Sounds." These stories offer various depictions of women contributing to the ongoing vitality of their communities. Though their work is necessary, the mental and emotional toll their labor entails affects the workers differently. For some, the impact of their contributions or their inability to contribute causes various degrees of emotional trauma, while others feel restored through their ability to support their communities. In this reading, I analyze the work required of three different African American female protagonists and investigate how the weight of their labor affects their identities.

Butler's short story anthology *Bloodchild and Other Stories* (2005) features narratives collected over a lifetime of work that emphasize stories of various African American women's experiences. A key feature to this collection is that following every story Butler provides a brief afterword with details about the creation of the text and her ideas about writing the work. Whether these brief glimpses into the mind of the writer provide effective information for interpreting the text is up for debate, but one key point these texts emphasize is the conscious thought of a writer reflecting on the importance of her work. Butler's metacommentary regarding her work further emphasizes the importance of Black women's work in her narratives. In her short stories, the value the individual women place on their work often distinguishes them from their peers, and this separation from their community proves problematic. Through an analysis of work and the moral value Butler places on work within her narratives, I explore the healing and trauma associated with Black women's work.

Butler's novels consistently center women's work and the value of that work, but she also presents feminist revisions of women's work within religion. Most clearly seen in *Parable of the Sower* through the character of Lauren Olamina, Butler criticizes Christianity and incorporates a revisionist image of women's roles through Earthseed. Through Lauren's journey, the role of women is moved from the margins to the center as she takes on a leadership role within her community and faith system. Additionally, in *Dawn*, the first novel of the Xenogenesis series, Butler again critiques women's roles in religion through her protagonist Lilith Iyapo. Butler reclaims Lilith from biblical lore and reinterprets her story with Eve's through Lilith's role as a mother to a new breed of human-alien hybrids. Lilith's work is required of her but is not always appreciated by her fellow humans. In "Migration, Spirituality, and Restorative Spaces: Shape-Shifting to Heal in Octavia Butler's *Wild Seed*," in this volume, Brianna Whiteside explores Butler's emphasis on Black women's bodies as sites for trauma and healing. Her reading explores the potential of liberation for Black women that is undermined by ignoring Black women's lived experiences. Butler's use of revisionist narrative strategies within religious contexts in her novels is well documented. However, this approach appears within her short stories, but they have not yielded robust scholarship. In this chapter, I hope to extend the critical conversations already occurring about the connection between the healing and traumatic impulses of work within Butler's novels to her short stories.

The God in Me: Battling Inner Conflict in "Crossover"

In "Crossover," Butler tells the story of Jane, a factory worker who is a single woman living alone. The reader understands Jane's isolation from the opening description of her work environment and her reputation at work. "At work that day, they put her to soldering J9 connectors into a harness, and they expected her to do twice as many as everyone else. She did, of course, but her only reward was resentment from the slower girls down the line because she was making them look bad" (113). Jane's introduction informs the reader of two key aspects of her identity before the story even presents the key conflict she shoulders throughout the story. The first is that Jane stands out. Her difference manifests through her commitment to hard work and her boss's reliance on her ability to outperform her colleagues. Yet this ability wins her no friends and contributes to her alienation from her peers. The second key point is that her hardworking nature gains her no benefits. Because she is expected to outperform her coworkers, her focus and productivity are considered a norm, one that she must maintain or face consequences. "If she did good work, other employees resented her and her lead man ignored her. If her work fell off, other employees ignored her and her lead man wrote 'bad attitude' on her work review" (113). Her strength then makes her a target for the disdain of her employer and colleagues. The result of this hostile working environment is an insular character that is dehumanized through her productivity and lacks meaningful human attachments at work and beyond. Since Jane has few people to talk to, she becomes insular and frequently considers her situation.

There is a lot going on inside Jane's head. She does not readily express herself to her colleagues or supervisors; nor does she seem to have many outlets for the frustration she feels in her day-to-day encounters. Butler negotiates this inner tension by creating a dynamic narrative that offers more questions than answers. After work, Jane visits a liquor store and is accosted by rude teenage boys and a wino, but she also has an encounter with a mysterious man with a scar. The liquor store initially appears as a minor detour on her way home, but it really presents a strategy for dealing with the stress in her work life. She uses alcohol to create relief. Alcohol is not the only way people seek to deal with the pain of day-to-day living; they also turn to religion. In "Crossover," when Jane is at the brink, the man appears as a manifestation of her innermost thoughts.

As Jane struggles to grapple with the difficulties in her waking life, she argues with the man with the scar about her status. The conversations she has with this man represent a crossover from the natural to the supernatural. The title "Crossover" suggests that there is a point of intersection in Jane's life. This juncture between the physical world and the space where the man exists is a territory that provides Jane with an outlet to voice her inner feelings and to unhinge herself from the societal expectations that encourage the monotony of consistent output at work. However, Jane does not seem comfortable with this man. Her relationship with him is complex. As she leaves the liquor store, a wino tempts her with alcohol and sex, offering to take her to his room, but she rebuffs him and instead "noticed someone standing in the narrow doorway. A man who had something wrong with his face. Something . . . She almost turned and went back toward the drunk, but the man stepped out and came to her during her moment of hesitation. She looked around quickly, her eyes wide with fear" (114). Her encounter with the man with the scar is another moment of isolation because no one seems to recognize or sense this figure. Though she initially avoids an encounter, she ultimately allows him to come into her apartment. Is this the moment Jane crosses over? Is this the moment where she has a spiritual or supernatural encounter with a nameless spirit? Religious lore is riddled with stories about angels, demons, and people entertaining angels unawares, but this man does not seem holy or demonic. Instead he seems like an old friend, and the familiarity he exhibits with Jane proves more provocative than the advances she experienced from the wino at the liquor store.

He knows her. This knowledge disturbs Jane and pushes her beyond the boundaries of acceptable behavior in the daily order of her life. After having a verbal argument with him on the street, she leads him to her apartment: "When they had eaten and made love, she sat head in hands trying not to think while he talked at her. She paid no attention until he asked a question that she wanted to answer. Don't you ever wish for a decent-looking guy to come and get you out of that factory and out of this dump you live in . . .

and away from me?" (116). Is this the dream for every woman to be rescued from a life of work and squalor by a noble husband or through her devotion to societal norms? The suggestion questions heteronormative ideals that encourage monogamy, marriage, and feminine submission, yet Jane does not submit to this line of thinking and instead lashes out.

As the man continues his line of questioning, he switches their conversation to the topic of drugs. "You still have that bottle of sleeping pills in your medicine cabinet?" (116). This allusion to drugs coupled with her visit to the alcohol store suggests a pattern of behavior for Jane. In the past, it seems Jane has controlled her feelings with a dependence on pills, but she has since "poured them down the toilet" (116). But some habits seem to reappear in her life, just as the man has reappeared again seemingly out of nowhere to question her happiness. This pattern of self-reflection forces Jane to face the uncertainties of her living situation and the grief of her unhappy work life. Instead of finding comfort in her work and hoping for the best, it seems that during moments of conflict Jane crosses over and ruminates on the hopelessness of her situation. This intense focus on her inner conflict creates the opportunity for her to express her innermost feelings and doubts. This expression can be volatile. For example, during her argument with the figure, "she threw the heavy glass ashtray beside the bed. It flew wide of him, dented the wall behind him and broke into three pieces. . . . She began to cry and she was not aware when the crying became screaming. Get out of here! Leave me alone! *Leave me alone!*" (117). This outburst triggers a series of events for Jane. First, her neighbor comes to check on her and offers to talk with her but is rebuffed. Second, the reader realizes that the man cannot be seen by the neighbor when the narrator says, "He came up behind her and stood there. She did not have to look around to know he was there. Still, she did not come near losing control until her neighbor said, 'You must be lonesome over here by yourself'" (117). The realization of her isolation in the midst of her mental exploration triggers action. She leaves the house in search of the wino to drink, have sex, and, most importantly, to forget.

What does the title "Crossover" mean for Jane's experience of self? Instead of seeing this man as a manifestation of God, a ghost, or demon, it seems more likely that it is a part of Jane's consciousness. Through Jane's narrative, Butler hints at the divine within humanity. Instead of turning to other people or an organization to give her a false feeling of hope in the midst of her turmoil, Jane turns inward and reflects on her difficulties. This inward reflection does not provide her with a solution and seems to exacerbate the trauma her work and loneliness afford her. When people see Jane, they do not see her inner turmoil or loneliness. Her colleagues see a Goody

Two-shoes that shows them up, her employer sees a workhorse, and the wino sees sex. All of these interpretations focus on Jane's physicality and fail to acknowledge the troubled spirit lying within. As Jane seemingly loses her grip on reality first by having conversations with manifestations of self-doubt and finally through alcohol and sex with a stranger, Butler questions the value of Jane's hardworking nature because Jane does not reap benefits from her work. Instead she feels isolated and dejected. As she desperately attempts to subvert these feelings, she makes self-destructive choices to prevent feeling the hopelessness of her situation. Thus, Jane's turn to alcohol and sex embodies the trauma of her pain.

Speak to My Heart:
The Power of Purpose in "Speech Sounds"

Like Jane, Valerie from "Speech Sounds" lives in an environment where sharing her innermost thoughts is unappealing if not dangerous. Valerie lives in a time where an illness has affected humankind's ability to communicate. "The illness was stroke-swift in the way it cut people down and stroke like in some of its effects. But it was highly specific. Language was always lost or severely impaired. It was never regained. Often there was also paralysis, intellectual impairment, death" (96). In Valerie's world, language was negatively affected in two key ways: people lost literacy or verbal speech. The world of words is particularly important to Valerie's identity and her work. As a former history professor, reading and writing were critical parts of her sense of self. "She had taught history at UCLA. She had done freelance writing. Now she could not even read her own manuscripts" (98). Valerie's impairment diminishes her sense of self because she loses a key skill that defines her value as a historian.

Like many of Butler's other works, such as *Parable of the Sower*, humans living within a dystopian reality must develop skills and new communities to survive a world that has transformed over time due to disease. "Transcendence and transformation additionally mark Butler's oeuvre. Her science fiction deals with boundary crossings that involve new and often traumatic-forms of being" (Lillvis 79). The illness in "Speech Sounds" exposes the cruelty of a world that devolves to savagery without the ability to communicate effectively. This valuable skill that human beings have lost as a result of the illness creates tensions between individuals who have maintained a portion of higher thought, critical thinking, and the ability to communicate and people who have lost all communicative ability. These tensions can manifest within an individual as the story indicates through the protagonist, Valerie Rye. Valerie loses much due to the illness. In addition to her lost literacy, she has lost her children and husband, who have died as a result. These losses transform Valerie from an educator striving to instill knowledge in the minds of pupils to a traumatized victim struggling to maintain her sanity in a dystopian nightmare.

Valerie's higher reasoning skills and her ability to speak create problems for her in the narrative. As a single woman, she is living a dangerous life of isolation in a community where brute strength overpowers kindness and empathy. Her dire situation compels her to take a journey to Pasadena to find her brother and nephews, but her journey is cut short when a fight erupts during her commute. The conclusion of the fight introduces a new character to the story, Obsidian. Obsidian in many ways fulfills a savior archetype within the story. The story is set in a future LA that has lost all social infrastructure. Police officers, firemen, and state officials are nowhere to be found, but during this moment of conflict on the bus, an authoritative man emerges to bring peace to the chaos.

Obsidian behaves differently from the aggressive, violent men in the story. He does not pick fights or threaten people with his gun; he uses his intellect to try and diffuse the dangerous situation on the bus. He also defers to Valerie and seeks to work with her in order to aid the people on the bus. Obsidian's behavior stands in stark opposition to the fighting men and the bus driver, who care very little for the well-being of the other passengers. He represents a past era of moral uprightness that seems distant from the violent reality of the story, but his difference commands attention, and his weapon ensures that even violent men respect him. His strength is both attractive and repulsive to Valerie.

For Valerie, her survival strategies have involved using her intellect to anticipate problems and plan meaningful solutions for these issues as they arise. The reality of her living situation forces Valerie to take some chances. Her first decision is to venture to Pasadena to reunite with her brother though she does not know whether he is still alive or if he would receive her. The second risky decision is to get in the car with Obsidian. She anticipates the opportunity of relying on his male strength and following him because he has behaved as a noble individual. Her loneliness and desire for security encourage her to turn outside of herself to find some sense of sanctuary in this savior figure.

Yet Obsidian is not divine, and it is his humanity that secures their bond. As they depart the scene of the bus fight, Obsidian and Valerie communicate. Though Obsidian has lost verbal speech, and Valerie has lost literacy, they are able to use body language to tell each other about their past lives before the illness. First, they begin by sharing names. Their identities are shared through the exchange of totems. Obsidian "slipped a gold chain over his head and handed it to her. The pendant attached to it was a smooth, glassy, black rock. Obsidian. His name might be Rock or Peter or Black, but she decided to think of him as Obsidian" (97). Obsidian directs their conversation in the car not through language but through actions. By opening himself up to Valerie, he wins her confidence and her affection.

After exchanging names, they have a physical encounter that allows Valerie to acknowledge the depth of her desire for touch. Before Obsidian physically touches her, he seeks to win her trust by allowing her to dictate their route. Once he turns over this bit of power to her, she feels comfortable opening up to him in a sexual way and envisioning a new life despite the chaos of their present environment. This momentary lapse in judgment allows her to fantasize about the security that Obsidian and specifically his masculinity provide. The blind hope that she puts into Obsidian, as if he were a God that could magically change her circumstances, distracts her from the reality of her situation. This distraction, though momentary, represents a criticism to the ways in which people use religion to deal with the reality of their problems. There is no quick fix for a pandemic. You cannot close your eyes and wake up in a different world no matter how close you are to the divine. The sanctity of relationship can only provide so much protection from the brutality of a world in decline.

After Valerie and Obsidian decide to return to her home, a domestic dispute shatters her dream of restoration. They witness a violent encounter between a man and a woman. The man kills the woman as Obsidian attempts to intervene. "He had bent to check the wounded man who lay still. But as Obsidian looked around to see what Rye wanted, the man opened his eyes. Face contorted, he seized Obsidian's just holstered-revolver and fired. The bullet caught Obsidian in the temple and he collapsed" (104). Obsidian's death is necessary for Valerie's survival. Valerie's strength had been her self-reliance and determination. Obsidian distracts her from the inner will she has to fight. By relying on his strength, she allows herself to become comfortable in a dangerous situation and relinquish the self-honed skills that ensured her safety. However, her brief relationship with Obsidian does affirm her humanity in a positive way.

Her self-reliance has empowered Valerie and allowed her to face the uncertainty of living in a dystopian nightmare, but she has lost a bit of her humanity through her disassociation with people. Obsidian brings that back to her. Instead of relying on his strength to withstand the loneliness and vulnerability of life as a single woman, she is able to find a new will to live on her own as a leader by claiming the children of the woman killed in the domestic dispute as her new family and students. Obsidian's death reawakens trauma from her past. She has again lost a chance for family and connection. After the deaths of Obsidian and the couple, "two very small children came out of the house . . . a boy and a girl perhaps three years old" (105). It is not Valerie's maternal nature that causes her to take pity on them and bring them home; it is their speech that creates this possibility. Valerie decides to take Obsidian and the dead woman home to bury, and the little girl protests by yelling, "No!" Frightened, her brother whispers, "Be quiet" (106). Their speech reaches Valerie, and their defiance does as well. These two children have a bond with the dead woman, and even in death they seek to protect her from Valerie. Their speech and bond with one another spark another idea of hope for Valerie. She begins to conceive of a world where she is able to utilize her skills in a different way by teaching these young people to survive. The ability to teach again fulfills a longing that Valerie has expressed throughout the story. Through her relationship with the children, she will be able to fulfill her life's work as a teacher without having to take a back seat to a man. She can demonstrate her leadership skills by preparing the future generation to survive the dangers of the present.

Her decision to take the children rekindles hope for Valerie and an opportunity for healing. In a world where there is no social order, Obsidian's role of pseudo-police officer seems silly at first to Valerie, but further reflection reveals the importance of having a purpose beyond oneself. These children provide Valerie with a purpose and revive her identity as a teacher. Perhaps she cannot teach history anymore, but she can teach something more important: survival skills. These children will be her pupils, and after many losses, including the loss of language, the loss of her job, and the loss of her family, she has a new life to live revived through the ability to teach once more.

Tell Martha Not to Moan:
The Parable of Work in "The Book of Martha"

"The Book of Martha" represents Butler's most critical view of women and religion within her body of short stories. From the beginning of the narrative, the reader empathizes with Martha's peculiar position as she is summoned by God to fulfill a task. In the story, Martha's reality changes when God calls on her to complete an assignment similar to the prophets of old. "This is what you're to do. . . . You will help humankind to survive its greedy, murderous, wasteful adolescence. Help it to find less destructive, more peaceful, sustainable ways to live. . . . If you don't help them, they will be destroyed" (192). At once, Martha understands that she faces an impossible task to come up with a solution to help steer all of humankind to a more productive, less destructive reality. Claire P. Curtis argues that "'The Book of Martha' sets up a utopian hypothesis by asking what it means to try to change the world for the better" (425). This question explores how human beings can constructively heal the world. God in this story offers Martha an opportunity to fulfill a request by making a change that will have a lasting impact on humankind, but she will face a penalty if she fulfills this task.

God instructs Martha to keep three biblical figures in mind while she contemplates the assignment: Jonah, Job, and Noah. These models, God says, should function as guides for Martha as she attempts to complete her work, but what do their narratives reveal about the expectations for Martha and women more broadly within religion? Butler answers this question through Martha's journey by critically analyzing the ways in which parables have been used to socialize her to adopt a submissive posture. Instead of seeing the biblical figures as models for effective leadership, Butler presents the narratives as parables of obedient workers. Each figure represents a worker who was tasked to fulfill an assignment, and their relative effectiveness and obedience affect their metaphorical significance to Martha. As she contemplates her ability to complete this assignment, her reflection on the biblical guides results in a feeling of powerlessness to defy God and encourages her submission.

While contemplating the models, Martha remembers how her mother used these biblical figures to teach her lessons about behavior. "When she was a girl, she had gone to church and to Sunday School, to Bible class and to vacation Bible school. Her mother, only a girl herself, hadn't known much about being a mother, but she wanted her child to be 'good,' and to her, 'good' meant 'religious'" (192). These lessons reinforce patriarchal ideas regarding hierarchy and power. For Martha's mother, Bible stories were meaningful tools to teach important traits to her child. These traits enforced ideals regarding behavior, including submission and obedience. To be good, then, references more than living a virtuous life; it resembles a child's obedience to adult figures. Martha behaves unlike the biblical mother Mary, who "patiently accepts what is decided for her. She is expected to, firstly, decide on a plan to change the life of her fellow beings in a positive way, and, secondly, act on that plan" (Archeolooei and Leon 139). She is told what to do, but she initially does not accept the command at face value. She questions God and through this questioning arrives at a decision on her own. Yet, like Mary, she is used as a vessel to heal the world by bringing about a great change. In this way, Butler has revised a traditional feminine trope within Christianity by infusing the character with agency and power.

Confused and afraid, Martha questions how she can fulfill this task and is told that she will "borrow some of my power" (193). The ability to access the power of God does not provide Martha with a feeling of strength; instead, she anticipates the danger that comes from the possible consequences of her actions. Martha's reflection on the consequences of power reveals her experiences as a Black woman. For Martha, as a marginalized figure, she understands how oppressive forces exercise their power for selfish means. This realization results in a feeling that opposes the freedom that God seems to offer. God proposes to Martha an ability to utilize his powers, but instead of feeling freedom, she feels burdened by the exercise. Martha, a Black, middle-class single woman, is charged with creating a solution to solve the problems of humankind, but she will not receive any benefits for this task. Instead, she will be reduced for her acquiescence to God. "When you've finished your work, you'll go back and live among them as one of their lowliest" (193). This seems more like a punishment than a reward. Unlike Job, whose riches were restored, Martha faces a decline in status by following the path that God sets out for her. Yet she submits.

Martha's submission seems to have been taught to her through social forces, including family and religion. However, in adult life she has rebelled against these forces by resisting traditional expectations for women to marry and have children. As a single woman and a writer, she has claimed a social stability connected to her work and ingenuity, but God seeks to diminish her individual power by enforcing a connection and responsibility to a larger community. Her response to fulfilling this assignment is to provide human beings with a fulfilled life through their dreams. "I want them to have the only possible utopia. . . . Each person will have a private, perfect utopia every night—or an imperfect one. . . . A private heaven every night, it might take the edge off their willingness to spend their waking hours trying to dominate or destroy one another" (204). Her innovative response to God's assignment births an attempt to empower other people. Instead of selecting a solution that would punish bad behavior, she proposes a cure for humanity's hunger for success and power. Possessing the desires of one's heart even in sleep, she muses, will lessen conflict on a massive scale. Yet this gift will harm her. As a writer, will people need to read stories if their fantasies are satisfied every night in bed? Martha is willing to accept the risk of losing her stability as a storyteller if her dream strategy improves the lives of many.

Martha's journey in "The Book of Martha" does not offer redemption; rather, through her compliance, she is punished. Religion in this story is connected to fulfilling the work of God, and Martha's assignment comes with a penalty. She articulates her doubt that God's assignment can ever truly be fulfilled due to humanity's hierarchal nature. This hierarchy is pronounced through her subject position. Her race and gender offer her a unique perspective. As a Black woman, who has attained middle-class status through her work as a writer, she understands the sacrifices it has taken to achieve a comfortable life. However, by fulfilling the will of God, she will lose the status that she has earned through her work. The task that God wants Martha to complete will not free her from the issues that she faces as a Black woman. Martha's elevation requires the destruction of traditional conceptions of religion that instill patriarchal and hierarchal values within society. To fulfill the will of God is to adopt a lower position in society.

The inner conflict Martha faces emphasizes the need for her perspective as a Black woman. Though her political perspective affords her experiential knowledge, this knowledge is not used to elevate her status but to diminish her further, which results in a traumatic fall from grace. Martha's work throughout her life has afforded her comforts that are taken away from her through her decision to follow God's orders. Her decision to submit to God's request exposes women's value within religion. Women's acceptance in society is connected to their ability to "be good" as Martha's mother points out in her childhood. But as a woman, Martha knows that these values are like a prison she must escape from. This prison is further reflected in the various representations of God throughout the story, first starting as a large, white glowing man and finally as a mirror image to Martha so that Butler shows how supposedly liberated minds are burdened by the socialization of church and family. Martha subconsciously equates masculinity and whiteness to power, but through her conversations, she begins to see the divine in herself.

The story would be a different one if it ended with the realization of the strength she has as a Black woman, but Butler does not afford her audience this simplistic view. Even though Martha understands her power and the systems in place from the time she was a child to diminish her sense of self, she still acquiesces to God's demands and provides him with a solution for his problem. By seeking to help others, she will receive the punishment of falling to a lower caste. Thus, her submission reinforces God's power and prevents a condition for her freedom and elevation. In the Combahee River Collective's manifesto "A Black Feminist Statement," they argue that "if Black women were free, it would mean that everyone else would have to be free since our freedom would necessitate the destruction of all the systems of oppression" (267). The story's conclusion ends with Martha asking God to erase her memory of their encounter because she could not deal with the burden of knowing her decision could have positive and negative impacts on people's lives. This ending is antifeminist. Throughout the narrative, Martha has questioned God and exposed the flaws within the system he made. By speaking her truth to power, she performs as a different kind of prophet. Her knowledge does not come from the divine but from within. Her experience affords her a nuanced perspective to critically observe the problems embedded in social institutions. But she is not provided with a true opportunity to change the world for the better. A real change would involve a destruction of God or the religious systems that use his presence for gain. God only provides her with an ability to amend his creation, but Martha is a writer and godlike in her ability to create worlds and people them. This God does not want revolution; he demands obedience and work. Through her limited capacity, Martha fulfills his request while trying to offer peace to herself and others.

Conclusion

Octavia Butler's fiction features imperfect protagonists who struggle to maintain a sense of autonomy in a world that denies them esteem. Their complex identities often intersecting issues of racism, sexism, and classism expose flaws embedded in society. Dorothy Allison comments, "Within the genre of science fiction, Butler is a realist, writing the most detailed social criticism and creating some of the most fascinating female characters in the genre" (471). What makes Butler's protagonists struggle to maintain balance impactful is not their success but their unwillingness to accept the world as it seems. What the world allows for many of Butler's women is a world of work. Historically, African American women have always worked, yet their contributions have not been valued. bell hooks notes that the "systematic devaluation of black womanhood led to a downgrading of any activity black women did" (70). As such, Black women have faced a struggle to not only survive but to be acknowledged for their contributions in society.

This lack of social consciousness surrounding their social and economic contributions relegates the work that Black women do to the margins. Katie G. Cannon theorizes that "the moral situation of the black woman in contemporary society is still a situation of struggle, a struggle to survive collectively and individually against the continuing harsh realities and pervasive adversities in today's world" (66). Many Black women have turned to faith to address the harshness of their lived experiences to no avail. Delores S. Williams explains, "We have seen how black women often used their religion to cope with and transform the negative character of some of these processes" (144). But there are few answers to Black women's degraded social status in church because of traditional Christianity's patriarchal structure. This foundation has been used to justify their lower status within the United States since the time of slavery. Black women's work continues, as their economic contributions are central to the economic stability of the Black community.

Black women continue to work because their survival depends on it, but their work is often overlooked even when it is exceptional. Though Black women have been taught in church that "his eye is on the sparrow," Butler challenges this idea in her essay "The Monophobic Response," stating, "At the moment there are no true aliens in our lives—no Martians, Tau Cetians to swoop down in advanced spaceships, their attentions firmly fixed on the all-important US, no gods or devils, no spirits, angels or gnomes" (415). Yet we look outside ourselves consistently for reassurance. Butler's characters do the harder work of looking outside and within while struggling to have their contributions acknowledged. While they rarely accomplish this goal, they continue to work. Their work gives them purpose, and this purpose quiets the inner conflict momentarily, which contributes in a big way to their survival.

WORKS CITED

Allison, Dorothy. "The Future of Female: Octavia Butler's Mother Lode." *Reading Black, Reading Feminist*, edited by Henry Louis Gates Jr., Meridian, 1990, pp. 471–478.

The Bible. Authorized King James Version, Oxford University Press, 1998.

Butler, Octavia E. *Bloodchild and Other Stories*. Seven Stories Press, 2005.

———. *Parable of the Sower*. Grand Central Publishing, 2000.

———. *Xenogenesis*. Guild America Books, 1989.

Cannon, Katie. *Black Womanist Ethics*. 1988. Wipf and Stock Publishers, 2006.

Combahee River Collective. "A Black Feminist Statement." (1977) *The Black Feminist Reader*, edited by Joy James and T. Denean Sharpley-Whiting, Blackwell, 2000, pp. 261–270.

Curtis, Claire P. "Rehabilitating Utopia: Feminist Science Fiction and Finding the Ideal." *Contemporary Justice Review*, vol. 8, no. 2, June 2005, pp. 147–152.

———. "Theorizing Fear: Octavia Butler and the Realist Utopia," *Utopian Studies*, vol. 19, no. 3, 2008, pp. 411–431.

The Holy Bible: Old and New Testaments Authorized King James Version. Thomas Nelson, 2003.

hooks, bell. *Ain't I a Woman*. South End Press, 1981.

———. *Sisters of the Yam: Black Women and Self-Recovery*. South End Press, 1993.

Williams, Delores S. *Sisters in the Wilderness: The Challenge of Womanist God Talk*. Orbis, 1993.

11

Shapers of God

Octavia E. Butler's Parable of the Sower *and*
Womanist Theological Practice

TARSHIA L. STANLEY

A Victim of God may,
Through learning adaptation,
Become a partner of God,
A Victim of God may,
Through forethought and planning,
Become a shaper of God
—*Parable of the Sower*

Critics, and book jacket writers, have often identified Butler's *Parable of the Sower* as the work in which she not only critiques traditional Western understandings of religion but the space in which she creates a new religion. Now that the world of *Parable of the Sower* has become all too familiar to those of us living just a few years away from the novel's beginning, and dealing with a global pandemic, this may be the time for reflecting on her work not as a new religion but as further acknowledgment of how religion is intertwined with economic, social, cultural, and historical practices. While not traditionally seen in the same vein as Black American theologians, Butler's work may be less the enactment of a new religion and actually offer a contemplative space to critique and re-create in the same ways as Black liberation theology and the subsequent womanist theology that follows. Rather than Butler creating a "new" religion, this kind of framing places her squarely within an African American intellectual tradition and community of thinkers who long ago began to shape their reaction to and relationship with God rather than completely re-create the concept.

As the clarion work in the oeuvre of the first African American woman to be lauded in the science fiction genre, *Parable of the Sower* has experienced a spectacular renaissance of interest more than a quarter century after its initial publication. Often described by critics as a story in which the novel's protagonist creates a new religion, *Sower* is much more conflicted in its depiction of the relationship between humanity and its need to believe in something beyond itself than the characterization of a new religion would suggest. So much of the current fascination with the novel is undoubtedly due to its prescient narrative and its accurate predictions. Although written in 1993, the narrative world of *Parable of the Sower* commences in the year 2024. When the book was first written, it was hard for its readers to imagine the United States of the story. The world of *Sower* is one in which a fascist president comes to power by leveraging fear and right-wing Christian fundamentalism, in which corporate influence in federal and local government render public works and services unattainable for the average citizen, and in which homelessness and drug addiction have escalated to nearly incomprehensible proportions. Citizens in that narrative world feel—and in most ways are—powerless in the face of these threats. Further, the novel is set against the backdrop of a drought-stricken California ravaged by wildfires, which are summarily the result of global warming.

The protagonist of *Parable of the Sower* is a young African American girl who lives daily with the knowledge that her home is only marginally safe because it is located in a walled community. Lauren Oye Olamina recognizes how fragile the wall and the concept of safety really are and constantly pleads with her father to prepare for the day when their wall is breached. Lauren's foresight and prudence are enhanced by her hyperempathy syndrome. As a result of in vitro exposure to a mind-altering drug, Lauren can feel the pain and pleasure of those around her, but only if she is aware of it. For instance, her brothers trick Lauren into bleeding by making her think they have been wounded when they actually have not. Lauren's hyperempathy is itself a character in the novel as it not only makes her physically and emotionally vulnerable, but it also liberates her from egocentrism in that it requires her constant contemplation of the safety of the collective in order to guarantee her own.

Lauren must constantly contemplate the well-being of the people around her because her own survival is in direct proportion. Lauren grapples with the notion of collective safety in her diary in the form of Earthseed. *Earthseed: The Books of the Living* is what Lauren entitles the sayings or tenets that she comes to understand as her belief system. They are her sacred verses or scripture that introduce and explain her understanding of the God they need to survive in the United States in 2024. Rather than a God who metes out judgment and only rescues and provides for those he deems fit, circumstances demand that

God is Power—
Infinite,
Irresistible,
Indifferent
And yet, God is Pliable—
Trickster,
Teacher,
Chaos,
Clay.
God exists to be shaped.
God is change. (*Parable* 34)

According to Lauren, her family and community are being handicapped by a Western Judeo-Christian concept of God that does not respond to the suffering in her world. This is especially pertinent as Lauren notes that the people who suffer are those most marginalized. She cannot reconcile this Western Christian depiction of a loving God when those in power continue to justify their position as ordained by God. Lauren's solution is Earthseed. Lauren reconstructs an understanding of religion that allows her to survive in the world in which she finds herself.

From the outset of the novel and from her earliest interviews, Butler's apparent contempt for religion is palpable. When Lauren writes in her journal, "At least three years ago, my father's God stopped being my God. His church stopped being my church. . . . My God has another name," we hear Butler's enmity (*Sower* 17). Butler famously described herself as a "former Baptist" and declared "I used to despise religion" (Brown 187). In her interviews, Butler's mind is made up about religion and its penchant and potential for destruction. However, in her fiction, she is often irresolute in her depiction of religion because while she wishes it was not so, she finds it inevitable. For instance, Lauren may not be able to worship her father's God, but she is still compelled to formulate her own construct of God. Butler, like many practitioners from theology to psychology, recognizes a deep human need to believe that there is something divine that gives meaning and may bring order to the chaos and mysteries of life. This ambivalence is conspicuous in the *Parable of the Sower*.

A deeper exploration of Octavia Butler's conflict with religion and the way it has been used to reinforce the hierarchical nature of humankind is revealed in an early interview with Rosalie G. Harrison. Butler comments on a science fiction panel discussing the tendency of the genre to either ignore, dismiss, or show contempt for religion. Butler warns against the simplification and trivialization of religion, deeming it unwise as she understands religion to be significant to the psychic survival of human beings. Paradoxically, while understanding religion to be essential to the life and mind of many human beings, Butler demonstrates the same kind of derision the science fiction genre traditionally leveled at all things religious. In the same essay, Butler surmised, "In some way, I wish we could outgrow it; I think at this point it does a lot of harm. But then, I'm fairly sure that if we do outgrow it we'll find other reasons to kill and persecute each other" (Harrison 9). More recently, Kimberly Rae Connor posits that religion and speculative fiction (the overarching category that includes science fiction, fantasy, horror, etc.) are strange bedfellows whose structure and yield are quite similar: "Still, the impulse behind both religion and speculative literature is the same. Each offers a conception of reality that inclines toward different explanations not just of human behavior but of divine (supernatural) behavior, and each suggests differing ideas about how to respond" (370). Although Butler muses about the dangers of religion itself, it may be that her deeper protest is how religion has continually been pressed into the service of the tyrannical. Yet both writers are clear that science fiction as a genre that reflects the sociopolitical practices of society has to respond to religion. Whether the response is for Butler a begrudging acquiescence or for Connor overdue recognition, the genre cannot ignore, escape, or scapegoat interactions with religion.

Parable of the Sower opens with a dream the night before Lauren's fifteenth birthday. We learn that she is a teenager struggling to find her own voice and her own way not just in her biological father's house but also in a house aligned with the Judeo-Christian concept of God, the Father. Lauren dreams of a door set in a wall that is ablaze. Because Lauren does not yet have the means to resist her biological father's insistence that she be baptized into his faith, her dream manifests a way of escape. As Lauren levitates and learns to fly in her dream, it is still too early for her to gain enough momentum and direction to avoid the wall of fire and escape through the door. This introduction to Lauren is an introduction to her community. The wall that is on fire in Lauren's room is the wall that surrounds her neighborhood. Lauren has explained to her father on multiple occasions that the community or at the very least her family should prepare for the day when the wall does not keep the predators out. The wall is more to Lauren and her community than a physical barrier; it is also psychological and spiritual. For the adults in Lauren's life, the wall represents safety from the things outside that they cannot control and from the things they have lost that they find too hard to acknowledge.

It also represents their faith. The leader of the community, Lauren's father, is a Baptist minister. For Lauren, the wall and their subsequent acquiescence to their traditional understanding of God form a barrier to their freedom and ultimately their survival because it represents a false sense of security.

Lauren has been adapting an understanding of faith that helps her order the world in which she finds herself. Lauren names her thoughts *Earthseed: The Books of the Living* because she deems her father's faith as all but dead. Lauren sees her father's Baptist faith as rigid and far too dependent on a "big-daddy-God, or a big-cop-God, or a big-King-God" (*Sower* 24). For Lauren, adaptability and willingness to change become the means to survival and therefore the thing in which she believes. For Lauren,

> All that you touch
> You Change.
> All that you Change
> Changes you.
> The only lasting truth
> Is Change.
> God
> Is Change. (*Sower* 13)

A turning point for Lauren is when Mrs. Sims, who has been a staunch proponent of trusting in faith, commits suicide. Lauren sees Mrs. Sims's inability to survive as the inability of her faith. Lauren becomes even more committed to the book of verses she has been writing and her dedication to sharing them with others.

It is important to remember that while Lauren Olamina reads as perhaps the most precocious fifteen-year-old in literary history, she is nonetheless a teenager when the novel begins. She is also still a hyperempath destined to think and feel more deeply than most about the collective welfare of her community. However, Lauren is unable to see that she is more like the adults around her than she would like to admit. She too sees things in a very rigid manner. Lauren does not always understand the nuances in the behaviors of adults in her community. For example, Lauren's friend Joann divulges that Lauren has been preparing an escape plan for when their community is attacked. As a result, Lauren is chastised by her father and warned not to scare the people. Rev. Olamina advises Lauren to teach the community techniques for surviving outside of the wall rather than scaring them, rather than making them gaze into the abyss. "You've just noticed the abyss," he continued. "The adults in this community have been balancing at the edge of it for more years than you've been alive" (*Sower* 76). For Lauren, this tactic is too slow, and her frustration is summed up when she writes the Earthseed tenet:

Drowning people
sometimes die
fighting their rescuers. (*Sower* 71)

While Lauren is right to warn that they may run out of time, Lauren does not see the ways in which she is the same as the people in her community. Lauren also cannot see the ways in which her religion may be akin to the one she eschews. In Robledo, on the road after Robledo, and in her eventual new home of Acorn, Lauren Olamina often reinvigorates the same framework of faith as the one purported by her father. This is neither a positive nor a negative but rather an opportunity to acknowledge that it is more difficult to create a new religion than she or Butler enthusiasts imagine. Lauren's faith is born of her circumstances. While it may indeed be a truth to be discovered, Earthseed is also a methodology for survival built in, for, and by the circumstance under which Lauren has had to forge a life. The economic and sociopolitical contours of Lauren's faith are proportional to their spiritual expression.

In his essay "Post-Racial, Post-Apocalyptic Love: Octavia Butler as Political Theologian," Vincent Lloyd surmises that Butler's critique of culture and religion is ultimately unsuccessful because it does not acknowledge the ways Earthseed mirrors what is already in place. He writes: "Earthseed is deeply invested in the very order it purports to reject. I do not mean this as a claim about the motivation of Butler's characters but rather as a claim about the set of ideas, practices, and more generally worldviews in which they are invested" (451). Lloyd primarily alleges that Butler's Earthseed "rests on the same basis as the neoliberalism she opposes" (463). Lloyd's critique is useful here for confronting Butler's supposition that Lauren sees religion in a revolutionary light. Butler often acknowledges the ways in which Earthseed reiterates the dynamics of many religions, including Taoism's Tao Te Ching, but does not always seem to see the ways it mimics the Christian religion it reacts against (Thrall 511). Earthseed has scripture, makes disciples, and declares itself to be the best truth—just like Christianity. Rather than a heaven as the end goal, Earthseed quests for Mars, declaring its Destiny is to "take root among the stars" (*Sower* 87). As a result, it is not the new religion that critics and even Butler have surmised. It can be, however, a truly political and social gospel in that it acknowledges that religion is never truly indistinguishable from either the economic or sociopolitical.

Butler's strong feelings toward religion are much more impassioned than just wishing that humanity could outgrow a need for it. The sentiment comes through in her own musing on her texts as well as in the responses of her protagonists. Butler's attitude is such that she does not acknowledge the ways in which speculative fiction, as a genre, or Earthseed, as a concept, echoes the premises of religion. In her 2000 interview with Charles Brown, Butler further delineates her understanding of religion as useful for marginalized and subjected peoples: "Religion kept some of my relatives alive because it was all they had. . . . I think that's what religion does for the majority of people. . . . They use it to keep themselves alive" (186). She goes on to reiterate an understanding of religion as the proverbial opiate: "I'm not talking about most Americans. We don't need it that way, most of us, now" (186). On the one hand Butler's understanding of religion and her desire to introduce it seriously into the science fiction genre in a respectful way are evident: "I didn't want to make fun of religion. Lauren's father, a Baptist minister, is neither a fool nor a hypocrite. He's a decent man who can't cope with the situation he's in" (See 41). Yet Butler can't help but seed her protagonist with her own conflict: "Lauren feels about religion the way I feel about writing. For her it's a positive obsession, even while she realizes it's ridiculous and impossible" (See 41). However, as Butler develops the journey of Earthseed through *Parable of the Sower*, Lauren does not see the writing of her holy texts and the acolytes she gathers as ridiculous or impossible but begins to believe deeply that Earthseed is the way forward for humankind.

In the section of *Sower* that marks the year 2027, Lauren describes Earthseed as "self-aware, questing, problem-solving. . . . We are that aspect of Earthlife best able to shape God knowingly. Earthlife fulfilling its purpose, its promise, its Destiny" (*Sower* 157). It is difficult not to hear the words of John Connor describing Skynet in the *Terminator* film series or recall the musings of every theocrat ever when Earthseed establishes itself as fully cognizant and privy to what the destiny of humanity should be. Yet Earthseed is more than a manifesto for displaced humans in a dystopian novel. For Lauren, Earthseed becomes the means of stopping the destruction of humankind by exploiting its apparent need for God. That Butler seems to see Earthseed as a way of shaping the human propensity for religion is not surprising; what does give pause is Butler's seeming to think that she is among the first to understand religion in this way. Perhaps that is why Earthseed is founded by such a young character. It many ways Lauren's age justifies this naiveté. But it may be Butler's painful past with religion that shapes her own response. According to Butler:

> I think I take advantage of the reality that there are no human communities without religion. I mean, there may be human communities

that don't acknowledge a specific god, but they've found some way of creating religion, either secular or sacred. And in this case, my character looks around and says, "Well, why shouldn't religion be used for something? Why shouldn't it be a tool? Why shouldn't religion take us where, perhaps, other things can't take us?" (Juan Williams 174–175)

Butler seems to believe that all humans blunder into religion with passions opened and eyes closed. While this may be true for many, history has borne countless examples of people who are making choices at least as conscious as the ones Lauren makes. Lauren is not the first to think of shaping humankind through its need for religion. Lauren is not the first to think of shaping an interpretation of God that gives credence to the lives of powerless and disenfranchised peoples. Butler is not the first to employ her craft to shape an understanding of God as indistinguishable from the cultural, economic, and sociopolitical positioning of the marginalized. There is, in fact, a significant tradition of real-world heroes (and villains) thinking of religion in this way. Nowhere is this tradition more relevant than in the African American community.

Shaping God: An Inheritance

Butler's critique and creation of religion can be read alongside a number of Black theologians who have for centuries "shaped God" in their attempt to survive in the United States. I want to be careful here not to describe Butler as a Black theologian in the traditional sense of those Black preachers, pastors, and scholars who studied and theorized Black theology. I want to place her in their company in that she engages in a similar improvisation on a theme. Butler is a marginalized African American woman who used her literary prowess to ask human beings to think more deeply and more comprehensively about what being human means in the present and therefore the future. Theologians like Howard Thurman, James Cone, Katie Geneva Cannon, and Jacquelyn Grant, among others, also ask us to think more deeply about what being human means now, in the future, and into eternity.

Vincent Lloyd's premise that Butler is a political theologian lends credence to her connection to other Black theologians. In particular, Butler is writing in the same tradition as the forebearers of Black liberation and womanist theology and similarly "construct[s] alternative theologies, religious communities and practices that embrace and negotiate difference as a means of securing the future of the human race" (McCormack 19). At the heart of

Earthseed is the acknowledgment of difference and that the acceptance of difference, perhaps even the leveraging of difference, will be necessary for the planet and the people on it to survive. Earthseed connects inclusion to a belief system. The theologian Howard Thurman was doing the same throughout his life of advocacy.

Born in the Jim Crow south at the turn of the twentieth century, the grandson of a formerly enslaved woman, this civil rights leader's most famous text is *Jesus and the Disinherited* (1949). In it, as in his other sermons, lectures, and writings, Thurman makes the case for a Jesus who is more like the subjugated Jews than he is the privileged citizens of Rome. Often labeled a mystic and a philosopher, Thurman's assertions about Jesus were radical at the time. To insist that Jesus had more in common with abused and marginalized African Americans than he did with privileged white America was inflammatory and revolutionary. It was revolutionary enough to inspire Martin Luther King, whose social justice platform was very clearly influenced by Thurman—his Morehouse College elder, mentor, and family friend. Like Butler, Thurman engages in a reenvisioning of sacred texts that speak directly to the circumstance of the poor and oppressed.

Thurman is engaged in alternative readings of scripture, a half century before Butler. Even the wall in *Parable of the Sower* is reminiscent of Thurman's principle metaphor in *Jesus and the Disinherited*:

> I can count on the fingers of one hand the number of times that I have heard a sermon on the meaning of religion, of Christianity, to the man who stands with his back against the wall. . . . The masses of men live with their backs constantly against the wall. They are the poor, the disinherited, the dispossessed. What does our religion say to them? (3)

For Thurman, the powerless have been pushed up against a wall from which they have no means of escape or retreat. As such he rereads religion, in this case Christianity, in the shadow of that wall and demands an adequate response. By the time Butler reimagines Thurman's wall, it is on fire and Lauren's questioning necessarily ends in her own reenvisioning, her own reinterpretation, of her father's religion into Earthseed.

Perhaps the Elisha to Thurman's Elijah is his fellow theologian James Cone. The originator of Black liberation theology pushes past Thurman's questioning of religion in the face of racial, economic, and social oppression to an answer. From Cone's 1969 book *Black Theology and Black Power* to *The Cross and the Lynching Tree* (2011), he propels further the connection between

Jesus and the oppressed. Perhaps his most bold contribution is at the heart of Black liberation theology. He reinvigorates Thurman's message by declaring:

> The meaning of this message for our contemporary situation is clear: the God of the oppressed takes sides with the black community. God is not color-blind in the black-white struggle, but made an unqualified identification with blacks. This means that the movement for black liberation is the very work of God, effecting God's will among men. (Cone 7)

Cone's understanding of religion is that it is active, not passive; it fights, it does not retreat; it liberates, it does not enslave. Cone's Black liberation theology enacts a reading of scripture that declares God is Black because God identifies completely with the oppressed. In many ways, Butler's conception of Earthseed is the revisioning of scripture to imply the same thing.

In a 2005 essay entitled "The Anointed: Countering Dystopia with Faith in Octavia Butler's *Parable of the Sower* and *Parable of the Talents*," Clarence Tweedy asserted that many of the critics who had read Butler's works in the context of religion "inadvertently minimized not only the revolutionary and historical impact of the Black theological tradition but also overlooked valuable insights that Butler's fiction provides about the use of religion as a means of self empowerment in the resistance of oppression" (Tweedy). The author goes on to link the text to the work of Cone when he writes: "The re-articulation and re-defining of God in Earthseed counteracts human suffering and humiliation through a doctrine of self-reliance. According to James H. Cone, 'There can be no black theology which does not take seriously the black experience—a life of humiliation and suffering'" (23). Lauren is a young Black woman dealing with the dangers of the world in a state of ecological and socioeconomic collapse. Her experiences as an African American are central in the creation of Earthseed's theology and its attempts to provide security, as well as hope, in a world on the edge of an abyss (Tweedy). While Tweedy's essay is an essential analysis rightly linking Butler's work to Black liberation theology, it stops short of situating Butler in the pantheon of womanist theology.[1]

Shaping God: A Womanist View

Jacquelyn Grant, Black womanist theologian and student of James Cone, published "Black Theology and the Black Woman" in 1979. Grant, a staunch critic of her professor James Cone's thoroughly masculinist rendering of Black liberation theology, "first examined the invisibility of black women in black theology, arguing that black women cannot 'continue to be treated as if they were invisible creatures who are on the outside looking into the . . . theological enterprise'" (Thurman 30). Grant's classmates at Union Theological Seminary in the early 1980s were Katie Geneva Cannon and Delores S. Williams.

They were particularly influenced by Alice Walker's *In Search of Our Mothers' Gardens: Womanist Prose.* Together in community, these three Black women students began to articulate theologically the quandary of Black women, adopting Walker's language of womanism. It seemed a fitting framework, since it "complemented and accentuated a way of knowing and talking about God that was indigenous to the flesh-and-blood realities of black women in the United States" (Thurman 30). Katie Cannon drew from the work of Zora Neale Hurston when she helped to lay the foundation for womanist theology.

> The Black woman's literary tradition delineates the many ways that ordinary Black women have fashioned value patterns and the ethical procedures in their own terms, as well as mastering, transcending, radicalizing and sometimes destroying pervasive, negative orientations imposed by the mores of the larger society. (Cannon 76)

Williams, Cannon, and others laid the groundwork for womanist readings of scripture that took into account oppression, racism, and sexism. Like Lauren, they needed a religion that corrected for their circumstances and would speak to them not just where they were but where they needed to be. According to the theologian Emilie Townes, womanist theology is a form of reflection that places the religious and moral perspectives of Black women at the center of its method. Issues of class, gender (including sex, sexism, sexuality, and sexual exploitation), and race are seen as theological problems. Womanist theology takes old (traditional) religious language and symbols and gives them new (more diverse and complex) meaning. This form of theological reflection cannot be termed "womanist" simply because the subject is Black women's religious experiences. The key for womanist theology is the use of an interstructured analysis employing class, gender, and race. The likening of Butler's literary practice to womanist theology is appropriate not just because of her subject matter but because of Butler's analytical and literary practices themselves. Butler's building of the world of *Parable of the Sower*, its centering on a woman of color, and its emphasis on other intersecting systems of oppression are at the center of Towne's notion of the "interstructured analysis" that is womanist theology.

In *Introducing Womanist Theology*, Stephanie Y. Mitchem declares that womanist theology "is a place of discovery, in faith, that analyzes both politics and culture" (46). She traces the pioneers of the practice and attributes the differing approaches of each as one of the primary strengths of womanist theology.

> Renita Weems employed a narrative methodology. Her approach to constructing womanist theology resonates with African American traditions of oral culture. Other womanist thinkers utilized literary tools in their methodology, as did Katie Cannon when she focused on Zora Neale Hurston's work. Towne's *Troubling in My Soul* is truly like a jazz improvisation, where each artist takes a solo on the theme. (80)

Mitchem helps to define womanist theology as a method of inquiry, analysis, and creativity that finds a way to interrogate and reinterpret religion by drawing on the literary and oral traditions of African American storytelling and lived practices. She goes on to write that "womanist theology must employ the interdisciplinary tools of history, ethnography, literary criticism, folklore, sociology, economics, and medicine. Uses of different disciplines are liberatory practices" (61).

Certainly Butler's construction of Earthseed, along with the very act of inserting herself into speculative fiction—the last bastion of whiteness and white maleness in the literary tradition—situates her work in the Parable series as liberatory practice. Lauren creates Earthseed as a means and mechanism for survival by writing it, sharing it, and living it. Black theology, Black liberation theology, and womanist theology demonstrate a similar method of interrogation and improvisation of religion to that of Butler in her writing.

The womanist theological presence in Butler's work does not begin or end with *Parable of the Sower*. Originally conceived as a trilogy, the second novel in the series is *Parable of the Talents*. Although *Talents* is not as popular, it is the crucible in which Lauren's religion learns to thrive. At the end of the *Sower* novel, Lauren and her disciples establish a home for themselves and call it Acorn. They live and thrive for several years before they are attacked by the fundamentalist group Christian America. Acorn is violently converted to a reeducation camp, and Lauren loses her husband and daughter as well as her extended family. The story is largely told through Lauren's journals and reactions to them by her daughter Larkin. Larkin, taken as a toddler and raised by Christian America members, does not learn Lauren is her mother until she is an adult.

Much of *Parable of the Talents* is a kind of epistemological struggle between mother and daughter. Larkin initially only knows Lauren through the rhetoric Christian America espouses about Lauren. Then Larkin is able to read some of Lauren's journals and some of Bankole's (Larkin's father) journal entries, while she studies *Earthseed: The Books of the Living*. Larkin is the researcher and the lost child in *Parable of the Talents*. She tries to gather knowledge—to distinguish what is truth, belief, and fiction about her parents. Larkin is skeptical and convinced that her mother becomes what Earthseed preached against—a human embodiment of God. When Larkin studies the tenet of Earthseed that posits God as "Indifferent . . . Trickster . . . Chaos," she writes: "This is a terrifying God, implacable, faceless, yet malleable and wildly dynamic. I suppose it will soon be wearing my mother's face" (*Talents* 60). For Larkin, her mother has become indistinguishable from Earthseed itself.

Although *Parable of the Talents* is a continuation of Lauren's story and the development of Earthseed, many readers find it more difficult to engage. The violence and loss are even more direct in *Talents* as readers watch the familial community of Acorn experience ravage, rape, kidnapping, and death. Lauren manages to survive and continue to spread the gospel of Earthseed until it is powerful and expansive. At the novel's end, an eighty-one-year-old Lauren watches as acolytes of Earthseed submit themselves to suspended animation and leave Earth in spaceships bound for the stars. Lauren's dream of Earthseed taking root among the stars comes true. In keeping with a womanist theological perspective, Butler continues to shape God in *Parable of the Talents* mostly in the form of shaping Lauren Oye Olamina.

Much of Larkin's critique of Lauren comes from a place of skepticism and doubt. She surmises, "If my mother had created only Acorn, the refuge for the homeless and the orphaned . . . if she had created Acorn but not Earthseed, then I think she would have been a wholly admirable person" (*Talents* 75). Yet Larkin's critique is framed from the point of view of a child who feels abandoned by her mother. Although Larkin was stolen from Lauren, it is clear that Larkin feels as if she did not matter to her mother. At their eventual meeting when Lauren makes it clear that she loves and welcomes her daughter, Larkin's upbringing has left her jaded by religion in the same ways as the young Lauren. Larkin's past and her understanding of Earthseed as the first priority in her mother's life ultimately shape her, and she cannot move into a loving relationship with her mother. Yet Larkin's analysis of Lauren's life and legacy is about more than the hurt of a lost child. It is the apt critique of Lauren and what she has become in the face of Earthseed. In many ways, and from her armchair perspective, Larkin judges her mother guilty of the same crime as many religious leaders, finding her to be godlike / like God and essentially betraying that for which Earthseed stands. Larkin talks about the wealth of the Earthseed movement and its influence in communities across the "United States, Canada, Alaska, Mexico and Brazil." Even Lauren says of herself: "So I've begun to reach people. I've reached so many people from Eureka to Seattle to Syracuse that I believe that even if I were killed tomorrow, some of these people would find ways to go on learning and reaching, pursuing the Destiny. Earthseed will go on." (*Talents* 397). Lauren's tone is familiar to the religious-wound weary and sounds suspiciously like that of a savior or, at the very least, a martyr.

Mitchem further delineates the purpose and power of womanist theology as "God-talk." Womanists generally view theology as "God-talk," a way of thinking that keeps the human dimension front and center. For womanists, God-talk must encompass both words and actions in divine-to-human and human-to-human contacts. This contrasts with the idea that theology can be a "study of God," a process that abstracts theology and blurs the lines of the activity. Womanist theology is a continuing project that participates in the ongoing, fully human effort to refine God-talk (Mitchem 143).

The character of Larkin functions as the conduit and catalyst of "God-talk" in Butler's development of Lauren as a character. Rather than leaving the reader with the selfless, near superhero Lauren represents in *Parable of the Sower*, Butler continues to develop Lauren as a young woman and then an old woman. We see Lauren suffer and survive and grow from the fringe leader of a would-be cult to the embodiment of a powerful movement. However, the original premise of Earthseed as shaping God then requires that the reader continually question Lauren's motivations—question Earthseed—via the character of Larkin. The practice of womanist theology requires God-talk—that religion be questioned in its motives to ensure it honors the people, all people—just as Earthseed requires God-talk to ensure its adherents remember that it was created to serve the people the novel's mainstream religion forgot. If Black liberatory theological practices reread and reinterpret scripture, Butler takes it further by rewriting sacred text via the character of Lauren. If womanist theology "re-envisions the sacred" through an interdisciplinary social analysis that makes "visible Black women's lived experiences," then surely the *Parable* novels engage in a similar practice (Mitchem 63–71).

Butler practices an economic and sociopolitical theology that demands a religion that sees and acknowledges the plight of the dispossessed. She, like more formally recognized theologians, practices in a reinterpretation of traditional American Christianity that meets the needs of the marginalized. Lauren's gospel, though fictionalized, is no less relevant and potent. Thurman's God is a poor and disinherited Jew. Cone's God is Black. God for Cannon,

Grant, Williams, and Townes is the embodiment of intersectionality. God for Lauren is Change. Though she cannot escape it completely, Lauren does not center her critique of faith in her oppression or Blackness or Black femaleness but in the "interstructured," in all the isms she experiences. In the beginning, Lauren's youthfulness does not allow her to be taken seriously. Her hyper-empathy is framed as a disability. She is disenfranchised and threatened by a destabilized planet because of global warming. While the framework of Lauren's need to shape God differs, the foundation is the same. Twentieth-century Black theologians shaped God for their sociopolitical moment just as Lauren does in the world of the Parables.[2] Butler's Earthseed is not an entirely new construct. It operates in keeping with a long tradition in African American liberation practices that are inseparable from African American faith. Reading *Parable of the Sower* and experiencing Lauren write Earthseed is to see a practice of womanist theology in action both within the novel and outside of the novel. Through Lauren, Butler enacts a resistance and survival strategy that reaches at least as far back as enslaved Africans imagining freedom in America. Earthseed is unique in that it invites a discourse between the religious and the sociopolitical, performs God-talk, in the speculative realm where readers are more comfortable considering that conversation. Religion in the world of *Parable*, as often in the real world, is so necessary yet so linked to economic and sociopolitical marginalization, to trauma and pain, that Butler has to both profess and refute, confirm and deny, its importance to give herself and her readers a viable way into the text. Ultimately, like her brother and sister theologians, she has to shape God in order to survive.

NOTES

1. I want to note the essay by Michael Brandon McCormack in that there is a similar premise that locates Butler's work within the framework of postmodern womanist theology. However, the essay names Butler's work Afrofuturism which for me is a theoretical construct inclusive of but also distinct from speculative fiction and an assertion that must be addressed in a longer work.

2. It is not clear whether Butler ever read Black theology. It is clear that she herself practiced the same kind of reworking rather than creating something entirely new. What is distinct from Christianity in Lauren's understanding of God is the impersonal nature with which God is regarded. "We do not worship God" (*Sower* 27). "God is neither good nor evil, neither loving nor hating" (*Sower* 251). This kind of distancing is different from the personal relationship with God that stands at the center of many expressions of Christianity—in particular Black Christianity. This is reminiscent of Buddhist philosophy and seems to dually function as a safety mechanism for Lauren. If God is not your friend or your father, if God cannot be worshipped or anthropomorphized, you are less likely to be vulnerable to him.

WORKS CITED

Brown, Charles. "Octavia E. Butler: Persistence." *Conversations with Octavia Butler*, edited by Conseula Francis, University Press of Mississippi, 2010, pp. 181–188.

Butler, Octavia E. *Parable of the Sower*. Seven Stories Press, 2016.

———. *Parable of the Talents*. Seven Stories Press, 2016.

Canon, Katie. *Black Womanist Ethics*. 1988. Wipf and Stock Publishers, 2006.

Cone, James H. *The Cross and the Lynching Tree*. Oribis Books, 2013.

Connor, Kimberly Rae. "The Speed of Belief: Religion and Science Fiction, an Introduction to the Implicit Religions of Science Fiction." *Implicit Religion: Journal of the Centre for the Study of Implicit Religion and Contemporary Spirituality*, vol. 17, no. 4, 2014, pp. 367–377.

Harrison, Rosalie G. "Sci-Fi Visions: An Interview with Octavia Butler." *Conversations with Octavia Butler*, edited by Consuela Francis, University of Mississippi Press, 2010, pp. 39.

Lloyd, Vincent. "Post-Racial, Post-Apocalyptic Love: Octavia Butler as Political Theologian." *Political Theology*, vol. 17, no. 5, 2016, pp. 449–464.

McCormack, Michael Brandon. "'Your God Is a Racist, Sexist, Homophobic, and a Misogynist . . . Our God Is Change': Ishmael Reed, Octavia Butler and Afrofuturist Critiques of (Black) American Religion." *Black Theology: An International Journal*, vol. 14, no. 1, 2016, pp. 6–27. *EBSCOhost*, doi:10.1080/14769948.2015.1131503.

McMickle, Marvin A. "A Look at James Cone and Black Theology." *Christian Citizen*, 6 June 2018. https://medium.com/christian-citizen/a-look-at-james-cone-and-black-theology-e4a3ae2c6938.

Mitchem, Stephanie Y. *Introducing Womanist Theology*. Orbis, 2002.

See, Lisa. "Publishers Weekly Interviews: Octavia E. Butler." *Conversations with Octavia Butler*, edited by Conseula Francis, University Press of Mississippi, 2010, pp. 38–42.

Thrall, James H. "Authoring the Sacred: Humanism and Invented Scripture in Octavia Butler, Kurt Vonnegut and Dan Simmons." *Implicit Religion: Journal of the Centre for the Study of Implicit Religion and Contemporary Spirituality*, vol. 17, no. 4, 2014, pp. 509–531.

Thurman, Howard. *Jesus and the Disinherited*. Beacon Press, 1996.

Townes, Emilie M. "Womanist Theology." *Encyclopedia of Women and Religion in North America*, edited by Rosemary Skinner Keller and Rosemary Radford Ruether, Indiana University Press, 2006, pp. 1165–1173.

Turman, Eboni Marshall. "Black Women's Wisdom." *Christian Century*, vol. 136, no. 6, 2019, pp. 30–34. *EBSCOhost,* search.ebscohost.com/login.aspx?direct=true&db=aph&AN=134877441&site=ehost-live.

Tweedy, Clarence W., III. "The Anointed: Countering Dystopia with Faith in Octavia Butler's *Parable of the Sower* and *Parable of the Talents*." *Americana: The Journal of American Popular Culture (1900–present)*, vol. 13, no. 1, 2014, http://www.americanpopularculture.com/journal/articles/spring_2014/tweedy.htm.

Williams, Juan. *Conversations with Octavia Butler*, edited by Conseula Francis, University Press of Mississippi, 2010, pp. 161–180.

Part III

Black Liberation and
Notions of Freedom

12

Octavia Butler's Xenogenesis Trilogy, *Bloodchild*, and the Androgynous Third

ALEXIS BROOKS DE VITA

Octavia Butler has built her religious explorations on traditional Yoruba theosophical and African and diaspora historical grounds, including Ifa and the mysteries of Gnostic Christianity. In Ifa, the binding, balancing, and spiritual uplift that result from unifying the mermaid Yemoja and merman Olokun is an entity with its own incarnation, the idealized androgynous Chief of the White Cloth, Obatala. Characters that recall Obatala's balance of male and female in a sexually powerful androgyne appear in Butler's Xenogenesis trilogy of *Dawn, Adulthood Rites,* and *Imago* and in her novella *Bloodchild.* Like Ifa's Obatala and early Coptic and Gnostic Christianity's Holy Spirit, what I call the Androgynous Third in Butler's Xenogenesis and *Bloodchild* embodies long-suffering, humility, wisdom, and commitment, bound in a tolerant and devoted love that brings female and male powers into harmonious community building and spiritual growth through sexualized union. Synergy of these qualities, as I suggest in my account of Xenogenesis, catalyzes revolutionary change in a mythic as well as physical reality, equalizing systemic imbalances of power.

The Androgynous Third can be seen as an Ifa religious force represented in Xenogenesis's Oankali ooloi, a necessary third sexual partner who makes peaceful human-Oankali hybrid families possible. Employing what Brianna Thompson in this volume calls "erotic pedagogy" in Olamina's teaching of Earthseed, androgynous ooloi reestablish the bonding, fertility, and viability of postapocalyptic heterosexual human couples as a foundational social structure through heightened lovemaking. The multigendered, interspecies-loving offspring brought into existence by Oankali-human three-way parenting stand in moral contrast to human resisters in Xenogenesis, who choose to incestuously mate a gang-raped mother with her own son while he is still a child, too young to give consent to this eugenic experiment. Thus, it is human resisters who perpetrate human rebirth at its own ethical peril. Concurrently, the Oankali racially subjugate humans. This chapter compares the interspecies egalitarianism, integration, and autonomy of the Androgynous Third in Butlerian textual spaces and the androgyne's resonance with precursive spiritual figures in Ifa and Gnostic mythologies, revealing this figure's moral and mythical functions.

The three books of Xenogenesis each focuses on one of the three types of beings who result from the Oankali's genetic trade with humans: humans, Oankali, and "constructs," or hybrids of the two. The trilogy focuses first on an adult female human imbued with traits of the Oankali, then on a genetically engineered "construct" male, and, finally, on an ooloi. The most obvious transition between the books and their respective protagonists is progressive exploration of gender. *Dawn* explores the experiences of a female, *Adulthood Rites* explores the life of a male, and *Imago* tracks androgynous ooloi. Xenogenesis's *Dawn* walks the reader through the female's new role in a blended-species repopulation of Earth, followed by the male's role in *Adulthood Rites*, before plunging into the shifting social positioning of ooloi in *Imago*. In this changing Oankali-human society, Butler posits that even the androgynous ooloi must adapt and evolve to fully assimilate humans into the Oankali's genetic and familial structures.

Merriam-Webster defines *androgynous* in negative terms, as "neither specifically feminine or masculine," rather than as a functionally necessary and sexually active third gender. Similarly, Butler is constantly explaining what the ooloi are by defining what they are not: neither male and female nor sexless. The third-gendered ooloi have neither male nor female genitalia but manipulate male sperm and female eggs with sense organs like unsheathed hands at the end of elephant-trunk second arms, in contrast to their "strength arms." Butler's ooloi are lustful, "thorny, possessive" (*Imago* 72). Highly sexed, ooloi undergo two metamorphoses to reach maturity after thirty. Oankali are accustomed to families with three parents when they encounter humans: the male contributing sperm, the female housing the fertilized egg, and the ooloi planted between husband and wife as they dream of copulation, intensifying their pleasures as it selects and combines their DNA. Oankali have traditionally married a brother/sister couple to an outsider ooloi who chooses and enhances DNA to bring forward while suppressing, repurposing, or destroying unwanted genes.

In hybrid human-Oankali families, ooloi are lynchpins. Each ooloi acquires two husbands, one human and one Oankali, a human and an Oankali wife, and children in whom ooloi combine desirable genes of all five parents. These construct children may metamorphose into any of their parents' three genders. Xenogenesis explores societal biases against and resistance to adjustments that humans, Oankali, and constructs must make, no matter how desirable, necessary, or sought after such changes may be. Xenogenesis prepares readers for Butler's explorations of survival and adaptation in *Parable of the Sower*, in which the world-rebuilding religion, Earthseed, has as its first tenet "God Is Change" (3). Brandon McCormack in this volume further explores the potentially negative consequences of positive change.

Because Xenogenesis explores bias and psychoemotional struggles necessitated by adaptation and cooperation, the trilogy confronts bigotry in three locations, metaphorically reflecting English slaveholding colonialism. *Dawn* opens in the Oankali sentient ship with the awakening of incubated human survivors. Oankali groom one human, Lilith Iyapo, to persuade other humans to cooperate with interbreeding. Because Oankali wish to blend their species with the humans they have rescued, they only gradually entrust autonomy to their human leader, or, as Lilith calls herself, their "Judas Goat." Lilith selects, awakens, and indoctrinates traumatized humans to repopulate the refertilized Earth with Oankali mates, providing a parallel social structure to that of colonial Europe's slavery systems in a creative exploration of familial, intercultural, and interracial domination. Cathy Peppers points out that "Butler's African-American Lilith is forced to live the 'choice' enforced during slavery" (12); thus, "the narrative of *Xenogenesis* relentlessly keeps the discourses of slavery and sociobiology in continuous dialogue" (17). Similarly, in Butler's *Kindred*, Dana, an African American woman, travels back in time and finds herself constrained to help her slaveholding ancestor rape her enslaved ancestress to ensure that Dana will exist. As sexual reproductivity facilitator, Dana mirrors Lilith's conflicted sexual surrender of humans to Oankali. Novella Brooks de Vita argues that Dana betrays and loses her idealism in performance of the androgynous sexual facilitation role thrust upon her. Securing the rape, Dana returns to twentieth-century freedom mutilated and disillusioned. Though Butler does not present the Oankali as a slave society as defined by Ira Berlin's "hateful embraces" in "dances of domination and subordination, resistance and accommodation" (4), and she denied *Bloodchild*'s being an allegory of slavery, Berlin's argument that "if slavery made *race*, its larger purpose was to make *class*" (5) may be applied to these Butlerian texts.

Once mated humans have earned passage back to Earth, fertilized and accompanied by three Oankali spouses, some rebel, refuse to bear construct children, and escape to form resister communities. Because resisters maintain their communities by disseminating misinformation about the Oankali, the second Xenogenesis text, *Adulthood Rites*, reflects ideologies of segregation. Once construct children have begun to mature, Butler demonstrates the social hypocrisy of the desegregationist Oankali, who are opposed to allowing a construct to become an ooloi, the most controlling and powerful of all Oankali family and community members. Thus, *Imago* becomes a vehicle for creative analysis of the third and most enduring pillar of European colonialism: racism.

In summary order, then, Xenogenesis explores social hierarchies in three shifting locations paralleling African American histories of chattel slavery, segregation, and integration. *Dawn* begins in the aliens' sentient ship, introducing the first mother of hybrid human-Oankali offspring, whom Butler has named after the Judeo-Christian first wife of Adam, who became the mother of demons rather than be made subservient: Lilith (Cavendish 1631). Citing sixteenth-century Judaic tradition as the origin of the monstrous Lilith, Sarah Wood argues, "Not only does Butler's naming of her character after this Lilith recall the original myth, but it also introduces the reader to the construction of the other woman as both radicalized and racialized" (88). Peppers explains that "because the text puts the origin story of African diaspora and slavery into dialogue with Biblical discourse," it becomes necessary that the "recovery of black women's identity must also take into account the fact that a potentially empowering goddess like Lilith was 'racialized,' 'became black' as part of aesthetic representation in the service of slavery" (14). As Lilith confronts humans' gendered racial biases while attempting to waken and orient humans, *Dawn* interrogates changes that would be necessary before a post-Eurocentric male globalist human society might accept an African-descent woman's leadership toward interracial survival in a state of alien domination. *Dawn* thereby contrasts biological and social roles of femaleness in a postapocalyptic society trapped in sexual colonization.

Adulthood Rites introduces a construct male, Akin, stolen in babyhood from Lilith's interspecies five-parent family by infertile human rebels. Resisters want to rebuild their civilizations by raising construct children as humans. This regressive, rebellious subversion of Lilith's progressive survivors' family and community supports Phyllis L. Burns's arguments in "Black Women's Prophecy" in this volume. Akin's name is an onomatopoeic allusion to Cain, the Judeo-Christian mythical first murderer, a fratricide. But Butler's Akin struggles to harm no one, hiding his poisonously tentacled tongue and refusing to speak when bullied by human raiders, knowing that his life has caused the death and attempted murder of his two human fathers. Akin was constructed by his ooloi parent from the sperm of his biological human father, who was murdered by the first humans Lilith awoke. Unable to kill or harm Lilith, a powerful woman made resistant to human attack by the Oankali, male humans instead bashed in Lilith's human mate's head to destabilize the Oankali's repopulation mission. When Akin is later kidnapped on Earth, his human stepfather is subjected to the same head bashing. Akin's distress signals reach the Oankali husband, who sustains the human husband until their ooloi mate can heal him, though he remains brain damaged.

Akin's story takes place predominantly in the resister settlement that buys him and tries to turn him against his mother, Lilith. Wood analyzes "the resisters' reading of Lilith" as "this monstrous, unruly, but also specifically Black female sexuality," reverting to a chattel slavery archetype that affords the resisters cultural familiarity and "substantiates their preferred understanding of 'reality' in this disordered and disorienting new world" (89). Wood finds that Lilith's fate "is to become both outcast and hated by the human community" because she "encapsulates, and is emblematic of, the potential threat that an undisciplined femininity poses to patriarchal order" (88). In this evolution of personal story interfacing community mythmaking, Lilith is "empowered, empowering, and subjugated" (89), an empathetic heroine "caught at the nexus of competing social, cultural, and religious discourses" as she becomes a "reflexive mythification" (135).

Human resisters distort kidnapped construct children's psychobiological development and alter their destinies. Resisters plot to cut off construct children's tentacles to make them look human—an operation analogous to removing a human's eyes—a metaphor for the mutilation of spirit taking place in Akin. Since Oankali and constructs marry their paired siblings, Akin has been kidnapped from the sibling who should have metamorphosed into the female he would marry. Because Akin and his paired sibling are kept from each other when they need to bond, their characters and bodies become distorted by dissonance. Akin and his paired sibling develop revulsion instead of spiritual kinship as Akin's wife-to-be metamorphoses instead into his brother.

But Akin's emotional mutilation results in his sympathy for resisters. In her comparison of Akin's tale in *Adulthood Rites* with the tropes of American captivity narratives as predominantly "the tale of a white, Western, civilized, Christian colonizer" (Magedanz 4), Stacy Magedanz translates Akin's name as Yoruba for "hero" (12–13). This translation of Akin's name explains his benevolent rescue of his kidnappers and allows a doubling of the significance of Lilith's name so that she reflects not only Old Testament Adam's demonized first wife but also the New Testament's mother of the Anointed One. Magedanz explains that, "Lilith has become the Second Eve, Mary, mother of a Savior who is both fully human and fully God-like alien," who alone can, "through his sufferings, redeem his lost people, the resister humans," in his role "as redeemer-archetype" (13). In a similarly transcultural reading, Ayana Rehema Abdallah finds that Butler's "transgressive creativity" renders her feminism "more akin to *malidoma* consciousness," a phrase of the Dagara people in Burkina Faso that means "making friends with the stranger or enemy," so that "Butler's fiction imbibes a larger cultural ideological construct that is African American cultural philosophy or Africentrism" (4161–4162). Akin becomes the construct leader who persuades the Oankali to refertilize human resisters and exile them to Mars. Exile to Mars is merciful because the Oankali plan to strip Earth of refertilized soil and hybridized plant life when they take their constructed population to find new peoples with whom to interbreed. Resisters and the raiders who prey on them would have found themselves stranded on a barren rock. Though onomatopoeically named for the biblical first fratricide, Akin becomes his human kidnappers' savior when he persuades the Oankali to allow resisters a safe place to self-segregate.

In the third text of Xenogenesis, *Imago*, the main protagonist Jodahs's name recalls the biblical Judas, the ultimate Christian symbol of betrayal. Jodahs, one of the youngest of Lilith's construct children, has grown up closest to the ooloi of its five-parent family. Ooloi parents are forbidden by Oankali society to construct hybridized ooloi children. Nevertheless, Jodahs learns upon completion of its first metamorphosis that it is becoming ooloi, not male, as expected. Jodahs's accidental metamorphosis into a construct ooloi is disastrous not only for Jodahs and its family but for the colonizing Oankali.

With Jodahs's metamorphosis into an unsanctioned ooloi, Butler explores the species racism underpinning Oankali domination of humans. Oankali have reserved the influential position of third-gender ooloi for themselves, not for constructs who might inherit human violence. By developing as its psychospiritual bond with its ooloi parent prompts it to do, Jodahs threatens Oankali social order. Jodahs's ooloi sexuality unmasks the hypocritical egalitarianism of Oankali society. Because those who dominate each family and take counsel together to resolve community issues are ooloi, ooloi make up the Oankali ruling class. Since humans are capable of only two binary sexes and therefore incapable of joining the ruling androgynous class, and constructs are forbidden admission to it, Oankali have ensured that only Oankali can dominate their new hybrid empire. Sarah Outterson appears to take the Oankalis' antihierarchical self-presentation at face value when she theorizes that "slavery makes us aware of freedom" just as the "path to any utopia of change" chez Butler "passes through pain" (454). Equally inconclusively, while acknowledging "the dominating, yet ostensibly benevolent"

Oankali, Christina Braid interrogates "pretenses of justice in which violence hides itself," asking, "Why do we still turn to violence as an answer to conflict?" (47). Classism based on racism and fortified by engineered extermination means that the Oankali will dominate humans into the foreseeable future. Conversely, Stacy Magedanz insists that "Oankali repeatedly deny the humans choice and self-determination" (10). Humans are relegated to a servile, sexually preyed upon helpmeet class, wanted for selective breeding and the hard labor of world building. Patricia Hill Collins explains that "intersecting oppressions rely on sexuality to mutually construct one another" (135). The plight of humans in the Oankali empire defamiliarizes and queries the sexual roles of people of African descent in "one drop rule" (Collins 133) racist English slave societies. Peppers states, "The narrative of *Xenogenesis* relentlessly keeps the discourses of slavery and sociobiology in continuous dialogue" (17) as the trilogy evolves "to contest the 'innateness' of a human nature based on violence, xenophobia and male dominance" (30). For, by Xenogenesis's conclusion, Butler brings characters and readers to imagine a resolution of institutionalized racism in favor of the disempowered.

What could persuade a dominant culture to allow those whose bodies and destinies they control and consume to have permanent entry into the ruling class? Butler foreshadows answering this question by establishing at the climax of *Dawn*, when awakened humans undertake a doomed rebellion aboard the Oankali's sentient starship, that ooloi are vulnerably bonded with their human sexual partners. Oankali-human bonds are socially sanctioned matehood. Mates provide lifelong unions for Oankali males and females, for ooloi who manipulate humans into joining them, and for the human partners who become addicted to the opiating sexual pleasures that only ooloi can provide. Though humans struggle with accepting Oankali, comparing them to tentacled sea creatures or giant slugs and running away from them to join resister settlements, humans continue to yearn for their ooloi sexual partners, who remain willing to take them back even after decades of abandonment.

Socially sanctioned exclusive sexual union between the Oankali ruling class of ooloi and their human mates is not analogous to the sexual misusage of African-descent captives in colonial English chattel enslavement. Paula Giddings tracks the legalization of sexual misusage of African-descent captives, from protections against the rape of enslaved women in nascent English colonies to denying enslaved women the right to identify who fathered their children, following U.S. independence and self-governance. Xenogenesis's socially sanctioned sexual unions between members of skewed power classes is therefore not comparable to foundational U.S. racist hierarchy building. But the first condition Butler predicates as necessary to a society's rejection of its racism is socially protected exclusionary lifelong sexual union between members of that society's most privileged class and those whom they dominate. In short, interspecies marriage and family are the first foundations of egalitarianism.

The next condition necessary to the eradication of racism is the rupturing of social barriers as Jodahs, the unintentionally metamorphosed ooloi, demonstrates. Jodahs's parent ooloi did not construct Jodahs to become ooloi; nor did Jodahs approach metamorphosis with the intention of emerging as ooloi but with the assumption of becoming male. Jodahs's paired sibling, Aaor, born to their Oankali mother shortly after Jodahs was born to their human mother, Lilith, grew up planning to become Jodahs's sister/wife. With Jodahs's metamorphoses as an ooloi, the family finds itself exiled from their settlement despite Lilith's extraordinary service to the Oankali empire, having facilitated human cooperation in construct family building. In exile, denied mates, Jodahs triumphs by wandering unsettled territory until stumbling on, healing, and seducing a human brother/sister pair, the ultimate Oankali prize. Victoriously claiming ooloi state and status complete with human siblings as mates, Jodahs returns to its family's camp to discover its previously destined sister/wife in crisis. Having lost its presumptive brother/husband when Jodahs became ooloi, Aaor has begun metamorphosing not into a female there is no longer any need for but into a second construct ooloi.

These tragedies lead Lilith's brood to their greatest triumph: the eradication of institutionalized Oankali racism against humans. Androgynous ooloi cannot survive without mating, the function for which they exist. Unmated—or having stung to death violent human mates in self-defense—ooloi die. Jodahs's duo-gendered resister mates, willing to be healed of their incestuously bred illnesses, are addicted to Jodahs's lovemaking, rendering Jodahs mated for life. Aaor is less fortunate. Heartsick and self-negating, Aaor disintegrates to the state of a giant amoeba before it is pulled from the waters in which it drifts, as its family attempts to keep it alive.

Aaor must become the ooloi its body destines it to be or degenerate into mindless particles of matter. Flesh must mirror spirit or release it. Fa'lokun Fatunmbi argues that it is in the union of Yemoja's having "guided early life forms into greater levels of complexity" in Olokun's "environment in which this transformation occurred" (*Yemoja/Olokun* 13) that these principles "exist in primal relationship to Obatala" (*Yemoja/Olokun* 11), the androgynous deity responsible for "generating consciousness and setting the standards for ethical behavior" (*Obatala* 9). Jodahs, an evolving ooloi, must overcome its jealousy and share its mates with its sibling or keep its mates to itself but transform its society if it wishes to save Aaor's life. According to Fatunmbi, the "patience and generosity" of Yemoja/Olokun nurture the "physical, psychological and spiritual growth" that are "established by the wisdom" of Obatala (*Yemoja/Olokun* 11). Jodahs's crisis between embracing its unanticipated nature by sacrificing its sibling or rescuing its sibling by defying its society's laws and suppressing its own possessive nature provides a balancing, upward opportunity of movement for Jodahs, as an individual, to effect sweeping social change.

Jean Doresse recounts "a wonderfully living witness to the literary activity of the Gnostics" (170) when "Pistis who is called Sophia" drew Chaos from jealous Darkness and Obscurity, leaving below the waters of the Spiritless abyss (165). Pistis-Sophia's terror evokes the male-and-female "child who is traversing places" (Doresse 166) in a tale mirrored in *Imago* by the watery life-and-death travels of the brother and sister, Jodahs and Aaor, who are becoming construct ooloi. Pistis-Sophia sets in motion a series of creations that result in "they who will judge and condemn the gods of Chaos and their powers" (Doresse 170). Just as the Oankali have judged and banished Jodahs and its family, they will be forced to judge themselves and reverse their initial judgments. Elaine Pagels recounts the Gnostic Genesis of spiritual sibling/mates as "the primordial Source," a male force, projecting "the beginning of all things" into "the primordial Silence," female, who conceives masculine Mind and feminine Truth, who produce masculine Word and feminine Life, giving birth to masculine Humanity and feminine Church, until "What-has-been-willed" is brought into being with his feminine counterpart Wisdom, known as Sophia. But Wisdom "plunged herself into a desperate search" for the primordial Source until, in danger of being dissolved into it, "the Power that sustains and preserves," the Limit, "restored and supported" her. Wisdom thus learned that Source is incomprehensible, and Source sent Christ with the Holy Spirit to teach that "none but the primal Mind could possibly comprehend God" (Pagels, *Adam* 74–75). Like Wisdom's disintegration into the primal Source, Aaor's body in the water "was trying to commit suicide" (*Imago* 158). Feeling "deeply, painfully afraid, desperately lonely" (*Imago* 157), Aaor "had to be brought back from drifting toward dissolution" (*Imago* 159). Valentinian Gnostics taught that suffering was "the first prerequisite for spiritual understanding" (Pagels, *Adam* 76); Wisdom joins Christ "to transform those sufferings" (Pagels, *Adam* 75) into light. Jodahs's, its mates', and Aaor's sufferings are being transformed into their society's enlightenment.

In struggles between self and society, the Gnostic text *Trimorphic Protennia* celebrates "feminine powers of Thought, Intelligence, and Foresight," calling its speaker the androgynous "'Invisible One within the All,'" both "'in the likeness of a female'" and "'the likeness of my masculinity'" (Pagels, *Gnostic Gospels* 55).

The Gnostic theologian Marcus was attacked for praying to feminine elements of the divine known as Silence, Wisdom, and Grace (Pagels *Gnostic Gospels* 59). The Gnostic *Thunder: Perfect Mind* declares, "I was sent forth from [the] power" (Robinson 297); Barbara G. Walker summarizes that "Sophia once represented God's female soul, source of his power," a role she compares to Kali-Shakti of the Hindu pantheon (951). Coincidentally, Oankali call their parents "Ooan" (*Imago* 27), which seems to translate as "Parent Kali," similar to Kali-Ma, "the Hindu Triple Goddess of creation, preservation, and destruction" (Walker 488), the "primordial female principle" Vishnu called the "material cause of all change" (Walker 490). Kali-Ma is the "primal Deep, or menstrual Ocean of Blood at creation" (Walker 491), a designation circling Kali and Butler's Oankali back to Yemoja as goddess of the waters. Aaor "swam in the river near our cabin for three days," the time needed for Christ's resurrection, before it attracted family members' attention by "forcing part of its body out of the water" (*Imago* 150, 151), a poignant Butlerian image of helpless return to the primordial source.

Jodahs and its mates rescue Aaor from devolution by sneaking with it into a resister settlement, risking all their lives. Jodahs's spouses are incestuously descended from Maria de la Luz, translatable as "Mary Light-bringer," and her son Adan, named in imperfect recall of Adam, the first man. These incestuously bred humans are grotesquely disfigured. Aaor manages to eat and alter its fill of human DNA by lustily healing guards and wounded villagers and securing as mates the two humans it falls in love with at first sight as soon as the raid begins, thus defining and healing itself.

Imago's construct pair of ooloi end resister rebellion by recruiting emigrants for the Mars colony established by their elder brother, Akin. Their most spectacular achievement for full acceptance back into Oankali society, however, is winning over almost the whole deformed, cancerous, and fertile resister human settlement as converts willing to interbreed with Oankali. Peppers summarizes, "*Xenogenesis* generates xenophilia in place of xenophobia" (40). In this way, Butler completes the three conditions necessary for overcoming institutionalized racism: the dominated must be in socially sanctioned family union with the dominant society's most powerful members; the dominated must breach the social barriers erected to keep them disempowered; and once in that breached position, the dominated must demonstrate that their racial qualities make them uniquely capable of supplying the dominant power with what it wants most of all but cannot secure for itself.

Jodahs's ultimately successful dismantling of Oankali institutionalized racism contrasts with the more futile struggles of Butler's other androgynous reproductive role-players. In *Fledgling*, vampiric Ina choose human symbionts with whom they enjoy sexual activity and upon whose blood they feed, allowing symbionts to mate and produce more of themselves for Ina to parasitize. The fifty-three-year-old female Ina who is *Fledgling*'s protagonist, Shori/Renee, practices Thompson's "erotic pedagogy" to groom her male and female symbionts into a family. Shori/Renee fights species racism among vampires as a dark-skinned vampire whose family and affianced allies are targeted for extermination. But Shori's battle of wits and wills with an older European male Ina are more reminiscent of gendered struggles for dominance in *Mind of My Mind* and *Wild Seed* than of Jodahs's determination that constructs should enjoy social ascendance as mated ooloi in *Imago*.

Jodahs manages to fully integrate constructs into Oankali society by demonstrating that construct ooloi can achieve what Oankali and their human leader, his mother, Lilith, cannot: persuading resisters to interbreed with Oankali. Now that resisters are emigrating to Mars and mating with ooloi, raiders will also have to emigrate, mate, or die. By emptying resister and raider settlements, Jodahs wins the revitalized Earth for the triffid Oankali empire. Thanks to Jodahs, Oankali sentient ships will not have to tear up the fertilized Earth to relocate to another planet unless and until the Oankali wish to find more genes to add to their DNA pool. Jodahs and Aaor have established construct ooloi as strategic agents of the empire's success, thereby delegitimizing the Oankali's previously exclusionary racist power structure.

Social upheaval in Xenogenesis is facilitated by Oankali embrace of change, a Butlerian constant. Perhaps Butler's character closest to Jodahs in Androgynous Third function is *Bloodchild*'s Gan. In *Bloodchild*, survivors of nuclear warfare have fled Earth and been colonized by scorpion-like beings called Tlic. The socially powerful position of the ooloi of Xenogenesis contrasts with the Androgynous Third's disempowered sexual misusage in *Bloodchild*. The Tlic believe they have constructed a moral and egalitarian interspecies society because they protect and preserve Terrans, who fled their suicidal Earthly apocalypse, while parsing Terrans out to Tlic who are ready to hatch new generations. Opiated on infertile eggs and coddled by their captors, N'Tlic human Terrans are raised to incubate fertilized Tlic eggs.

Gan is a Terran/human male, prized for incubating Tlic eggs. Linda Brent explains that men of African descent, as well as women and children, were sexually misused by slaveholders in American chattel slavery society, confirming *Bloodchild*'s historical realism. *Bloodchild* follows Gan the night he goes from being the Tlic-favored Terran child of his hybrid family to being ovipositor implanted with his adoptive mother's fertile eggs, risking an agonizing death if the grubs hatch and eat through his body.

Gan's sex is immaterial to his reproductive role as an N'Tlic, rendering him androgynous in their reproductive relationship. If Gan refuses to be implanted, his adoptive mother will implant Gan's sister. But Terran girls are not the Tlics' preferred incubators because they are needed to remain alive and healthy enough to bear more Terrans. In *Bloodchild* as in Xenogenesis, the remnants of Earth's depleted human population are highly desirable among alien families for purposes of self-regeneration. Terrans are told their symbiotic relationship with the Tlic is mutually beneficial, which Gan believes until he watches a Terran man get his Tlic's ravenous parasitic grubs cut out of him.

Aware of his peril, Gan cannot meet the second of Jodahs's conditions for destabilizing Tlic society's racist hierarchy. Gan tries threatening his Tlic with a contraband gun, but he cannot engineer a sustainable breach of the barriers the Tlic have constructed around Terran social standing as incubators, forced to be the talking animals that Africans were medically defined as in English chattel slavery societies (see drapetomania). Gan therefore surrenders to the third stage of supplying the Tlic with what they cannot supply for themselves: incubation.

Outterson's analysis demonstrates that for *Bloodchild*'s Gan and Xenogenesis's Lilith, Akin, and Jodahs, "education in Butler's work is violent in both senses," involving "physical harm and suffering" and serving as "a metaphor for more fundamental bodily boundary-violation," both of which are "necessary to the teaching and learning" processes (437). Following his failed armed standoff, Gan makes the morally sacrificial but emotionally self-important choice to protect his sister and prolong his favored status by agreeing to have his adoptive mother's eggs laid in him, reflecting the story of Maria de la Luz and her son Adam in Xenogenesis. The reader comes away from this tale with faint hope that Gan can change his society to an egalitarian one unless he inspires the threat of mass suicide among Terrans. All that Gan has gained during his day of awakening is an understanding of his very limited choices in his bleakly unspiritual world.

The Androgynous Third is a passionate and detached spiritual actor, receiving and nurturing the gene pools of its binary sexual partners, to whom it has devoted the fortress of its body, while offering the love of its hungering soul. This spiritually enlightening and potentially liberating gendered role is tragically depicted by Butler in *Bloodchild* and triumphantly in Xenogenesis. Lilith's construct brood, the most vulnerable members of the Oankali empire, assure everyone's survival by ensuring their own. This enlightening and liberating third gender presages the real-world qualities of leadership that Shelby L. Crosby's chapter in this volume finds in the Parables.

WORKS CITED

Abdallah, Ayana Rehema. "Africantric Transgressive Creativity: A Reader's Meditation on Octavia Butler." *Dissertation Abstracts International, Section A: The Humanities and Social Sciences*, vol. 62, no. 12, 2002, pp. 4161–4162.

Achachelooei, Elham Mohammadi, and Carol Elizabeth Leon. "The God-Human Relationship in Octavia Butler's 'The Book of Martha.'" *Journal of Language Studies*, vol. 16, no. 3, 2016, pp. 129–143.

Berlin, Ira. *Many Thousands Gone: The First Two Centuries of Slavery in North America*. Belknap Press of Harvard University Press, 1998.

Braid, Christina. "Contemplating and Contesting Violence in Dystopia: Violence in Octavia Butler's *Xenogenesis* Trilogy." *Contemporary Justice Review*, vol. 9, no. 1, Mar. 2006, pp. 47–65.

Brent, Linda. *Incidents in the Life of a Slave Girl*. Harcourt, Brace, Jovanovich, 1973.

Brooks de Vita, Novella. "Beloved and Betrayed: Survival and Authority in *Kindred*." *The Griot: Journal of the Southern Conference on African American Studies, Inc.*, vol. 22, no. 1, Spring 2003, pp. 16–20.

Butler, Octavia. *Adulthood Rites: Book Two of the Xenogenesis Series*. Warner Books, 1988.

———. *Bloodchild and Other Stories*. 2nd ed., Amazon Digital Services, Open Road Media Sci-Fi and Fantasy, 2012.

———. *Dawn: Book One of the Xenogenesis Series*. Warner Books, 1987.

———. *Fledgling*. Grand Central Publishing, 2007.

———. *Imago: Book Three of the Xenogenesis Series*. Warner Books, 1989.

———. *Kindred*. Doubleday, 1979.

———. *Mind of My Mind*. Warner Books, 1977.

———. *Parable of the Sower*. Warner Books, 1993.

———. *Wild Seed*. Warner Books, 1980.

Cavendish, Richard, ed. *Man, Myth and Magic: An Illustrated Encyclopedia of the Supernatural*. Marshall Cavendish, 1970.

Collins, Patricia Hill. *Black Feminist Thought: Knowledge, Consciousness, and the Politics of Empowerment*. 2nd ed., Routledge, 2000.

Doresse, Jean. *The Secret Books of the Egyptian Gnostics*. MJF Books, 1986.

Fatunmbi, Fa'lokun. *Obatala: Ifá and the Chief of the Spirit of the White Cloth*. Original Publications, 1993.

———. *Yemoja/Olokun: Ifá and the Spirit of the Ocean*. Original Publications, 1993.

Giddings, Paula. *When and Where I Enter: The Impact of Black Women on Race and Sex in America*. Bantam Books, 1988.

Magedanz, Stacy. "The Captivity Narrative in Octavia E. Butler's *Adulthood Rites*." *Extrapolation: A Journal of Science Fiction and Fantasy*, vol. 53, no. 1, 2012, pp. 45–59.

Outterson, Sarah. "Diversity, Change, Violence: Octavia Butler's Pedagogical Philosophy." *Utopian Studies*, vol. 19, no. 3, 2008, pp. 433–456.

Pagels, Elaine. *Adam, Eve, and the Serpent*. Vintage Books, 1988.

———. *The Gnostic Gospels*. Vintage Books, 1989.

Peppers, Cathy. "Dialogic Origins and Alien Identities in Butler's *Xenogenesis*." *Science Fiction Studies*, vol. 22, no. 1, 1995, pp. 47–62.

Robinson, James M. *The Nag Hammadi Library in English.* Members of the Coptic Gnostic Library Project of the Institute for Antiquity and Christianity, translators. HarperSanFrancisco, 1990.

Walker, Barbara G. *The Women's Encyclopedia of Myths and Secrets.* Castle Books, 1996.

Wood, Sarah. "Subversion through Inclusion: Octavia Butler's Interrogation of Religion in *Xenogenesis* and *Wild Seed.*" *FEMSPEC: An Interdisciplinary Feminist Journal Dedicated to Critical and Creative Work in the Realms of Science Fiction, Fantasy, Magical Realism, Surrealism, Myth, Folklore, and Other Supernatural Genres,* vol. 6, no. 1, 2005, pp. 87–99.

13

Erotic Pedagogy in *Parable of the Talents*

Freedom and Community through Touch

Brianna Thompson

Octavia Butler's 1997 postapocalyptic novel *Parable of the Talents* imagines a 2030s United States that is plagued by sociopolitical and environmental ills eerily resonant with our current moment. *Talents* involves a conservative, nationalist president who endorses military violence while neglecting public safety, schools, and health care. In response, the novel's protagonist, Lauren, invents a new religion called Earthseed that preaches interconnectedness and equality. Earthseed levels hierarchy and claims that "God is Change" (92). However, inciting transformation through religion is no easy task. As Lauren laments, "The thing that I want to build is so damned new and *vast*! I not only don't know how to build it, but I'm not even sure what it will look like. . . . I'm just feeling my way" (51). The phrase "feeling my way" illuminates the way Earthseed draws on human touch to create new intimacies and communities that liberate followers from the devastation of a competitive, patriarchal world.

I show that in *Talents* "erotic pedagogy"[1] is a physical embodiment and enactment of the equitable, reflexive, and interconnected world Lauren wants to create through Earthseed. Building on womanist theology, the history of the Black sermon, and the French psychoanalyst Didier Anzieu, who provides the theory that the skin is the site of psychic well-being, I argue that through erotic pedagogy Lauren frees her pupils from the oppression of postapocalyptic America. I use Aimee Carillo Rowe's phrase "erotic pedagogy" to describe the process through which Lauren ministers Earthseed to individual women because it emphasizes the way that Lauren's intimate teaching taps into creative potential. Working with Audre Lorde's classic "Uses of the Erotic," Rowe writes that the erotic "is not reducible to one thing, but works at the nexus of the body, desire, love, and the spiritual" (1032). My use of erotic pedagogy to describe Lauren's teaching practices signals this understanding of the erotic as a loving, transformative force. I also wish to convey that these women use vulnerable, intimate touch to cultivate a kind of love that is not limited to the realm of the sexual, the romantic, or the platonic. To highlight the inextricable overlaps between Lauren's teachings about survival (often through Earthseed), her comforting, and her preaching, I call this process pedagogy rather than just ministry.

A critical reader might point out that Lauren's ministerial efforts to spread Earthseed recall womanist theology, the Black feminist critique of Black liberation theology, and this reader would be correct. Butler wrote *Talents* after living through the civil rights and Black power movement. She was a prophet of doom and solutions informed by the same historical events that influenced womanist theology. Stacy M. Floyd-Thomas writes that "a womanist theologian . . . calls for the church to transform embodied relationships by taking society from domination to partnership" (49). The preoccupation in *Talents* with religion, female intimacy, and revolutionary politics rooted in bodily intimacy that dismantles hierarchy does indeed, I would argue, mark Earthseed as a womanist theology.[2] While situating Earthseed within its womanist theological genealogy is important, I do so by way of looking at what women *do* when they are learning about Earthseed.

Parable of the Talents is the second book in Butler's Parable trilogy, following the 1993 *Parable of the Sower*. *Talents* is a compilation of the deceased Lauren Olamina's diary entries from the 2030s, of commentary by her daughter Larkin, and of verses from *Earthseed: The First Book of the Living* (a text written by Lauren to instruct her followers). Lauren's diaries chronicle the era known as "the Apocalypse," which involves crises of patriarchal religion and neoliberalism,[3] such as the persecution of religious difference, social stratification, privatization, and nationalism (7–8). The destruction endorsed by the white supremacist Christian America president Andrew Jarret drives Lauren to create Acorn, a commune in California where she and her husband farm, take in families, and practice Earthseed. Although Lauren's race doesn't play a prominent role in the narrative, it factors into her understanding of her father as a minister. While Lauren cultivates religion differently than her father's traditional Black Baptist ministry, she does not identify Earthseed with a particular race. Lauren's religion preaches adaptability, communal caretaking, and that "the destiny of Earthseed / Is to take root among the stars" on a new planet (276). Eventually "Crusaders," followers of President Jarret, attack

Acorn, where they enslave or murder Lauren's community and send children to Christian orphanages (208). Three years later Lauren escapes enslavement to preach Earthseed and search the northwest for her kidnapped daughter. To articulate the way that Earthseed is a liberating religion that Lauren ministers through erotic pedagogy, I first address how she crafts a religion that upends Abrahamic ideology and the Baptist ministry she grew up hearing her father preach.

Hortense Spillers observes that while the Black sermonic tradition is rooted in Abrahamic masculinism, it signifies differently than Anglo Protestant sermons (252). For enslaved and free African Americans, Christianity was a humanization strategy; learning and modifying the codes of the dominant culture allowed them to congregate, encode messages, and organize revolt (263). "Through the African-American's sermon of exhortation," Spillers writes, "'I' improve; 'I' 'hear'/'have' the Word, at last, in a gesture of intervention" (252). If hearing the word is having liberation in an older tradition of Black sermon and church, Lauren's method of holding women (of any race) while sharing Earthseed with them signals two crucial things. First, Lauren's method registers that in her view the Black person has become human and, second, that all humans need to get close to one another to survive. This first aspect of Earthseed might seem colorblind, taking for granted the fact that Black people in the United States were once property who could not ward off the violence of unwanted intimacies.

Some critics agree, accusing Butler's Parable novels of condoning the hollow neoliberal discourses of multiculturalism. Vincent Lloyd claims that the Parable series narrates a "post-racial" celebration of diversity (as difference rather than necessitating justice) that is part of a politically evacuated "neoliberal love" (452). In his critique, Lloyd draws on Carl Schmitt's *Political Theology*. Predicated on the necessity of authority, Schmitt's theory of sovereignty suggests that political systems that adopt a secularized model of the divine can inspire secular change (*Stanford Encyclopedia of Philosophy*; Lloyd 449–450). In Lloyd's understanding, Earthseed ignores worldly differences like race to focus on survival, community building, and human intimacy (457). This thinking, Lloyd argues, fosters an undesirable "environment where the flux of sameness and difference, defining identity, displaces contest over visions of how the economy ought to be organized and how politics ought to be organized" (456).

In my reading, Earthseed frees its followers from suffering and oppression because it is predicated on a critique of neoliberalism as the destructive apotheosis of patriarchal, racist capitalism. Lauren's religion most certainly does aim to cultivate a world in which the "contests" of avarice and hierarchy have no role. Although I disagree with Lloyd's claim that Earthseed is neoliberal, he is right to suggest that Earthseed envisions a world without the brutalities of competition and authority. When Lloyd decries the loss of a transcendent authority figure in Earthseed, he is finding fault with *Talents* for parting ways entirely with systems of authority and sovereignty. Butler's novel refuses a secular theology of an authoritative God just as she challenges the Abrahamic tradition. When Lloyd claims that *Talents* endorses a postracial politics since "race and capital are no longer linked," he misreads the novel's relationship to race, religion, and authoritative hierarchy (457). In particular, Lauren is operating from a religious understanding in which Black people are humanized and thus can depart from Abrahamic and Black sermonic conventions. Because Lauren considers Black people to be human, she opts out of the traditional engagement in Black Protestantism that, in spite of its legacy of humanizing Black people, is also rooted in Abrahamic values.

Liberation from Patriarchy

We can better understand Earthseed's commitment to community and freedom by exploring how Lauren's religion departs from Abrahamic traditions and her father's ministry in particular. Through readings of the biblical parable of the talents in the novel, I show that Lauren's religious vision differs from her father's. In particular, she rejects top-down authority, and she finds religion's power in vulnerable intimacy. In *Talents*, before Acorn is attacked, Lauren dreams of her father preaching the biblical parable of the talents. This parable has often been interpreted as a story that "encourages the faithful to invest" in the praise of God and as a warning against the slothful failure to "share the riches of God's revelation" (Brisson 308; Kistemaker 124). In the Bible, the parable is a story about a rich man who travels away from home and distributes his "goods," eight talents, or eight units of currency, among three of his servants. He gives two of his servants multiple talents, and a third servant gets one talent. The first two servants invest or trade their share, eventually doubling it. The servant with one talent, however, buries it in the earth. When their master returns, he praises the servants who doubled their riches and castigates the "wicked and slothful" servant who failed to increase his share (*King James Bible*, Matthew 25.14–30).

The biblical parable is an important intertext that signals Earthseed's departure from Christian patriarchy and its masculinist hierarchies. Lauren clarifies how her religion differs from her father's in her portrayal of him as an immovable, conservative patriarch. In a journal entry, Lauren writes of having a recurring nightmare. She describes being back home in her dream, seeing her father "in his church robes: tall, broad, stern, straight—a great black wall of a man with a voice you not only hear but feel on your skin and in your bones. There's no corner of the meeting rooms that my father can't reach with that voice" (10). In this description, Lauren's father personifies masculine might as immovability, and his racial and his robes' blackness are linked with his commanding voice. Lauren locates in her father an under-standing of Black sermon as one that privileges sound, the word, and the ear. Spillers writes that in "the African American's sermon of exhortation," "the listening *ear* becomes the privileged sensual organ" (252).

Lauren continues describing her dream, recalling that in spite of the fact that her father disappeared shortly before her family's home was destroyed, "in my dream, things have come right again. I'm at home, and my father is preaching" the parable of the talents (10–11). Lauren repeatedly interrupts her father's sermon, quoting him in fragment and interspersing his narration of the parable of the talents with her own commentary. She relates a few sentences from her father's recitation of the parable, following them with her observa-tions. After another two lines of her father's preaching, Lauren interjects her own remarks again (14). Indicating her aspiration to minister and protect her community differently than her father, Lauren comments on her father's reci-tation of the parable but does not hear his discourse on it: "There is preaching between the bits of the parable, but I can't quite understand it. . . . I can't catch the words—except for the words of the parable" (14). This fragmented nightmare implies that Lauren does not just associate her father's ministry with a parable that encourages saving souls through ministry but that he failed to "save" her family from the destruction of the Pox. Lauren's father preaches the last sentences of the parable: "But from him that hath not shall be taken away even that which he hath," and then she writes that "when my father has said these words, my mother vanishes" from the dream (15). This marks the dream's transition into a nightmare in which her family members disappear. Her narrative suggests that losing her family and home has something to do with her father's ministerial inadequacy.

In Lauren's dream, her mother disappears immediately after her father speaks the parable's final, ominous warning. She seems to be "taken away" as a result of her husband or his language, a real-time playing out of the parable that demonstrates what happens to religious patriarchs who fail to boldly invest their faith. Due to the sequence of events in Lauren's dream, it is clear that she partially holds her father responsible for not rising to the occasion to protect his family. In Larkin's later commentary on Lauren's journals, she writes of her mother that "she [Lauren] saw her father's error when he could not see it—his dependence on walls and guns, religious faith, and a hope that the good old days would return" (138). His decision to remain in a walled city and rely on faith alone, rather than the initiative to move or change, reflects a lack of risk that Lauren repudiates. Just as Lauren interrupts her father's preaching in her dream, Earthseed interrupts her father's understanding of religion and survival to attempt something different, something itinerant and risky. Her ministry is predicated on freedom from authoritarian, patriarchal immovability, privileging instead action, risk, and eventual itinerancy that leads to erotic pedagogy.

However, Lauren does not just challenge her father's religion. Her desire to minister differently than her father is also a desire to minister differently than Christian America, in part because both her father's and Christian America's ideologies are rooted in patriarchal Abrahamic hierarchy. Lauren points out that the "demagogue" "Jarret . . . has a voice that's a whole-body experience, the way my father's was. . . . Jarret was once a Baptist minister like my father," explicitly drawing attention to their likeness (20). Lauren's father's ministry and Christian America are different expressions of a similar hierarchical, masculinist might; Lauren's father is static and immoveable, while Christian America (its ideology in general and the Crusaders in particular) is actively violent and destructive.[4]

Earthseed resists this masculinist violence by embracing change, vulnerability, and collective equality. Such qualities are modeled through leadership and worship. Acorn residents host weekly Earthseed gatherings, and the sermon is given by volunteers who read verses and initiate discussion rather than giving a sermon (347). When Lauren's Christian brother Marc visits Acorn, he is critical of Earthseed's God, Change. He corrects a follower, saying, "Even you believe your God doesn't change. Your God promotes change, but he stays the same," which elicits community responses like "God *is* change," "God *promotes* nothing," and "Our God isn't male. Change has no sex" (150; italics in original). At the level of grammar, Earthseed followers correct Marc's vision of God from a sovereign entity that does or acts upon to a God that is the action. They emphasize that Change does not differentiate subject from predicate, illuminating the hierarchies summoned when someone or something is separated from what it acts upon. Insisting on a pure God maintains the Christian foundational story that positions God as supreme authority, separate in his position above all.

Earthseed challenges masculinist might and exclusionary binaries through vulnerability as Lauren refuses to be static and is unwilling to be contained. Before the Crusaders attack Acorn, Lauren and her husband, Bankole, conceive their first child. Bankole suggests they move to the safer walled city of Halstead, but Lauren will not leave Acorn to be cloistered in an enclosed city. This is unsurprising, considering that Lauren wrote the Earthseed verse "Ignorance / protects itself. / Ignorance promotes suspicion . . . Suspicious, afraid, / Ignorance / Protects itself, / And protected / Ignorance grows" (207). Lauren's husband thinks she is irrational for refusing to move to the "long established, yet modern, familiar, and isolated" city; her friend advises her to go for her baby's sake (139, 146). Unmoved, Lauren reasons that "Halstead is like Robledo with a better wall" (145). As Lauren writes in Earthseed, walled cities embody the "Ignorance" that defends itself by keeping out difference and change. This is the stasis embodied by her father, the same fear of difference or change that characterizes walled cities. Instead of reforming society, Christian American and thus Abrahamic ideology foster privatized, walled cities and then police a boundary between (heathen) outsider and insider.[5] Lauren values the work she does in Acorn above any promise of increased security; as she reflects, "I wouldn't walk away from it [Acorn] any more than I'd walk away from the baby I would soon be having" (145). Counter to values that would equate child-rearing with privatized safety, Lauren refuses the fixed security that would also separate her from the outside world or her community.

Before addressing another appearance of the parable of the talents in the novel, I turn briefly to a scholar who also takes an interest in Lauren's relationship to her father. Whereas I argue that Lauren challenges the traditional ministry of her father, Mathias Nilges insists that Earthseed is an escapist, "nostalgic" movement that in mourning the loss of stability (the "laws of the father") re-creates totalitarian authority (1340). Nilges writes that Lauren is "the leader of the group, filling the role of the absent father herself. As the leader of the group, Lauren makes decisions, assigns roles, and provides the group with structure and order" (1343–1344). Here, Nilges conflates leadership and ambition with masculinity or the paternal. On the other hand, I see Lauren leading her community because she believes Earthseed is humanity's only chance to survive and because the religion is her invention. Nilges's reading is predicated on his understanding of Earthseed as a capitulation to "post-fordist"[6] instability that frames Earthseed's embrace of change as complicity with the violent chaos of the Pox. In my view, however, Earthseed's acceptance of flux upends the rigidity of Abrahamic hierarchy. If Lauren's religion valued the disorder of post-Fordist culture, as Nilges suggests, then it would support the Crusader raids, the sex slave trade, and the anarchic violence that Earthseed opposes. In fact, Earthseed is Lauren's solution to these problems; not only does Lauren attempt to comfort and teach individuals who have been traumatized by postapocalyptic violence, but Earthseed doctrine counters anarchic, amorphous violence and the abstract, unregulated greed that fuels it.

We can see these doctrines by attending to another appearance of the parable of the talents in Butler's novel. Here, the parable offers insight into the way that Earthseed privileges finite material bodies and rejects the abstraction of value. Analysis of the parable here clarifies Earthseed's valuation of material life and imminent bodies, anticipating the way that touch and holding are Lauren's dominant modes of ministry, as opposed to her father's use of commanding sound, authority, and the appeal to triumph. The last pages of *Talents* are a journal entry from 2090 followed by a scriptural citation of the parable of the talents. In this journal entry, the eighty-year-old Lauren watches rockets filled with Earthseed followers blast off to fulfill the Destiny (living on another planet). Lauren writes in this last scene that "the Destiny of Earthseed is to take root among the stars, after all, and not to be filled with preservative poisons, boxed up at great expense . . . and buried uselessly in some cemetery" (407). Then, Lauren's journal entry ends, and the italicized parable of the talents concludes the novel: "*For the kingdom of heaven is as a man traveling into a far country, who called his own servants, and delivered unto them his goods*" (407). The parable is printed in its entirety, complete with citation: "The Bible/Authorized King James Version/St. Matthew 2:14–30" (408). It's unclear whether the parable is reproduced by Lauren in her journal, whether it is appended at the end by Larkin (who compiles Lauren's journals), or whether an even farther removed, implied narrator provides this reiteration. We ought to pay attention to the irony of biblical scripture cited from an "authorized" source by a narrator who is difficult to identify. Earthseed has no interest in knowledge that comes from the top of the hierarchy or from a sovereign figure whose claim to be the source of that knowledge is exclusively his or her own. Here we can see *Talents*' rootedness in womanist theology, as Earthseed contests traditional Christian epistemologies that categorize and hierarchize Western religions as such.

This final reference to the parable of the talents underscores Earthseed as an imminent, material religion committed to preserving yet moving bodies by holding them on Earth and sending them to other planets. Lauren's interpretation of the parable offers us a critique of neoliberal capitalism in which intimacy and touch redeem the idea of keeping or holding. This critique is evidenced by Lauren's statement that "my talent . . . is Earthseed. And although I haven't buried it in the ground, I have buried it here in these coastal mountains" (21). A literal, pecuniary interpretation of the parable (rather than a theological reading that emphasizes the investment of transcendent faith) reveals that the talent, or whatever is invested, holds its value through scarcity. As a unit of currency, the talent has a finite limit (however large that limit may be) since capital is predicated on material existence and thus eventual scarcity. Such an interpretation reveals that Earthseed understands bodies to be limited since they are threatened by Crusaders and the conditions of the apocalypse. When Lauren writes that she buried her talent in the mountains at her commune Acorn, she highlights the fact that Earthseed is designed to maintain rather than increase these valuable bodies. *Talents* does not see the third servant's burial of his talent as a mistake. Earthseed redeems the third servant in its critique of the neoliberal capitalism that thrives on the abstraction of value. Since Lauren's religion privileges materiality, it is not interested in potential interest that creates abstract surplus value; nor does it care for projected or speculated increase. Earthseed reflects Lauren's attempt to relieve the world of the devastation of patriarchal, neoliberal capitalism in that rather than valuing the surplus that can be gained from bodies, Earthseed values the bodies just as they are in their precarious scarcity.

Erotic Pedagogy and the Freedom of Reflexive Touch

Once the Crusaders attack Acorn, they turn it into a labor gulag called Camp Christian. When Lauren escapes, she disguises herself as a man for safety and travels north with the traumatized Len. Len tells Lauren that, earlier, she had been kidnapped for ransom. Her "captors had kept her awhile for sex" and then deserted her since her family did not care enough to pay for her release (345). Len asks ashamedly, "Do I seem normal to you?" To which Lauren answers, "We're survivors, Len. . . . We're all wounded. We're healing as best we can. And no, we're not normal. Normal people wouldn't have survived what we've survived" (346). When Len begins to cry, Lauren "just held her. . . . When had anyone last held her and let her cry? I held her" (346). Lauren's emphasis of the word "held" reveals how important touch, bodily support, and intimate comfort are to erotic pedagogy. Lauren knows that part of Len's pain is not just the trauma itself but bearing it alone for so long. Her embrace assures Len that Lauren can comfort her and relate to her. It models the basis for cultivating community out of loss: the two women are in intimate proximity, vulnerably physical together and no longer isolated. To shape others and God as Earthseed instructs, Lauren suggests, one must start by literally embracing and shaping other women. Immediately after being held, Len asks about Earthseed: "'If God is Change, then . . . then who loves us? Who cares about us? Who cares for us?' 'We care for one another,' I [Lauren] said," and then Lauren goes on to quote Earthseed (347).

The scene in which Lauren embraces Len primes the reader for the episode that follows shortly after with Nia. Lauren repeats her erotic pedagogy, serving as a metaphorical skin ego for Nia by providing her comfort and support. Eventually, Len and Lauren arrive at the house of Nia Cortez, who takes them up on their offer to do yard work for food. After doing work in Nia's garden, Lauren as a man offers to draw Nia. Lauren is a "sharer," which means that she was born with "hyperempathy syndrome," the "neurochemically induced illusion" that she feels the pain or pleasure that she sees someone else experience (11–12). So "drawing someone gives me [Lauren] an excellent excuse to study them and let myself feel what it seems to me that they feel. . . . Drawing a person helps me *become* that person, and . . . it helps me manipulate that person" (366; italics in original). Lauren writes that "she was lonely, Nia was. And she was taking an uncomfortable interest in me-as-a-man" (367). Lauren takes advantage of this, since it gives her "a chance to talk about Earthseed without seeming to proselytize. I [she] quoted verses as though quoting poetry to her" (367). The next day while Nia cooks in the kitchen, Lauren reveals that she is a woman. This deeply disappoints Nia, who was under the impression that Lauren was a compassionate man who might stay as a romantic partner (370). Lauren writes, "I went to her and hugged her and held her. Like Len, she needed to be hugged and held, needed to cry in someone's arms" (371). Again, Lauren emphasizes holding, demonstrating the bodily quality of the comfort that helps her free lonely, suffering women from the pain with which their postapocalyptic world has saddled them.

Lauren's embrace serves as a skin ego for Nia, since Lauren's body provides literal relief while also modeling conceptually the support of the community that Earthseed promises. Nia "needed" to be hugged and "to cry in someone's arms," because, in the language of Anzieu, the skin ego is the "mental image" of oneself "as an Ego containing psychical contents on the basis of its experience of the surface of the body" (40). Skin is the center of emotional well-being, responding to the psychic need for an "envelope" that contains and can accumulate a sense of fulfillment and safety (40). Nia "needed" to cry in Lauren's arms, Lauren suggests, because part of Nia's suffering is bearing her pain without any support. Lauren physically ameliorates this pain by moving to contain both Nia and her loneliness. As Lauren holds Nia, she separates Nia from a world that has become too difficult for her to process. In essence, Lauren envelops Nia's pain to give her a reprieve from having to sustain her own nurturance. Since the skin ego functions not just as a protective shield but as an interface, Lauren's embrace is both a supportive boundary as well as a means of communication with Nia (40). By virtue of wrapping Nia in a sense of safety, Lauren's embrace also signals to Nia that she can rest, that she can be comforted. This message also opens up an embodied space for Lauren to introduce Earthseed.

Erotic pedagogy's enveloping embrace plays on the semantic overlap of holding and shaping, tipping us off to the way that Earthseed's doctrine privileges a reflexivity that blurs the boundaries between people as separate subjects. In common usage the concepts of holding and shaping may sound like static and active words, respectively. While shaping connotes fashioning, or forming, holding suggests a seemingly passive support. But shaping a believer by holding her physically and emotionally takes advantage of the support of holding. In effect, holding is a strategic way of shaping in that one holds a less active entity with one's own exertion and in the shape of or at least dependent on the holder's body. To hold is to support physically and emotionally, and it is also to contain or mold. Lauren's erotic pedagogy models the reflexivity of Earthseed's principles, blurring the boundaries between herself and Nia. The way that Lauren serves as Nia's physical container reminds us that Earthseed, like the skin ego, is predicated on the dual function of shaping and being shaped. Where Earthseed proclaims that shaping the world involves being shaped by the world, the skin ego bears the traces of that which it protects the subject from, along with vestiges of the subject itself. The skin ego's receptivity to the world from which it shields its subject endows it with a reflexivity that models Earthseed's values. By virtue of embracing, Lauren and Nia are bound in mutual relation. As Nia's metaphorical skin ego, Lauren intends to make Nia feel protected from the world. Nevertheless, Lauren's touch is an interface, a surface onto which Nia too may "inscrib[e]" (Anzieu 40).

Such a mutually intimate relationship leads to an intimacy in which the women seduce each other. With Nia, Lauren's erotic pedagogy necessitates Lauren "becoming" Nia by gazing at her and then empathizing. She capitalizes on both Nia's feelings and her own hyperempathic abilities. When Lauren sketches Nia while reciting Earthseed verses to her, Nia is so charmed that even when she discovers that Lauren is a woman, Nia is disappointed and still wants to go to bed with her (371). As Lauren holds the crying Nia, she thinks "under different circumstances, I might have taken her to bed. . . . I had never been tempted to want to make love with a woman. Now, I found myself almost wanting to. And she almost wanted me to" (371). Instead, both women go on to have dinner with Len and discuss Earthseed. The next day, Lauren "kisses her [Nia's] lonely mouth" before leaving (373). Erotic pedagogy stirs sexual desire that Lauren decides to not act on in order to continue focusing on her ministry. This process begins at the level of separate gazing bodies, moves to reflexive gazes and feelings as self and other are integrated, and then culminates with intimately touching bodies, mutual desire, and a departing kiss. Once Nia is emancipated from her heavy feelings, and once the women mutually desire one another, Nia is absorbed into Lauren's Earthseed community.

Lauren reflects that "[by] the time we [she and Len] did leave, she [Nia] was as much with me as Len was" (372).

The doctrinal importance of the material body in Earthseed suggests that erotic pedagogy will do its more creative, important work through touch and that Len and Nia are "with" Lauren because Lauren held their bodies and feelings in ways that made her as vulnerable to them as they were to her. Rather than transcendent ideologies, imminent touch models physically the way Earthseed frees women of pain by bringing bodies together through reflexive trust. Bodies touch as touched beings who cannot interact without becoming part of a relation that alters them. Although Lauren initially shapes women by holding them, she is shaped as she embraces them, in effect being changed by them just as she changes them. While her father's religion privileged static transcendence and physical separation from the outside world, Lauren's ministry reflects the doctrinal outlook that physical separation from problems and suffering does nothing to fix either of them. Earthseed, via erotic pedagogy, insists that material problems call for material answers. One of these answers is freedom from traumatic suffering, freedom brought about by engaging first in tactile and then emotional intimacies that affect oneself as much as they affect others.

Standing in stark contrast to the conditions of the 2030s, Earthseed offers a sustainable, equitable way of life that liberates believers from the destructive, patriarchal hierarchies of *Talents'* postapocalyptic United States. Lauren ministers Earthseed to other women through erotic pedagogy, a practice of physical comfort and instruction that demonstrates the way skin, as a site of emotional well-being, offers a surface for releasing pain, offering protection, and modeling reflexive, trusting community building. As a wandering comforter-teacher-preacher, Lauren frees suffering women from the traumas of postapocalyptic life. Touching these women changes Lauren as much as it changes the women themselves, and through the reflexive intimacy, erotic pedagogy models Earthseed's value of the material body. Although Lauren's insistence that her religion will "take root among the stars" to colonize Mars seems to work against Earthseed's modality of comfort, the victory of the novel is that Lauren plants her sociopolitical seed of change on Earth rather than on Mars (276). Through erotic pedagogy, Lauren has given the conceptual stuff of Earthseed materiality. This frees her followers from their suffering, giving them the tools for a new way of life on Earth that has no need for hierarchy or rigidity. At the end of *Talents*, a wizened Lauren ruminates on the success of her religion: "Earthseed was always true. I've made it real, given it substance" (405). But Lauren is too modest; Earthseed was real, existing in the physical plane, the moment she began ministering to other women by touching them.

NOTES

1. This term is Aimee Carillo Rowe's.

2. Earthseed diverges from womanist theology in its embrace of the experiences of all women rather than privileging women of color only. As Keri Day notes, "Black feminist and womanist discourses have highlighted the material and cultural experiences of poor women of color around the world as these women disproportionately experience the fallout of neoliberal capitalism" (13). *Talents*, however, focuses on the experiences of white women and women of color.

3. Although the term *neoliberalism* signifies broadly, I define it as a move away from state provision and toward free market. Neoliberal policy allows market forces to control the economy. A concomitant shrinking public sector leads to privatization, increased competition, and widening social stratification as "social and economic inequality was [considered] necessary as a motor for social and economic progress" (Jones 9; see also Brown 21–22, 33; George; and Steger and Roy 1–5).

4. Marlene D. Allen notes, "Butler ingeniously depicts the white Jarret as the dark shadow of the black Laurence, reversing traditional gothic associations of blackness with evil, for it is Jarret who represents the more sinister aspects of historical Christianity" (1361).

5. As Gloria Azaldua has written, "borders and walls . . . are supposed to keep the undesirable ideas [and bodies] out. . . . The only 'legitimate' inhabitants are those in power" (101).

6. Although post-Fordism refers to an era after industrialization that coincides with neoliberalism, Nilges's affiliation he uses "post-fordist" rather than "neoliberal." I suspect that he uses "post-fordist" to describe the period as a phase in the history of capitalism, since his methodology is rooted in the Marxist French regulation school (Nilges 1333).

WORKS CITED

Allen, Marlene D. "Octavia Butler's Parable Novels and the 'Boomerang' of African American History." *Callaloo*, vol. 32, no. 4, 2009, pp. 1353–1365.

Anzieu, Didier. *The Skin Ego*. Yale University Press, 1989.

The Bible. Authorized King James Version, Oxford University Press, 1998.

Brisson, Carson E. "Between Text and Sermon: Matthew 25:14–30." *Interpretation*, vol. 56, no. 3, 2002, pp. 307–310.

Brown, Wendy. *Undoing the Demos: Neoliberalism's Stealth Revolution*. Zone Books, 2015.

Butler, Octavia. *Parable of the Sower*. Grand Central Publishing, 1993.

———. *Parable of the Talents*. Grand Central Publishing, 1998.

Day, Keri. *Religious Resistance to Neoliberalism: Womanist and Black Feminist Perspectives*. Palgrave Macmillan, 2016.

Floyd-Thomas, Stacey M. "Womanist Theology." *Liberation Theologies in the United States: An Introduction*, edited by Stacey M. Floyd-Thomas and Anthony B. Pinn, New York University Press, 2010, pp. 1–15.

Jones, Daniel Stedman. *Masters of the Universe: Hayek, Friedman, and the Birth of Neoliberal Politics*. Princeton University Press, 2014.

Kistemaker, Simon J. *The Parables: Understanding the Stories Jesus Told.* Baker Books, 1980.

Lloyd, Vincent. "Post-Racial, Post-Apocalyptic Love: Octavia Butler as Political Theologian." *Political Theology*, vol. 17, no. 5, Sept. 2016, pp. 449–464.

Lorde, Audre. *Sister Outsider: Essays and Speeches.* Crossing Press, 1984.

Nilges, Mathias. "'We Need the Stars': Change, Community, and the Absent Father in Octavia Butler's *Parable of the Sower* and *Parable of the Talents.*" *Callaloo*, vol. 32, no. 4, 2009, pp. 1332–1352.

Rowe, Aimee Carillo. "Erotic Pedagogies." *Journal of Homosexuality*, vol. 59, no. 7, 2012, pp. 1031–1056.

Spillers, Hortense J. "Moving on Down the Line: Variations on the African American Sermon." *Black, White, and in Color: Essays on American Literature and Culture,* University of Chicago Press, 2003, pp. 251–276.

Steger, Manfred B., and Ravi K. Roy. *Neoliberalism: A Very Short Introduction.* Oxford University Press, 2010.

Vinx, Lars. "Carl Schmitt." *The Stanford Encyclopedia of Philosophy* (Fall 2019 Edition), https://plato.stanford.edu/archives/fall2019/entries/schmitt/.

14

Black Women's Prophecy

O. E. Butler's Parables

PHYLLIS LYNNE BURNS

am going to indulge myself for just a moment, and I am not asking permission to think wistfully—I am pretty thoroughly convinced the "E" might possibly, could instead be "Extraterrestrial." Doesn't it just feel like Octavia E. Butler's imaginative visions suggest her personal acquaintance with outer-worldly entities and realms that exist beyond our confined notions of finite space and linear time? It would not surprise me at all to read an Octavia E. Butler biography to hear a relative or close family friend recall how elders would declare with surety—"She's been here before"—to describe their young one's aura. I choose to believe those of you who have "been here before" make return trips to this plane of existence to help us survive, if not find pathways out of this damned cultured Hell.

Within Octavia E. Butler's worlds, the complexity of Black women and girls is neither diminished nor made backdrop because we do not exist simply to help others find the importance of themselves at our expense. With Octavia E. Butler's science fiction and dystopian narratives *I am, we are*, active decision makers who comprehend the necessity of collective work and partnership. Octavia E. Butler is the first Black woman science fiction / fantasy author I ever read, and like most of you who have gravitated to this collection of contemplations about Butler's *oeuvre*, I was mesmerized by her imagination. It was also Butler's stories that inspired me to reconsider the speculative and dystopian literary genre.

I understand dystopian literature to feature key elements: The story is set in a distant, distinct future whose inhabitants are anxious about a lamented past. When we enter the narrative, society has already nose-dived into an abysmal, if not apocalyptic, state because we have persistently failed to learn from mistakes of our own making; thus, readers are immediately situated amid an aftermath. The protagonist is driven by the twin forces of fear and hope because they desperately forge on, usually by their lonesome, to escape the sinister reality. And while the dystopian narrative could be mistaken for a prophetic, cautionary tale, it instead depicts present-day atrocities steeped in the uncanny and unfamiliar. Dystopian texts are observations or critiques about the here and now. Yet something curious, perhaps even contradictory, emerges with a dystopian narrative. This time displacement of the contemporary world prompts a safe distance while inviting the reader to move in closer to understand the main character's existential crisis. I think it is fair to assert that the reader is expected to comprehend what compels the protagonist, to hope the main character finds some solace or that the hellscape will eventually dismantle. Thus, I feel for and sit with Winston (*1984*) who waits panic-stricken in the Ministry of Love while he thinks about the individualized, made-to-order terrors that reside in Room 101. When the man and boy (*The Road*) trudge through the bitterly cold glaucoma-dimming world, my fear is gratefully, although briefly, abated once the father "finds everything" to extend their survival. The Christian, white-supremacist regime's state-sanctioned misogyny (*The Handmaid's Tale*) engineered by the Old Testament–based Sons of Jacob enrages me. Dystopian literature implores us to acknowledge the myriad ways our humanity can be threatened, presently and potentially. Moreover, the dystopian narrative announces that we are all in *this* together or that our shared humanity dictates we should be. These tales are about our shared and equally troubled humanity, our universal humanness. The meditation and inquiry regarding empathy foreground these narratives, which attempt to depict our affinity, our universality.

However, when I read dystopian texts by white authors, I am contorted. I am compressed. I have to somehow squeeze my complex Black female self into narratives in order to accommodate an affinity that is never reciprocal for Black female identities. Dystopian narratives offer pronouncements about our shared human predicaments, but within these expressions concerning humanity's salvation, depictions of Black females as reduced entities are so ubiquitous it seems that North America's ritualized misogynoir is sanctioned rather than contested. Moya Bailey coined the term "misogynoir," and Butler's literature rescues us from the textual barracoon situated in dystopian literature. So if and when a dystopian novel is authored by a Black woman, and a Black woman or girl provides the central voice and perspective, I sigh with some relief even while immersed within chaos.

I am compelled to think about how a Black feminist analysis of Butler's novels redirects, even calls out, the universal utility of Black women within contemporary, celebrated dystopian narratives that focus on the oppression of women within theological structures. We can discuss how Lauren Oya Olamina of Butler's Earthseed series is a nuanced persona whose innate empathy empowers her to simultaneously speak for her individual self and respect everyone's personhood. This Black female protagonist relies on interdependency to cocreate solutions, and Lauren Oya Olamina refuses to serve as savior for everyone else except herself.

Keeanga-Yamahtta Taylor, in *How We Get Free: Black Feminism and the Combahee River Collective* (CRC), helps clarify these assertions, which will also be supported by a close read of Lauren Oya Olamina (*Parable of the Sower* and *Parable of the Talents*). And, since I read Butler's Earthseed series as dystopian text to be compared to dystopian narratives authored by white authors who depict Black women transfixed in a theocracy, I focus on Margaret Atwood's characters Rita and Cora (*The Handmaid's Tale*) and Rebecca Eckler (*The Year of the Flood* and *MaddAddam*). Of course I'm aware Rita, Cora, and Rebecca are not main characters. The three characters are so similar they warrant our attention given this line of inquiry. Equally, reaching into these texts about the future that consider humankind's fate though a woman's perspective provides space to compare how Black women either flourish or wither, respectively, within the pastoral, spiritual, and religious-based communities of Butler's Acorn and Atwood's Gilead and God's Gardeners.

Taylor explains how the name Combahee honors Harriet Tubman's emancipation activism and, in particular, Tubman's ingenious strategy that made possible the successful 1853 raid on South Carolina's Combahee River, which liberated 750 enslaved people of African descent. Tubman, as we know, freed herself, and her self-liberation enabled her to lead numerous women, men, and children out of chattel bondage. Akin to Tubman, CRC women, who organized in 1974, focused on crafting theory to help identify and navigate escape routes for Black women in the United States. CRC women understood that a recognition of the multiple oppressions imposed on Black women living in a white-supremacist–patriarchal regime has been obscured through various attempts to challenge white-male dominance. White feminism is culpable when it consigns sexism to be universally applied in equal measure and, in doing so, ignores white women's racial privilege, a move that conceptualizes sexism to be unmediated by racism. Within this frame, we should recall Audre Lorde proclaiming to white feminist how "the master's tools will never dismantle the master's house." Taylor also discusses how mainstream discourse co-opts, as it conveniently ignores vocabulary originally articulated by Black women activists to specify systemic oppressions imposed specifically on *all* Black women. Taylor takes the example of mainstream appropriation and sometimes recognition of Kimberley Crenshaw's coined term "intersectionality." Taylor points out for our edification that

> the CRC did articulate the analysis that animates the meaning of intersectionality, the idea that multiple oppressions reinforce each other to create new categories of suffering. The CRC described oppressions as interlocking or happening simultaneously thus creating new measures of oppression and inequality. In other words, Black women could not quantify their oppression only in terms of sexism, or racism, or of homophobia experienced by Black lesbians. They were not ever a single category but it was the merging or enmeshment of those identities that compounded how Black women experienced oppression. (Taylor 00:08:01–00:08:52)

CRC's concept of "interlocking oppressions" has theoretical antecedents. Taylor acknowledges Frances M. Beal's "double jeopardy" definition of Black women's predicaments, which, in turn, is preceded by Anna Julia Cooper's 1892 insight: "The Colored woman of today occupies a unique position in this country. She is confronted by both a woman question and a race problem, and is as yet, an unknown or unacknowledged factor in both" (Taylor 00:09:12–00:09:32).

Lauren Oya Olamina is compelling. She is a dynamic and nuanced Black female character whose multiple dimensions are rare in dystopian narratives. Equally important, this Black female identity attempts to comprehend the world according to her unique perspective. We are introduced to Lauren through first-person narration while she writes in her journal. Lauren, who "lives in a tiny, walled, fish-bowl cul-de-sac community," further explains how the world restricts her life, and through this assessment, she both dreams and theorizes (Butler 00:20:49–00:20:54). From the beginning the fifteen-year-old Black girl evaluates the surrounding world in order to consider possible escapes. Our protagonist begins her story in Robledo, California, in the year 2024—a distant future from when Butler published *Parable of the Sower* in 1993. Lauren tells us that her multicultured community eventually organizes nightly, armed patrols to protect residents and property that are all situated in a cul-de-sac. The community is literally and figuratively backed up against a wall and residents desperately try, to no avail, to defend their lives against outside predations. While Lauren describes how the world beyond her walled community is physically lethal, she also details what perils her interior life.

Death and destruction always lie in wait beyond the cul-de-sac. One early morning, when members of Lauren's community arm themselves and ride their bicycles to venture into the ominous "out there" to attend church for her baptism, she remembers seeing so many unhoused people sleeping and waking up on the "cracked streets." She writes how during this journey she saw "*at least* three people who weren't going to wake up again, ever. One of them was headless" (Butler 00:12:30–00:12:37; italics added). She also sees within this ghastly tableau "a woman, young, naked and filthy," who, appearing to be either drunk or dazed, stumbles pass the churchgoers, which prompts the fifteen-year-old Lauren to surmise: "Maybe [the woman] had been raped so much she was crazy. I heard stories of that happening" (00:12:45–00:13:03). Lauren's life within the cul-de-sac is made difficult because her father is both a Baptist minister and pastor of the "tiny, walled-in, fish-bowl community." Although Lauren wants to please her father by being baptized, the religion and ritual have become hollow for the preacher's daughter. Lauren's world perceptions, mediated by her innate (dis)ability, lead her to disavow Christianity. Lauren cultivates a new spirituality that she names Earthseed, and its text, *The Books of the Living*, contains, for lack of a better word, comprehensions, not scriptures, about the connection and continuation of life. Lauren understands that all within the natural world are transformative. All life is united, cyclical, and therefore eternally interdependent. The primary Earthseed comprehension articulated within Lauren Oya Olamina's *Books of the Living* asserts, "All that you touch you change. All that you change changes you. The only lasting truth is change. God is change" (Butler 00:01:19–00:01:34).

Lauren, as I note earlier, writes about a recurring dream. This repeated vision of "terror and joy" symbolizes her ongoing struggles to control how she is able to both exist and move in the world. It is important to note that within her dreams Lauren is teaching herself how to stand upright and float above the ground. She is teaching herself because Lauren lives in a society where no one exists to help her make her life anew, to adapt to possibility, to be self-empowered and untethered to a theology or world structured to restrain her. Lauren notes how in each dream episode she is able to improve her ability to rise above, to transcend. Yet when she attempts to escape the room by floating through a doorway that glows with cool, pale light, she instead loses control and gravitates into a wall of fire that swallows her.

Lauren says she is "the most vulnerable person she knows" (00:19:51–00:19:54). This proclamation about herself is not a self-absorbed utterance of teenage angst. Lauren inherited from her mother the (dis)ability to "collect other peoples' misery" *and* pleasure. Lauren is able to speak for and about herself: "I feel what I see others feeling or what I believe they feel. Hyperempathy is what the doctors call an organic delusional syndrome. Big shit. It hurts, that's all I know" (Butler 00:20:03–00:20:15). Ironically, a capacity to connect with others makes hyperempaths social pariahs. On one hand, empaths have to hide their ability because they exist in a sadistic culture. Pain is omnipresent in a nation where people are frightened prey. On the other hand, hyperempaths, or "sharers," are taught to be ashamed about their condition. Lauren and other sharers developed hyperempathy syndrome during gestation. Their mothers became addicted to the "Einstein" designer drug developed to boost the users' mental capacity. I contend that Butler created hyperempathy syndrome, in part, to critique one of the many ways American culture routinely vilifies and afflicts Black women. Beginning in the 1980s, Americans, lay and medical, bemoaned the arrival of "crack babies"—infants born by Black women who struggled with an addiction to crack cocaine. And when the "crack epidemic" was generally considered yet another testament to Black people's degenerative nature, it gave rise to racist government policies, which paved the way for an increased police state and incarceration rates all designed to devastate our Black communities and families. And guess what? Black crack babies never materialized, but their imagined existence was all that was needed to feed and replenish the racist-sexist psychosis of white America. Summarizing her empathy syndrome, Lauren proclaims, "I get a lot of grief that doesn't belong to me and it isn't real, but it hurts" (Butler 00:20:26–00:20:32).

Toni Morrison provides incisive analysis regarding the United States' literary landscape. Morrison theorizes that white authors often engage a "code." The white literary imagination proceeds from a premise that it is "unraced," which affords white authors the privilege to "take for granted the centrality of their experience because it is white" (Morrison 23:46–23:51). At the risk of making the term circular, this *universal* whiteness within literature is not vacuum sealed since the code echoes societal expectations, which Brittney Cooper describes as follows:

> Before we learn to fully love ourselves all People of Color in the United States learn we are supporting characters and spectators in the collective stories of white peoples' lives. The stories we watch and read ask us to put aside their whiteness and relate to their very universal struggles around conflicts with the world, the self and others. The problem is that only their experiences are treated as universal. (01:17:38–01:18:03)

Let us consider how Cooper's analysis can be placed in stark relief through contemplation of Lauren's hyperempathy syndrome. According to Cooper, "before we begin to fully love ourselves," Black people in the United States are expected to relate to the concerns and dilemmas of whites. Tucked inside this idea of relatability to whiteness are deplorable images of blackness. The idea of whiteness is built upon a rejection of blackness. Hyperempathy syndrome forces Lauren's body to share, to take in, the pain and pleasure of others. The condition makes Lauren become relatable, even if the relatable occurrence is horrifically antithetical to her being. For example, when white men, members of Jared's Crusaders, enslave Acorn residents, they begin raping Acorn women and girls. Lauren, if she is raped, will simultaneously experience her pain *and* the pleasure the assailant(s) derive(s) from brutally assaulting her personhood. Therefore, to "relate" to whiteness as Cooper defines it, also includes a level of self-negation for Black people. Moreover, within the white-as-universal mind-set, echoed in the white literary code, Black people are put to work. According to Morrison, Black characters "appear in a scene for no reason other than to provide the tension that might suggest illegal sexuality or violence" (Morrison 24:31–24:45).

Before we begin to unpack how Morrison's and Cooper's analyses applies to Atwood's characters, I want to emphasize the code's operation. Black characters are most often introduced as Black and this state of blackness reverberates. If the white character, similar to the author, is universal and unraced, the reader is made aware of a "nonwhite" character's racial designation quite deliberately during the initial introduction of the nonwhite character. Equally, this position of nonwhiteness makes the character hyperstatic—even beyond conventional formulations of a flat character. The nonwhite character only exists, I assert, as an unrelatable, perpetually isolated, antiuniversal character. Rita, Cora, and Rebecca are virtually interchangeable. All three women are domestic workers consigned to a life of constant servitude—a state of being for Black women that has, historically, comforted mainstream America. (I wonder how many American households still keep Aunt Jemima in their kitchens?) Our introduction to Rita and Rebecca announces their race and/or ethnicity. Cora, Rita, and Rebecca each exists in a world wherein her exclusion is an integral part of the world order. When they appear, their presence is utilized, as Morrison emphasizes, to evoke unspeakable sexual transgressions and assaults on human bodies. These assertions invite close reads.

Offred descends the staircase, stops in front of the mirror, looks at herself, but doesn't make note of her own whiteness. Yet when Offred enters the kitchen, she describes how she and Rita possibly mirror each other because of their Handmaid and Martha uniforms. It is through this uniformity that Offred explains Rita's difference of nonwhiteness: "[Rita] puts on the veil to go outside, but nobody much cares who sees the face of a Martha. [Rita's] sleeves are rolled to the elbow showing her brown arms" (Atwood, *Handmaid's Tale* 00:12:34–00:12:45). Later in the chapter, Offred laments an imagined past. Offred recalls a supposed past when women, all women, equal in rank and station, were able to easily, leisurely sit around a kitchen table, no less, to share with one another. Offred wants to join Rita and Cora in conversation, despite calling Rita "surly." Offred also wants to know what takes place in Gilead households, and to this end, in adherence to the code, she explains:

> The Marthas know things. They talk among themselves, passing the unofficial news from house to house. I've heard them at it some-times, caught whiffs of their private conversations. "Stillborn, it was." Or, "Stabbed her with a knitting needle right in the belly. Jealousy, it must have been, eating her up." Or, tantalizingly, "It was toilet cleaner she used. Worked like a charm, though you'd think he'd of tasted it. Must've been that drunk; but they found her out all right." (Atwood, *Handmaid's Tale* 00:16:22–00:17:04)

Again, the code is followed within Rebecca's introduction. Readers are introduced to Rebecca through the narrator's focus on Toby, a young white woman, when she recalls her conversation with Rebecca, an older Black woman. Rebecca warns Toby about their manager, who is a serial rapist:

> Rebecca Eckler, who worked Toby's shift, told her about him right away. "Stay off his radar," she said. "Maybe you'll be okay—he's doin that girl Dora, and he mostly does just the one at a time, and you're kinda scrawny and he likes the curvy butts. But if he tells you to come to the office, look out. He's really jealous. He'll take a girl apart."
> "Has he asked you?" said Toby. "To the office?"
> "Praise the Lord and spit," said Rebecca. "I'm too black and ugly for him, plus he just likes the kittens, not the old cats. Maybe you should wrinkle yourself up, sweetheart. Knock out a few of your teeth."
> "You're not ugly," said Toby. Rebecca was in fact beautiful in a substantial way, with her brown skin and red hair and Egyptian nose.
> "I don't mean ugly like that," said Rebecca. "Ugly to deal with. He knows I'd get Blackened Redfish onto him, and they're one mean gang. Plus, maybe the Wolf Isaiahists. Way too much grief." (Atwood, *Year of Flood* 01:02:46–01:03:53)

Atwood's descriptions of Rebecca border on the comically flat—her "brown skin and red hair and Egyptian nose" and her overwhelming "ugliness"—

especially in contrast with the rich interior and morally complex exterior lives of Butler's protagonists. Lauren Olamina, Lilith Iyapo, and Butler's other Black female characters bring life to the complexities and beauty of Black female experience rather than ciphering it as a contrast bringing life to other characters. The richness of these characters brings full life to Butler's dystopian fiction.

WORKS CITED

Atwood, Margaret. *The Handmaid's Tale.* Narrated by Claire Danes et al., Audible, 2012. Audiobook.

————. *The Year of the Flood.* Narrated by Bernadette Dune et al., Audible, 2009. Audiobook.

Butler, Octavia E. *Parable of the Sower.* Narrated by Lynne Thigpen, Recorded Books, 2009. Audiobook.

————. *Parable of the Talents.* Narrated by Patricia R. Floyd et al., Recorded Books, 2009. Audiobook.

Cooper, Britney. *Eloquent Rage: A Black Feminist Discovers Her Superpower.* Narrated by Brittney Cooper. Audible, 2018. Audiobook.

Morrison, Toni. *The Source of Self-Regard: Selected Essays, Speeches, and Meditations.* Narrated by Bahni Turpin, Random House Audio, 2019. Audiobook.

Taylor, Keeanga-Yamahtta. *How We Get Free: Black Feminism and the Combahee River Collective.* Narrated by Renee Pitts. Audible, 2018. Audiobook.

15

The Violence of Making America Great Again

Religion, Power, and Vulnerable Bodies in Octavia Butler's Parable of the Talents

Michael Brandon McCormack

Choose your leaders
   with wisdom and forethought.
To be led by a coward
   is to be controlled
   by all that the coward fears.
To be led by a fool
   is to be led
   by the opportunists
   who control the fool.
To be led by a thief
   is to offer up
   your most precious treasures
   to be stolen.
To be led by a liar
   is to ask
   to be told lies.
To be led by a tyrant
   is to sell yourself
   and those you love
   into slavery.
      —*Parable of the Talents*

During the unlikely campaign, and after the unimaginable election, of Donald J. Trump, popular online media outlets published an array of articles insisting, "Octavia warned us!": "When Science Fiction Becomes Real: Octavia E. Butler's Legacy" (Caldwell), "Octavia Butler Predicted a Trump Presidency 20 Years Ago" (Jones), and "Octavia Butler's 1998 Dystopian Novel Features a Fascistic Presidential Candidate Who Promises to 'Make America Great Again'" (Open) were just a few of the titles that sprung up on the internet in the aftermath of the election. As such headlines suggest, most of these journalistic articles focused on Butler's stunning "prediction" of Trump's presidential candidacy and election. On the day after the election, one writer opined, with somewhat understated astonishment, "This might be the worst day of the year, and late science-fiction writer Octavia Butler predicted this day would come" (Jones). Shortly after the inauguration, another writer presented a far more dramatic account: "We are living in a nightmare. . . . Is this fiction or reality? Thank the goddesses of clear-eyed prophecy for the black science-fiction writer, Octavia Butler, who foresaw this moment and created guidance for us" (Brown).

To be sure, Butler's description of social and political realities in *Parable of the Sower* (1993) and *Parable of the Talents* (1998), which mirror certain aspects of the present historical moment, seems almost clairvoyant. Set in a postapocalyptic United States, between 2032 and 2035, *Parable of the Talents* is a dystopian narrative of the rise of a violently repressive right-wing religious extremist movement. Radicalized members of the Far Right religious sect Christian America, mostly young white men (though there were significant minority exceptions), who were previously fringe members of society, are emboldened by the rise of their leader, Texas senator Andrew Steele Jarret. As a former fundamentalist preacher turned fascist presidential candidate, Jarret's xenophobic campaign rhetoric threatens to banish ungodly "pagans," "heathens," and "savages" and promises to "Make America Great Again." Inspired, or incited, as it were, by the Jarret campaign's rhetorical violence against those it demonized as reprehensible others, and cast as enemies of the state, Jarret supporters enact all manner of vigilante and mob violence. The horrifying results are beatings, burnings, rape, raids of minority communities, captivity, concentration camps, forced separation of children from their parents, new forms of technologically enhanced slavery, and death.

Considering the violently xenophobic discourses, practices, and policies associated with Trump's presidential campaign and administration, and the emboldening of his white/Christian/nationalist supporters, it is not surprising that casual readers and critics alike have described Octavia Butler's Parables using the religious language of prophecy. However, Butler resisted descriptions of her Parables as prophecy. With reference to *Parable of the Talents*, Butler insisted, "This was not a book about prophecy. . . . This was a cautionary tale, although people have told me it was prophecy. All I have to say to this is: I certainly hope not" (337). Alternatively, Butler claimed, "The idea in *Parable of the Sower* and *Parable of the Talents* . . . is to look at where we are now, what we are doing now, and to consider where some of our current behaviors and unattended problems might take us" (337). Not prophecy but "cautionary tales," warnings of what *might* come to pass "if this continues"— if we should fail to make radical sociopolitical interventions and fundamentally reimagine what it means to be human *in the here and now.*

In the public imagination, prophecy is often conceived, narrowly, as a religious mode of predicting the future. It is not surprising, then, that Butler would be wary of such ascriptions of prophecy. She had no pretentions of divine foresight; nor did she make claims to divinatory powers of fortune-telling. Perhaps, however, more scholarly descriptions of prophecy—especially those that emphasize its historical development as a performative mode of sociopolitical and cultural criticism that has been strategically deployed in Black religious, political, intellectual, and artistic traditions—might be better aligned with Butler's own description of her literary work in the Parables. For instance, in *American Prophecy: Race and Redemption in American Political Culture*, George Shulman reminds us that biblical prophets "speak in registers of announcing, bearing witness, and warning to address crucial dimensions of politics" (14). But Shulman goes further to trace an American tradition of prophecy that includes such figures as Martin Luther King Jr., James Baldwin, and Toni Morrison, whom he sees as "not only 'American' critics recasting prophecy to oppose white supremacy, but political thinkers reworking redemptive language to foster political life" (178). Shulman's American prophecy involves a tradition of intellectuals and artists who draw on and rework prophecy as poetic, political, and performative speech acts that warn the nation of impending doom, while also challenging the nation to live up to its best possibilities.

When conceptualized as poetic performances that critique contemporary issues of oppression and suffering, as well as practices of bearing witness to the possibilities for alternative futures, the adjectival rendering of "prophetic" seems to be an apt description of Butler's work, indeed. After all, even if her aim was not prediction, Butler was most certainly asking us to gaze with her into her vision of possible futures. Through her Parables, Butler asks us to consider, "What sort of future are we creating? Is it the kind of future you want to live in? If it isn't, what can we do to create a better future?" (*Sower* 341). Consistent with the central argument developed throughout this volume in different ways and across sections and individual chapters, I argue that Octavia Butler offers a prophetic vision of the interplay between religion, violence, healing, and liberation that not only warns of potentially apocalyptic fates but also offers possibilities for more liberating futures.

Along these lines, this chapter explores Butler's prophetic vision in *Parable of the Talents*, focusing particular attention on her warnings concerning the violent interplay between fundamentalism and fascism. More specifically, the chapter draws on the "affective turn" in the academic study of religion in order to explore Butler's representation of the violent ways the relationships between religion, power, and (vulnerable) bodies are *felt* in *Talents*. The significance of such a reading becomes clearer considering the protagonist Lauren Olamina's hyperempathy syndrome, which heightens her experiences of the ways affects, emotions, and physical sensations (especially pain) surge through bodies. Finally, the chapter draws on the postmodern womanist theology of Monica A. Coleman and the writings of the activist-healer adrienne maree brown, to briefly sketch Butler's prophetic imaginings of possibilities for survival, care, and healing in the wake of violence and death.

In *Parable of the Talents*, Butler warns of unimaginable violence unleashed on the bodies of those rendered vulnerable by the interplay between religious and political extremism. Though the violence of Christian America culminates in futuristic modes of enslavement, torture, rape, burning, and slaughter of "alien" bodies, *Talents* narrates the perpetuation of a centuries-old violence bound up with the very conceptualization of religion and the hierarchical categorization and domination of its racialized Others. As such, Butler's vision is consistent with the insights of critical theorists of religion, who have deconstructed the ideological workings of religion as a supposedly *sui generis* phenomenon ascribed to the "civilized" and used to denounce as "savage" those "primitives" imagined to be lacking the morality presumed to be inculcated through religion.

Critical theorists of religion have demonstrated the violent history of how "religion worked in lockstep with the very idea of differentiating the civilized from the primitive (a distinction critical to the discourse of race in the Western world)" (Glaude 19). On the later parenthetical point, Eddie S. Glaude Jr., a scholar of African American religion, notes "the very concept of religion played a critical role in fortifying racial meanings about newly encountered people" (19). In other words, contact, conquest, captivity, and colonizing have been deeply intertwined with the categorization and valuation of religion and with the racialization, demonization, and subjugation of religion's/religious Others.

Parable of the Talents offers a prophetic critique of near-futuristic developments of this centuries-old form of violence. Christian America perpetuates such violence through religious discourse and practices that signify as Other, inferior, and dangerous those who do not conform to an extremely narrow categorization of "Christian" belief and practice or assimilate to an equally narrow conceptualization of "America(n)" identity. In *Talents*, Christian America represents an ethno-nationalist religious extremist movement intent on resisting "change," which is symbolized by the perceived "invasion" of racialized religious Others. "Change" is a central trope throughout *Parable of the Sower* and *Parable of the Talents*. According to Lauren Olamina's alternative religion, Earthseed, "God *is* Change." Change is both inevitable and irresistible; change is to be embraced and shaped. While Earthseed deifies Change, as integral to its understanding of theology, ethics, and community, Christian America's fundamentalist theology emphasizes the immutability or "changelessness of God" (and country). As such Christian America demonizes and resists change—especially demographic and cultural changes associated with race, ethnicity, sexuality, and religion—as not only ungodly but also antithetical to notions of American "civilization." Thus, Butler's representations of Christian America warn of resurgent formations of (white) Christian nationalism that support and enable violently repressive authoritarian regimes.

The violence of the Trump administration's rhetoric of "Making America Great Again" is captured in Christian America's rhetorical construction and representation of religious and racialized minorities as "pagans," "heathens," and "witches" responsible for the decline of, and preventing the restoration of, American greatness. Unlike Donald Trump, however, prior to his presidential candidacy, Andrew Steele Jarret developed a significant following as a charismatic religious leader. As founder of Christian America, Jarret's sermons were widely circulated and voraciously consumed by his followers, cultivating hatred and resentment among the "faithful."

In a representative sermon, Jarret waxes nostalgic about a golden age when the United States enjoyed global dominance, presumably secured by divine favor. According to Jarret, "America was God's country and we were God's people and God took care of his own" (88). Arguing for a theocratic politics of American identification bound up with theological claims of divine election, Jarret subsequently describes a filthy, godforsaken America that has betrayed its covenant with God through its tolerance of "heathens." Thus, Jarret decries the presence of "pagans" in America, denouncing them "as destructive as bullets, as contagious as plagues, as poisonous as snakes to the society they infest. They kill us, Christian American brothers and sisters. They kill us! They rouse the righteous anger of God against us for our misguided generosity to them" (88).

Jarret's American jeremiad not only casts these Others as unrepentant sinners, deserving of the wrath of God, but ontologizes and politicizes their condemnation by judging them as "*natural* destroyers of our country" (89; emphasis added). Jarret's non-Christian scapegoats are stereotypically represented as always already inherently guilty "seducers of our children, rapists of our women, drug sellers, usurers, thieves, and murders!" (89) Moreover, Jarret insinuates, if not incites, violence against those he demonizes by posing leading rhetorical questions, such as "And in the face of all that, what are we to them? Shall we live with them? Shall we let them continue to drag our country down into hell? Think! What do we do to weeds, to viruses, to parasitic worms, to cancers? What must we do to protect ourselves and our children? What can we do to regain our stolen nation?" (89). In an interview about *Talents*, Butler sounds a cautionary note concerning real-world responses to such rhetoric: "Some people know that if they can only find the people responsible for all the chaos and punish them, stop them, kill them, then all will be well again" (412).

Framing his scapegoats as menacing threats to law, order, and public safety, Jarret infers to his base what must be done—these racialized religious Others must either be eliminated or forced to assimilate to the tenets of Christian America. Inevitably, Jarret's rhetorical violence gives way to the physical violence carried out by his supporters. Initially, "heathen houses of devil-worship" become sites of domestic terrorism and eventually concentration camps. In the end, "savages" are subjected to technologically enhanced forms of slavery, violence, and death (19).

Of course, presidential candidate Jarret, much like the current president of the United States, claims no responsibility for the violence his vitriolic speech acts set into motion. In prescient words that could have easily been written about the Trump administration's tepid responses to Charlottesville, El Paso, and any number of other hate crimes committed in the wake of his campaign rallies, Butler's protagonist, Lauren Olamina, notes, "Jarret condemns the [violence], but does so in such mild language that his people are free to hear what they want to hear" (19). Here, Olamina's further reflections on the effects and affects of Jarret's religiopolitical rhetoric are worth quoting at length:

> His speeches during the campaign have been somewhat less inflammatory than his sermons. He's had to distance himself from the worst of his followers. But he still knows how to rouse his rabble, how to reach out to poor people, and sic them on other poor people. How much of this nonsense does he believe, I wonder, and how much does he say just because he knows the value of dividing in order to conquer and rule? (89)

Describing her portrayal of Andrew Jarret and other tyrannical leaders, Butler offers commentary that all too accurately captures the machinations of the Trump campaign and administration: "He turns his true believers—his thugs—loose on those he chooses as scapegoats and he looks around for an external enemy to use as an even bigger scapegoat and a diversion from the reality that he doesn't really know what to do" (412). According to Butler, because of inept but dictatorial and divisive leaders like Jarret—and it is no exaggeration to extend this critique to the current presidential administration—"innocent people lose their freedom, lose custody of their children, lose their lives" (412). Jarret's scapegoating, Butler warns, is not merely rhetorical but incites real physical violence. Thus, Butler's cautionary tale echoes the prophetic warnings of Toni Morrison's Nobel Prize speech: "Oppressive language does more than represent violence, it is violence; does more than represent the limits of knowledge, it limits knowledge" (104).

If Butler warns of the violent *effects* of religiopolitical oppression, she also calls attention to its *affects*. Recently, scholars of religion have turned to affect theory to describe, among other things, the relationship between religion, bodies, and power. It is beyond the scope of this chapter to detail the multiple trajectories within this burgeoning field of inquiry. However, in *Religious Affects*, Donovan O. Schaefer offers a relatively succinct mapping of the "affective turn" in the study of religion: "Religious studies begins in a constellation of theoretical moments . . . in which prelinguistic affect was put forward as the cradle of religion as such. Affect theory turns back to these resources, but, building on the linguistic turn, radically redraws the map of theoretical engagements between religion and emotion by explicitly linking affects to frames of power" (*Religious Affects* 59). Schaefer calls particular attention to "how affects connect political, religious, and cultural spheres to bodies" (*Religious Affects* 59). Among other analyses, Schaefer uses affect theory to read and interpret conservative evangelical movements, American Islamophobia, and other religious phenomena as particular formations of power that work in, on, and through bodies. Schaefer's work, deeply informed by Sarah Ahmed's notion of "affective economy," resists the "linguistic fallacy" that power circulates *primarily* through thoughts and language but rather "as a 'thing of the senses' that feels before it thinks" (Schaefer, "It's Not What You Think").

Schaefer's conception of the relationship between affect, power, and bodies is useful for reading Butler's representation of the violence wrought by Christian America (as well as Trump's America). Conversely, Butler's literary imagination offers a richly descriptive account of what affect theorists argue discursively. Throughout *Talents*, Butler is especially attentive to the affective dimensions of religious and political discourses and practices. In a sermon, for instance, Jarret proclaims, "There was a time, Christian Americans, when our country ruled the world," but then demands, "Now look at us. Who are we? What are we? What foul, seething, corrupt heathen concoction have we become?" (*Talents* 88). Butler's literary prose warns of manipulative appeals to the emotions in order to achieve particular affective responses, which her protagonist describes, in this case, as "inflammatory" (*Talents* 89). An affective analysis, however, requires more than a content analysis of such use of language in sermons and political speeches. Schaefer theorizes the point Butler describes above: "Whereas rhetorical analysis asks how affects are being mobilized to achieve certain political objectives, affect theorists argue that politics is being done in order to achieve certain affects" (Schaefer, "It's Not What You Think").

Scholars working through the affective turn in religious studies claim, "Affect can help us make sense of the relationship between virtual and physical violence," such as "the response of a group of individuals to a sermon, to a political speech, to a ritual, and be licensed to speak about the visceral response of individual bodies and social bodies at once" (Kluchin 257). In an attempt to make such theorizing more concrete, I want to call attention to a particular point and example:

> What affect theory shows is that a political formation is best understood not as a package of more-or-less coherent ideas but as a swirling vortex of emotions. This goes as much for the incoherent rage-fests of a Trump rally (the lust for hatred, the desire for strength, the refusal of shame) as it does for the soaring and optimism and calls for a more just society of a Sanders speech: both are avenues for the production of affects. (Schaefer, "It's Not What You Think")

Along these lines, we might emphasize the ways oppressive religious and political discourses involve what Schaefer calls the "hedonicity of hate," or "the desire to cast scorn, the lush, self-absorbed pleasure in erasing another body's face" (Schaefer, *Religious Affects* 123). Drawing on the literary theorist Sharon Patricia Holland's concept of "the erotic life of racism," Schaefer describes how forms of racism and religious intolerance thrive "not because of ignorance or a lack of information, but because of a set of compulsions that drive bodies to generate and police the boundaries of their social worlds" (Schaefer, *Religious Affects* 123). To be sure, there is a perverse interplay between politics, power, and pleasure on display in the feedback loop between Trump and his supporters. Trump rallies, for instance, can be understood in similar terms Schaefer uses elsewhere to describe "a technology for the production of affects, a site to splash around in rage" (Schaefer, *Religious Affects* 137).

But Trump rallies are also a site to "splash around" in *pleasure*, or "the hedonicity of hate." This is evident when smiling crowds cheer as the president mocks and derides minorities, women, the disabled, and those marked as Other to his framing of American identity. Likewise, when he incites his base to chant "build that wall," "lock her up," or "send her back," crowds of supporters appear to be almost giddy at his performances of derision and insult. Butler and affect theorists alike press us to consider that interventions in the violence of "Making America Great Again" require not only resisting "ignorance," "hate," and dangerous policies but also struggling against MAGA's "affective economy," including the *pleasure* derived from participating in such performances of violence.

Of greater concern is Butler's prophetic warning concerning the ways Jarret's supporter's seemingly innocuous "delight of disdaining" the Other gradually morphs into a more sadistic taking of pleasure in unconscionable acts of physical violence. At various points throughout Olamina's captivity and torture, she describes the "fun," "amusement," and the "orgy of abuse and humiliation" that characterized her captors' affective disposition while brutalizing the bodies of racialized religious Others. In perhaps the most graphic account, Olamina describes the perverse pleasure her captures take in the infliction of pain, and specifically the pain of "lashings" inflicted through technologically advanced "slave collars" imposed on the bodies of vulnerable women: "The son of a bitch smiled and pressed his button over and over as though he were fucking me, and he grinned while he watched me groaning and thrashing" (*Talents* 228). Concerning the pleasure taken in the pain of sexualized violence, Olamina recounts, "There are a few men here . . . who lash us until they have orgasms. Our screams and convulsions and pleas and sobs are what these men need to feel sexually satisfied. I know of three who seem to need to lash someone to get sexual pleasure" (*Talents* 233). Butler's description of these men's use of slave collars for sexual pleasure can be understood as a quite literal instance of what affect theorists have referred to as "technologies for the production of embodied affects" (Schaefer, *Religious Affects* 130). More subtly, however, the *erection* of border walls, prisons, detention centers, and other sites of policing are examples of technologies for the production of embodied affects, both in vulnerable bodies and bodies socialized to feel the pleasures of privilege in relation to "deviant" bodies.

This points to another relevant conversation among scholars working in this trajectory of religious studies. In this vein, analyzing religion vis-à-vis affect involves thinking about how not only violence but the subject positionality and experience of being rendered *vulnerable* to various modes of violence is *felt* in bodies—especially those rendered marginal by various workings of power. According to thought leaders in this trajectory of academic inquiry:

Vulnerability is more than just an economic, political, or social location. Its impact is felt in the bodies it enfolds. Thinking about
how vulnerability feels is a way of mapping the effects of power. Racialized, religious, gendered, sexualized, and classed vulnerabilities
interact to form unique dynamics of marginalization, frustration,
alienation, and pain.[1]

In *Talents*, the xenophobic rhetoric of Christian America renders certain
bodies (already vulnerable to the viscous effects of corporate capitalism and
ecological disaster) targets for the resentful violence of Jarret's most zealous
supporters. In Trump's America, such vulnerability is felt in the bodies of
those traumatized by everything from the daily microaggressions and gas-
lighting of those emboldened by his unrepentant racism to the hate crimes,
police brutality, ICE raids, and acts of domestic terror unleashed on the bodies of those targeted by such unpredictable and unaccountable violence.

Butler also reminds us that one need not be the *direct* victim of such violence to be made to feel vulnerable to its workings. The development of her
protagonist's "hyperempathy syndrome" warns of the ways affects can circu-
late between and across vulnerable bodies, as powerful forces (i.e., fear, angst,
humiliation, shame, and especially pain) surge through them. As a "sharer,"
Lauren Olamina feels these powerful affective forces, especially pain, surge
across, between, and through vulnerable bodies into her own. As such, Olamina and other sharers are particularly vulnerable in Christian America. As
she puts it, "They treat known sharers as objects of contempt, suspicion, and
ugly amusement. They're so easy to torment" (*Talents* 226).

As the "objects of . . . ugly amusement," sharers are particularly vulnerable
to the "hedonicity of hate." When their abusers take pleasure in causing pain
in those they hate, sharers feel the intensity of both their abuser's pleasure and
their own pain. While Olamina describes the Christian America concentration camps as "a university of pain," where she has been forced to learn to
protect herself and others, she laments, "Somehow, though, it never occurred
to me that I had to protect myself from the pleasure of my 'teachers'" (*Talents*
233). Reflecting on the experience of feeling the pleasure experienced by a
"teacher's" lashing, Olamina recalls her visceral response: "The first time it
happened—or rather, the first time I understood what was happening, I threw
up" (*Talents* 233).

Butler warns not only of the immediate visceral effects of violence but
also of the continuing affects and effects of traumatization felt in vulnerable bodies. Bodies traumatized by the abuse of power and those who
"share" the pain of the abused are rendered particularly vulnerable to various

manifestations of physical and mental illness. Over time, victims of violence in *Talents* become increasingly suicidal. Even children (especially those who experienced abduction from their "heathen" parents and forcible division from their "heathen siblings" to be raised in "good middle-class Christian America homes") were subject to depression, madness, and suicide. Significantly, even after Olamina and her surviving Acorn comrades eventually escape their concentration camp, their bodies still carry the memories of slavery, and they continue to live in fear and the felt vulnerability of reenslavement or random acts of violence. For Olamina, "Remembering [how 'long we had been filthy slaves in filthy rags cultivating filthy habits in the hope of avoiding rape or lashing'] wasn't safe. You could lose your mind, remembering" (*Talents* 269–270). In the affective aftermath of their enslavement and their frustrated attempts to "put ourselves together as respectable human beings again," Olamina recalls:

> We were together at last, comforting one another, and yet I think each of us was alone, straining toward the others, some part of ourselves still trapped back in the uncertainty and fear, the pain and desolation of Camp Christian. We strained toward some kind of release, some human contact, some way into the normal, human grieving that had been denied us for so long. It amazes me that we were able to behave as sanely as we did. (*Talents* 269)

Conclusion

In her brief essay "Peril," the late Toni Morrison insists, "Certain kinds of trauma visited on peoples are so deep, so cruel . . . only writers can translate such trauma and turn sorrow into meaning, sharpening the moral imagination" (ix). To be sure, Morrison's words speak to the profound significance of Octavia Butler's prophetic literary work. Throughout this chapter, I have described the ways Butler's *Parable of the Talents* offers prophetic warnings concerning the violence of religious and political extremism and the ways such workings of oppressive power are *felt* upon and across bodies rendered vulnerable to such violence. I want to conclude by very briefly gesturing toward some ways of thinking about how Butler's *Parable of the Talents* "sharpens our moral imaginations" through her prophetic imaginings of survival, healing, and liberation in the wake of such violence. This brief gesturing signals toward a fuller treatment, in the next chapter, of further implications from Butler's writings for ongoing struggles for liberation.

In the face of religious extremism and political fascism, Lauren Olamina's alternative religious and political commitments to survival and thriving engender in her a determined hope against hope, leading her to insist, "We will survive. I don't yet know how. How is always a problem. But, in fact, we will survive" (*Talents* 185). Olamina's stubborn insistence on survival can be understood in terms of what the womanist scholar of Africana religions Monica A. Coleman refers to as a postmodern womanist theology of "making a way out of no way." Building on womanist theology's long-standing tradition of reflecting on the historical, social, cultural, and religious experiences of Black women, "making a way out of no way" insists "the way forward was not contained in the past alone. . . . A way forward, a way toward life, comes from another source. It comes from unforeseen possibilities" (Coleman, "Making" 188).

This (Afro)futurist orientation leads Coleman to draw on Black women's science fiction, and especially Butler's work, as a significant resource for "making a way out of no way" and for third-wave womanist religious thought (Coleman "Womanist"). For Coleman, Butler's Parables are "prophetic literature that both [warn] the current world of the dangers that lie ahead and [offer] proposals for how we can 'make a way out of no way'" ("Making" 126). As Coleman reminds us, central to Butler's prophetic vision is "the value of imagination in the process of creative transformation" ("Making" 127). In her popular work *Emergent Strategy: Shaping Change, Changing Worlds*, adrienne maree brown—who describes herself as, among other things, a social justice facilitator, healer, and doula "called to lead . . . from spirit to liberation"—echoes Coleman's womanist valuation of imagination and creative transformation, not only for understanding Butler's work but also for doing contemporary justice and healing work (12). Along these lines, brown makes her reliance on Butler's work explicit: "Octavia Butler appeals to me because she wanted to prepare us for inevitable consequences of human behavior . . . Change is coming—what do we need to imagine as we prepare for it?" (58). Taken together, Coleman's "making a way out of no way" and brown's "emergent strategy" call attention to the implications of Butler's writings for ongoing struggles for liberation in the Trump era.

Monica Coleman describes postmodern womanist theology as "a quest for health and wholeness in the midst of violence, oppression and evil" ("Invoking" 188). adrienee maree brown considers "emergent strategy" as a model of relational leadership and way of being in the world that emphasize "critical, deep, and authentic connections," which allow us to be adaptive as we work collaboratively to "transform a world that is, by its very nature, in a constant state of change" (14). Both consider Octavia Butler's writings to be "prophetic" and thus turn to her work as a critical resource for their own. Both find resonance in Butler for alternative strategies of spiritual activism—as a mode of healing, as well as imaginative and creative transformation—that draw on the plurality of Black women's religious experiences. Finally, both thinkers draw out implications from Butler's work that insist on the significance of the interplay between power, affects, and bodies engaged in liberation struggles.

As this concluding gesture suggests, Coleman and brown remind us that in the midst of her often-grim, apocalyptic, cautionary tales, Octavia Butler's prophetic vision also offers us profound possibilities for survival (i.e., "making a way out of no way") and thriving (i.e., "emergent strategy"). While this conclusion has been a mere gesturing toward such possibilities, in the final chapter of this volume, "Practicing the Future Together: Earthseed as a Tool for Black Liberation," Shelby L. Crosby further develops the implications of Butler's work for ongoing struggles for liberation. In anticipation, perhaps it is appropriate to conclude this chapter with Lauren Olamina's words to her comrades struggling to survive Jarret's violent efforts to "Make America Great Again": "Jarret will pass, and we will still be here. We know more about survival than most people. The proof is that we have survived. We have tools that other people don't have, and that they need. The time will come again when we can share what we know" (*Talents* 274).

NOTE

1. This is an excerpt from the abstract for a panel entitled The Felt Life of Vulnerability, presented by the Religion, Affect, and Emotion workgroup at the American Academy of Religion. The abstract was drafted by Donovan Schaefer and Gail Hamner. In November 2017, I presented a paper on this panel.

WORKS CITED

brown, adrienne maree. *Emergent Strategy: Shaping Change, Changing Worlds*. AK Press, 2017.

———. "Re-read: Octavia Butler's *Parable* Series." *The Portalist*, https://theportalist .com/re-read-octavia-butlers-parable-series. Accessed 19 Aug. 2019.

Butler, Octavia E. *Parable of the Sower*. Grand Central Publishing, 1993.

———. *Parable of the Talents*. Grand Central Publishing, 1998.

Caldwell, Ellen C. "When Science Fiction Becomes Real: Octavia E. Butler's Legacy." *JSTOR Daily*, 3 Oct. 2016, https://daily.jstor.org/when-science-fiction-becomes -real-octavia-e-butlers-legacy/. Accessed 19 Aug. 2019.

Coleman, Monica A., ed. *Ain't I a Womanist Too? Third Wave Womanist Religious Thought*. Fortress Press, 2013.

———. "Invoking Oya: Practicing a Polydox Soteriology." *Polydoxy: Theology of Multiplicity and Relation*, edited by Catherine Keller and Laurel C. Schneider, Routledge, 2011, pp. 186–202.

———. *Making a Way out of No Way: A Womanist Theology*. Fortress Press, 2008.

Corrigan, John, ed. *Feeling Religion*. Duke University Press, 2017.

Glaude, Eddie S., Jr. *African American Religion: A Very Short Introduction*. Oxford University Press, 2014.

Jones, Heather. "Octavia Butler Predicted a Trump Presidency 20 Years Ago." *Wear Your Voice*, 9 Nov. 2016, https://wearyourvoicemag.com/culture/octavia-butler -predicted-trump.

Keller, Catherine, and Laurel C. Schneider. *Polydoxy: Theology of Multiplicity and Relation*. Routledge Press, 2011.

Morrison, Toni. *The Source of Self-Regard: Selected Essays, Speeches, and Meditations*. Knopf, 2019.

Open. "Octavia Butler's 1998 Dystopian Novel Features a Fascistic Presidential Candidate Who Promises to 'Make America Great Again.'" *Open Culture*, 21 July 2016, http://www.openculture.com/2016/07/octavia-butlers-1998-dystopian-novel -features-a-fascistic-presidential-candidate-who-promises-to-make-america-great -again.html.

Schaefer, Donovan O. "It's Not What You Think: Affect Theory and Power Take to the Stage." https://dukeupress.wordpress.com/2016/02/15/its-not-what-you-think -affect-theory-and-power-take-to-the-stage/. Accessed 19 August 2019.

———. *Religious Affects: Animality, Evolution, and Power*. Duke University Press, 2015.

Schaefer, Donovan, and Gail Hamner. The Felt Life of Vulnerability panel. Religion, Affect, and Emotion workgroup at the American Academy of Religion. November 2017.

Schulman, George. *American Prophecy: Race and Redemption in American Political Culture*. University of Minnesota Press, 2008.

16

Creating New Worlds

Earthseed as a Tool for Black Liberation

SHELBY L. CROSBY

The dedication to *Octavia's Brood: Science Fiction Stories from Social Justice Movements* invokes Octavia E. Butler's connection to and inspiration for activism and social justice: echoing Earthseed's founding tenet, "all that you touch you change," adrienne maree brown and Walida Imarisha explicitly draw a connection between science fiction—or what they term "visionary fiction," which is "science fiction that has a relevance toward building new, freer worlds and encompasses all of the fantastic with the arc always bending toward justice" (4)—and social activism.

> To Octavia E. Butler, who serves as a north star for so many of us. She told us what would happen—"all that you touch you change"—and then she touched us, fearlessly, brave enough to change us. We dedicate this collection to her, coming out with our own fierce longing to have our writing change everyone and everything we touch. (brown and Imarisha)

brown and Imarisha point to the "fierce longing" for change and the actions that brown calls "science fictional behavior," meaning that activists are imagining new ways and new paths for the current world, even if they may not be around to see and benefit from the changes. Borrowing from the term *visionary fiction*, I call this type of activism *visionary activism*. Visionary activism is concerned with and builds toward a freer world that focuses on social justice for all, regardless of race, class, gender, sexual orientation, and so on. The iconic visionary Dr. Martin Luther King Jr. is a prime example; in both the "I Have a Dream" speech and the "I've Been to the Mountaintop" speech, he reimagines the United States as a new place, a place where Black and brown people are considered citizens and can be free and safe. In the opening paragraphs of the "Mountaintop" speech, King takes a "mental flight" through the ages to witness the great moments of freedom and then asks to be allowed to see even just a "few years in the second half of the 20th century" so that he can see how the great push for human rights might turn out. He prophetically knows that he may not get to the other side with us, but that is all right because "he's allowed me to go up to the mountain. And I've looked over. And I've seen the Promised Land. I may not get there with you. But I want you to know tonight, that we, as a people, will get to the Promised Land" (King). Like the Earthseed Destiny to "take root among the stars," King has no idea if he can make it to the Promised Land—but that is not the point. The point is to have the vision to "shape change," to constantly strive to create a world where his "four little children will one day live in a nation where they will not be judged by the color of their skin but by the content of their character" (King). Shaping Change, as Butler's Earthseed calls, demands that its followers recognize that

> there's power in knowing that God can be focused, diverted, shaped by anyone at all. But there's no power in having strength and brains, and yet waiting for God to fix things for you or take revenge for you. . . . God will shape us every day of our lives. Best to understand that and return the effort: Shape God. (*Sower* 220)

Shaping God is exactly what activists are promoting and participating in: they are shaping the world into what they imagine it could and should be. And in the process of shaping God, people are empowered to take charge of their lives and destinies, to imagine and dream of new worlds, new ideologies, and (ultimately) liberation. Visionary activism is King's mental flight and adrienne brown's belief in "emergent strategies." Both of these perspectives mean being able to take that mental flight—to have hope, belief in a better, more just world. It is the imagination to see and build a new world out of the chaos and violence we see around us. This is the power of Butler's fiction, and it is what makes her work visionary fiction. In the Parable series, she provides the tools to imagine a new world and possible future through Earthseed and its belief system. Earthseed's rugged pragmatism provides followers a focus and guidance to build a world in the here while working toward the Earthseed Destiny, which is to take root among the stars. As noted above, Dr. Martin Luther King

Jr., adrienne maree brown, Aaron Robertson, and Melissa Simpson all provide examples of visionary activist work.

Claiming Butler as a "north star" demonstrates how important Butler's work, and particularly Earthseed, are to Black liberation activists with a visionary strategy. Following the North Star is how many a slave found their way north and to freedom; the North Star never changes position and is always pointing north, which made it a very reliable map. For visionary activists like brown and Imarisha, Butler is an author whose work points toward the path to get free. Like the North Star, Earthseed enables activists to move toward freedom, and Butler's fiction creates a new path of resistance and possibility. Reading Butler's canon as one that explores the "intersections of identity and imagination, the gray areas of race, class, gender, sexuality, love, militarism, inequality, oppression, resistance, and—most important—hope" (Imarisha 3), activists regard Butler and Earthseed as an essential component to any social justice movement whose aim is the liberation of Black and brown peoples.

What is it about Earthseed, and Butler's fiction more generally, that offers this foundation? With the publication of *Parable of the Sower* in 1993, Octavia Butler solidified her exploration of the continuity of change with the religion Earthseed. Earthseed, the creation of her protagonist Lauren Olamina, is a religious ideology based entirely on the idea that God is Change. Once this concept is accepted as truth, it can alleviate the fear and anxiety in the apocalyptic world of the novels: "All that you touch, / You change. / All that you Change, / Changes you. / The only lasting truth / Is Change. / God is Change" (*Sower* 79). Within the novel, Earthseed grows because it helps followers cope with their current world while also giving them a vision of a new world where they can be free and the space to reimagine what their world could look like. Much like other religions, it provides comfort and hope. Its hope lies in the collaboration and collective work of humanity. As a religious ideology based on the notion that God is Change and that its followers can shape change and, therefore, shape God, Earthseed is inherently an ideology of social justice and activism.

While the Parable series has been critically successful, it has also created new ways to consider activism and political change. adrienne marie brown links Earthseed and political activism explicitly in her text *Emergent Strategy: Shaping Change, Changing Worlds*. According to brown, "we are constantly impacting and changing civilization—each other, ourselves, intimates, strangers. And we are working to transform a world that is, by its very nature, in a constant state of change" (14). Thus, activism fueled by Earthseed can create new worlds "that transition ideologies and norms, so that no one sees Black people as murderers, or Brown people as murderers, or Brown people as terrorists and aliens, but all of us as potential cultural and economic innovators" (18–19). Using Butler's concept of change, brown builds a new way to consider and enact social justice movements. Using science fiction as a possible way to think outside of one's current world, brown claims that "science fiction is simply a way to practice the future together" (19). Building on brown's ideation, this chapter will explore how activists are using Butler's Earthseed to further the cause of Black liberation and take what brown calls a "time-travel exercise for the heart" (19). A time-travel exercise for the heart is like King's mental flight to visit his oppressed but thriving ancestors—a way to look at past, present, and future simultaneously, a way to see all of human existence rather than the limited view from our singular perspective and therefore to be able to create conditions for social and political change. Butler takes readers on time-travel exercises for the heart in the Parable series, where she shows us our present conditions and our possible futures.

At the center of Butler's time-travel exercise is the idea of change; moreover, change has been adopted as a mode of transformative political practice by activists like brown, Grace Lee Boggs, and Aaron Robertson. These activists are practicing an Afrofuturist political activism; according to Ytasha Womack, Afrofuturism is "an intersection of imagination, technology, the future, and liberation" (9). These activists believe that "we are dreaming new worlds every time we think about the changes we want to make in the world"; thus, they are shaping change. Shaping change from an Earthseed perspective is being prepared for the inevitable changes that will take place because "God is Change, and in the end, God prevails" (*Sower* 220). Essentially, to shape change requires hard work and dedication to the Destiny of Earthseed, which is "to take root among the stars." This Destiny provides a focus to followers' lives—gives them something to do and something to work toward amid the daily grind for liberation.

In *Emergent Strategy: Shaping Change, Changing Worlds*, brown develops the idea of emergent strategy, noting Butler as "one of the cornerstones of my awareness of emergent strategy" (6). Emergence is "the way complex systems and patterns arise out of a relatively simple interaction"; emergent strategy is a "strategy for building complex patterns and systems of change through relatively small interactions," and it provides a "potential scale of transformation that could come from movements intentionally practicing this adaptive, relational way of being, on our own and with others" (2–3). Emphasizing "critical connections over critical mass, building authentic relationships, listening with all the senses of the body and the mind," emergent strategy and its focus on shaping change are a way to see the world in a new way, a way to "understand how we humans earn a place on this precious planet" and "get in the right relationship with it" (5): a goal that Butler argues for explicitly in the Parable series, "To make peace with others / Make peace with yourself; / Shape God / With Generosity / And compassion. / Minimize harm. / Shield the weak. / Treasure the innocent. / Be true to the Destiny. / Forgive your enemies. / Forgive yourself" (*Talents* 153). Earthseed requires that one strive to be in right relationship with one's self and others; this practice reflects brown's emergent strategy. Emergence is also a "plan of action, personal practice and collective organizing tools that account for constant change and rely on the strength of relationship for adaptation" (brown 23). For brown, collaboration, embracing change, and being able to imagine a new future (beyond the status quo) are the cornerstones of emergent strategy and the future of social justice movements.

Shifting how movements are structured and organized is important to being in "right relationship" with the world and in being effective as an organizer and social justice activist. Developing movements that are more collaborative and cooperative while acknowledging that there will be "micro-hierarchies in a collaborative environment," brown argues against the "individualistic linear organizing (led by charismatic individuals or budget-building institutions), which intend to reform or revolutionize society, but fall back into modeling the oppressive tendencies against which we claim to be pushing" (8). Again, brown is thinking about Butler and her character development: "Octavia's leaders were also decentralized, and they were generative—resilience and solutions came from that decentralization; the collective response was possible because no one person held the power" (22).

As a model of collective action and decentralization, Earthseed teaches ideas disseminated through discussion, questioning, and individual interactions, both at weekly gatherings and through individual teachings. The first Earthseed community that Olamina establishes is Acorn; nestled in the hills of Oregon, Acorn is an intentional community created by Olamina and the groups she gathers on her walk from Southern California. The group is determined to build a safe community in which people will help and support one another and use Earthseed as its guiding principles. One such principle is weekly gatherings that help the community come together, organize, and unify. Acorn gatherings support brown's call for a collaborative decision-making process through debate, questioning, and critical thinking; they "involve questions, challenges, and argument" designed to clarify thought and move the community to action. There is even an Earthseed verse outlining the value of these Gatherings:

Once or twice
each week.
A Gathering of Earthseed
is a good and necessary thing.
It vents emotion, then
quiets the mind.
It focuses attention,
strengthens purpose, and
unifies people. (*Sower* 214)

Questioning and unity go hand in hand with building community and social movements. Earthseed's focus on gatherings and shared governance also appears in how new converts and children are taught. It is not a faith based on one person having the power to disseminate knowledge; rather, it is a communal sense of learning and sharing, as Lauren Olamina states, "As for the title, in Acorn, all the children call me 'shaper.' It was the title that seemed right for one teaching Earthseed. Travis, too, was called shaper. So was Natividad" (*Talents* 284). These two acts—the gatherings and the decentralization of preacher/teacher—ensure that Earthseed will not become an individualistic linear organization; instead, it strives to be more communal and in right relationship with the earth and one another. Olamina practices what Brianna Thompson calls "erotic pedagogy"—the "queer process of touching, teaching, preaching, and comfort" that Olamina employs when converting and teaching folks the ways of Earthseed. This concept privileges the nonlinear, nonpatriarchal ways to organize and create social movements and community rather than the linear patriarchal model that limits spiritual and political growth.

Creating a supportive, intentional community becomes one way that Olamina promotes and grows Earthseed. These communities are both physical spaces, like Acorn, and a broader and larger community that Earthseed reaches through the teaching and dissemination of *Earthseed: The Books of the Living*:

I must build . . . not a physical community this time. I guess I understand at last how easy it is to destroy such a community. I need to create something wide-reaching and harder to kill. That's why I must teach teachers. I must create not only a dedicated little group of followers, not only a collection of communities as I once imagined, but a movement. I must create a new fashion in faith—a fashion that can evolve into a new religion, a new guiding force, that help humanity to put its energy, competitiveness, and creativity to work doing the truly vast job of fulfilling the Destiny. (*Talents* 297)

While Acorn cannot survive as a physical space in the apocalyptic world of the Parable novels, its spirit becomes the basis of a social movement that is designed to focus humanity on a purpose higher than themselves: on the Destiny of Earthseed to "take root among the stars."

Butler's influence also appears outside of the literary world and imagination through the Wild Seed Community Farm and Healing Village. Located in upstate New York, Wild Seed (named for Butler's novel of the same name) is an intentional community, "an emerging Black and Brown-led, feminine-centered, queer-loving, earth-based intentional community, organic farm, healing sanctuary, and political and creative home" (Wild Seed Community Farm and Healing Village). Wild Seed is a social justice community that is part of a larger social justice movement focused on the collective responsibility humans have for the earth and how that responsibility reflects a larger responsibility to all human beings. Wild Seed's guiding principles reflect many of Earthseed's principles and many of the ideas that brown proposes in *Emergent Strategy*.

> Embodying the World We Dream Of; healing present and ancestral trauma; confronting institutional, interpersonal and internalized oppression; ecological guidance and reverence for the Earth; dignity and self-determination; communal intimacy and interdependence; radical imagination and courageous artistry; liberatory economics; transformative and restorative justice; accessibility and inclusivity; movement building and education; and intergenerational responsibility. (Wild Seed Community Farm and Healing Village)

Embodying the world we dream of is in conversation with brown's emergent strategy and Butler's Earthseed. As brown explores, it is the "science fiction" of imagining and then working toward and embodying that world, much like Wild Seed's first principle. Earthseed's followers are always preparing for the world of their Destiny; they are shaping the world in which they want to live. Earthseed promotes communal intimacy and interdependence, as does the Wild Seed community. This intimacy and interdependence create communities that work together to build a better world, the world they dream of:

> Earthseed offers its own rewards—room
> For small groups of people to begin new lives and

new ways of life with new opportunities, new
wealth, new concepts of wealth, new challenges to
grow and to learn and to decide what to become. (*Talents* 324)

It is through community that Earthseed can imagine and work with "new challenges to grow and to learn and to decide what to become." Whether a physical space like Acorn or the larger intellectual community that Olamina builds after Acorn's destruction, communities like Wild Seed are essential to social transformation. brown, like Wild Seed, calls forth the ideas of interdependence and communal intimacy: "The idea of interdependence is that we can meet each other's needs in a variety of ways, that we can truly lean on others and they can lean on us" (87). Wild Seed is an intentional community that embodies the visionary activism that Butler supports and that brown promotes in her social activist work.

In adrienne maree brown's adopted hometown of Detroit, visionary activism is working hard to revitalize the city's impoverished areas through cultural production and economic activities. The Detroit Afrofuturist activist Aaron Robertson argues that Detroit can imagine and enact a new future using an Afrofuturist or visionary activist lens:

Often the work of Afrofuturists, whether they are artists or engineers, is performed in a metaphorical underground. It tries to make abstract and material technologies relevant by giving blacks opportunities to understand, use, critique, resist, and design them. It reimagines technological processes and the economic and political systems that created them.

One such program happening is the Oakland North End (ONE) Mile Project; it is a collaborative community program developed in an effort to reinvigorate, rather than gentrify, neighborhoods that have been struggling economically and culturally. It does this by encouraging the use of local Oakland and North End business, the development of community gardens, the launching of a local magazine, and the development of cultural events featuring only artists from the communities. The investment in community creates an interdependence and communal intimacy in the middle of a city. Like Wild Seed, Oakland and North End are creating an intentional space that supports members of the community and the larger Detroit vision of the future.

Butler, King, brown, Robertson, and Wild Seed are all "practicing the future together," practicing how a new world can be shaped, how a new world can even be imagined. It is in the ability to imagine that freedom exists; it is through a visionary activism that change will happen. Visionary activists are practicing a healing behavior when they can "look at something so broken and see the possibility of wholeness in it" (brown 19). Using Octavia Butler as a guide or North Star, activists are adopting aspects of Earthseed's religious ideology as a way to reimagine and heal the world.

WORKS CITED

brown, adrienne maree. *Emergent Strategy: Shaping Change, Changing Worlds*. AK Press, 2017.

brown, adrienne maree, and Walidah Imarisha, eds. *Octavia's Brood: Science Fiction from Social Justice Movements*. AK Press, 2015.

Butler, Octavia. *Parable of the Sower*. Warner Books, 1993.

———. *Parable of the Talents*. Warner Books, 1998.

King, Martin Luther. "I Have a Dream by Martin Luther King, Jr; August 28, 1963." The Avalon Project, Yale Law School, avalon.law.yale.edu/20th_century/mlk01.asp. Accessed 10 Nov. 2020.

———. "I've Been to the Mountaintop by Martin Luther King, Jr.; April 3, 1968." American Rhetoric, https://www.afscme.org/about/history/mlk/mountaintop.

Robertson, Aaron. "The Future Was Already Here: Detroit's Afrofuturist Enclaves." *Detroit Metro Times*, Culture, 10 Aug. 2016, Metrotimes.com/Detroit/the-future-was-already-here-detroits-afrofuturist-enclaves/content?oid=2459448.

Wild Seed Community Farm and Healing Village. Wild Seed Community Farm, wildseedcommunity.org. Accessed 20 Sept. 2019.

Womack, Ytasha. *Afrofuturism: The World of Black Sci-Fi and Fantasy Culture*. Lawrence Hill Books, 2013.

Contributors

Alexis Brooks de Vita, with a Ph.D. in comparative literature studying the works of African and diaspora women in English, French, Italian, and Spanish, is the author of numerous analyses of African, diaspora, and women's literatures, analyses of supernatural film including horror and science fiction, and the single-author texts *Mythatypes: Signatures and Signs of African/Diaspora and Black Goddesses* (Praeger, 2000), the creative nonfictional account *The 1855 Murder Case of Missouri versus Celia: An Enslaved Woman* (Mellen Poetry Press, 2010), and the novels *Left Hand of the Moon* (Double Dragon ebooks, 2012) and the Books of Joy trilogy: *Burning Stream* (Double Dragon ebooks, 2011), *Blood of Angels* (Double Dragon, 2015), and *Chain Dance* (Double Dragon, 2011). Brooks de Vita is the author of poetry and short stories in such collections as *Candle in the Attic Window, Forced from the Garden: Poetry by Women*, and *Safari: African American Stories, Parables and Tales*, as well as the editor of the short story anthologies *Takes in Firelight and Shadow* and *Love and Darker Passions*.

Phyllis Lynne Burns, originally from Detroit, is Associate Professor of English and Director of the Race and Ethnic Studies Program at Otterbein University in Ohio. Her teaching and research focus on Black women's literature, African American literature, Black liberation theory and narrative, and Black speculative fiction. Burns's publications have appeared in *Criticism: A Quarterly Journal for Literature and Art, World Hustler: Critical Essays and Reflections on the Works of Donald Gaines, Black Camera: An International Film Journal* and *Proud Flesh*.

Shelby L. Crosby is Associate Professor at the University of Memphis. Her research spans mid-nineteenth-century to the early twentieth-century African American literature, representations of womanhood (particularly Black womanhood), and critical race theory. It threads together critical race, Black feminism, and literary historical frameworks to interrogate an American national story. She has published articles in *College Language Association Journal* and numerous edited collections. She is currently working on an edited volume on Black women and popular culture, specifically the proliferation of Black women on TV, such as in *How to Get Away with Murder, Claws, Being Mary Jane*, and such films as *Girls Trip*.

Ebony Gibson is Assistant Professor of English at Georgia Gwinnett College and teaches first-year writing, creative writing, and the occasional literature class. She has an MA in English from Morgan State University, an MFA in fiction from Columbia University, and an MA in African American studies from Georgia State University. She is also completing a Ph.D. in English at Georgia State University with a focus in twentieth- and twenty-first-century African American literature. She plans to write her dissertation on seminal Black antiheroines in literature and popular culture, primarily focusing on Olivia Pope (*Scandal*) and Lilith Iyapo (Butler's Xenogenesis series).

Mary M. Grover, after earning her Ph.D. in English literature at the University of Texas, Austin, served as Writing Programs Coordinator at Wheelock College in Boston for six years. She now teaches writing and public speaking at the University of California, Berkeley. Her essays and poems appear in *Salon, Memorious, Calyx*, and *Poem, Memoir, Story*.

Gregory Hampton was Professor of African American Literature and Director of Graduate Studies in the Department of English at Howard University. Hampton held a BA in economics and African American studies from Oberlin College, an MA in African American studies from Yale University, and a Ph.D. in comparative literature from Duke University. He published articles in the *English Journal*, the *CLAJ* (*College Language Association Journal*), *Children's Literature in Education: An International Quarterly*, *Obsidian III*, and *Callaloo*. His most recent courses were invested in the problematic of the Black body and its portrayal in literature and film, as well as literature across cultures (African, British, Native American, Caribbean, and Asian). His book *Changing Bodies in the Fiction of Octavia Butler: Slaves, Aliens, and Vampires* (Lexington Books, 2010) was the first monograph of literary criticism invested in examining the complete body of fiction produced by Octavia E. Butler. Hampton's most recent monograph, *Imagining Slaves and Robots in Literature, Film, and Popular Culture: Reinventing Yesterday's Slave with Tomorrow's Robot* (Lexington Books, 2015), is an interdisciplinary study that seeks to investigate and speculate about the relationship between technology and human nature. In addition to African American speculative fiction, Hampton's fields of interest included nineteenth- and twentieth-century American and African American literature as well as gender studies.

Jennifer L. Hayes is Associate Professor of English and Women's Studies at Tennessee State University in Nashville, Tennessee. Her research interests include pedagogy, Black drama, travel narratives, contemporary Black women's literature, and Black feminist theory. Her current book, entitled *Teaching African American Literature through Experiential Praxis: African American Writers in Europe* (Palgrave, forthcoming), considers teaching African American literature using study abroad. In addition to courses on African American literature, she teaches women's studies courses that foreground an intersectional approach that encourages the combination of theory and praxis. Her research has also been published in *South: A Scholarly Journal*, *South Atlantic Review*, and *A Critical Companion to Lynn Nottage*.

Christopher Kocela is Associate Professor of English at Georgia State University, where he teaches contemporary U.S. literature, theory, and popular culture. He is the author of *Fetishism and Its Discontents in Post-1960 American Fiction* (Palgrave, 2010), and his essays and articles have appeared in the journals *Postmodern Culture, Genders, Comparative Literature and Culture, LIT,* and in critical studies on the work of Thomas Pynchon and David Foster Wallace. His current research examines intersections between Eastern thought (especially Buddhism) and the depiction of racial and gender difference in contemporary U.S. novels.

Michael Brandon McCormack, Ph.D. (Vanderbilt), is Assistant Professor of Pan-African Studies and Comparative Humanities (Program in Religious Studies) at the University of Louisville. His research interests include the intersections of religion, popular culture, and political activism; religion and black youth culture (i.e., hip-hop); Black and womanist theologies of liberation; African diasporic religions; and the politics, poetics, and performance of the Black preaching tradition in America. His work has been published in the *Journal of Africana Religions, Black Theology: An International Journal, Practical Matters: A Journal of Practical Theology and Religious Practice, Ox-*

ford Bibliographies in African American Studies, and the *St. James Encyclopedia of Hip Hop Culture*, as well as several book chapters in edited volumes.

Aparajita Nanda, recipient of a Visiting Associate Professorship to the Departments of English and African American Studies, University of California, Berkeley, and a Fulbright faculty teaching scholarship, now teaches at the University of California, Berkeley, and Santa Clara University. Her book publications include *Black California* (2011), *The Strangled Cry: The Communication and Experience of Trauma* (2013), *Romancing the Strange: The Fiction of Kunal Basu* (2004), and *Ethnic Literatures and Transnationalism: Critical Imaginaries for a Global World* (2014). She has published several book chapters, most recently with Cambridge University Press and Modern Language Association (MLA). Her articles have been published in peer-reviewed journals, including *Callaloo* and *Ariel*, while her academic treatises (by invitation) are available in *Oxford African American Studies*, edited by Henry Louis Gates.

Charlotte Naylor Davis is a biblical scholar affiliated with the National Coalition of Independent Scholars. She specializes in the history of biblical interpretation and the translation of ancient texts. She is interested in the interaction between culture and the interpretation of the Bible, and particularly the language and symbols of gender. This has come together in her publishing on heavy metal music as a form of biblical exegesis and gender representation in heavy metal lyrics. A love of heavy metal, science fiction, and academic textual scholarship has led her to her current research on the way religious texts work as cultural artifacts—texts as living things within culture with which the reader is in relationship.

Keegan Osinski is Librarian for Theology and Ethics at Vanderbilt University. She earned her bachelor of arts in philosophy and theology from Point Loma Nazarene University, her master of library and information science from the University of Washington, and her master of theological studies from Vanderbilt University. Her research interests include ritual theory, liturgical and sacramental theology, and phenomenology and continental thought.

Chuck Robinson is a lecturer at University of Nevada, Reno, where he teaches core writing and the occasional literature class. Chuck's research focuses on science as it appears in nineteenth-century U.S. literature and its connection to the apocalyptic motifs and science fiction that arise at the end of the century. Beyond his home base of nineteenth-century realism and naturalism,

Chuck reads widely and deeply in (global) science fiction and contemporary scientific nonfiction. He is currently developing two related projects, one that focuses on the ambiguous uses of "speculation" in mid-nineteenth-century American prose and another focusing on the career of "catastrophism" and "uniformitarianism," two competing geological theories from the early nineteenth century that have a vibrant afterlife in the cultural imaginary from the late nineteenth century to today. Chuck has previously published on Octavia Butler in *Science Fiction Studies*.

Tarshia L. Stanley is Dean of the School of Humanities, Arts, and Sciences and Associate Professor of English at St. Catherine University in Saint Paul, Minnesota. She has written articles on Black women's iconography in African American and African cinema and American popular culture. She edited *The Encyclopedia of Hip Hop Literature* (Greenwood Press, 2008) and the forthcoming volume *Approaches to Teaching Octavia E. Butler in the Academy* (MLA Press, 2018). Stanley is founding president of the Octavia E. Butler Literary Society. She received her Ph.D. and MA in English from the University of Florida and AB from Duke University.

Brianna Thompson is a Ph.D. candidate in the English Department at Cornell University. Her areas of interest are nineteenth- and twentieth-century American literature, African American literature, gender, queer studies, religion, and critical theory. She is working on a dissertation in which she develops erotic pedagogy as an analytic for intimate teaching practices between female characters and their alternative kinship structures in Elizabeth Stuart Phelps's *The Gates Ajar*, Susan Warner's *The Wide, Wide World*, Octavia Butler's *Parable of the Talents*, and Toni Morrison's *Paradise*.

Briana Whiteside is Assistant Professor of English at the University of Nevada, Las Vegas. Her research interests include science fiction, popular culture, natural hair, and Black women's narratives. She is particularly interested in the ways in which Black women have endeavored to heal from physical and psychological traumas, as well as how African American literature by women has represented this struggle. Her work also explores the ways in which notions of imprisonment have shaped understandings of the prison system—an interest resulting from her experience teaching within both medium- and maximum-security prisons. As evidence of her commitment to fostering intellectual growth within the prison classroom, she created a library within a maximum-security prison in Alabama. Her work has been published in several edited volumes and journals, including the *College Language Association Journal*.

Index